JAMES V. CAPUA &
COL. CARL M. KRUGER (USA, RET.)

JÄGER
Europe's First Special Operations Forces

History, Organization, Arms & Equipment of the
Austro-Hungarian Empire's Elite Light Infantry to 1866

Copyright © 2020 by James V. Capua &
Col. Carl M. Kruger (USA, RET.)

All rights reserved. This book or any portion thereof may not be reproduced or used in any manner whatsoever without the express written permission of the publisher, except for the use of brief quotations in a book review.

ISBN 978-1-7345814-0-9 (Paperback)

ISBN 978-1-7345814-1-6 (Hardcover)

Cover design & book design by Noah Adam Paperman

Cover illustration: *The Battle of Santa Lucia*, by B. Bachmann-Hohmann, 1849

From a lithograph after Franz Kollarz

Heeresgeschichtliches Museum, Vienna

To our grandsons

*"And how can man die better, Than facing fearful odds,
For the ashes of his fathers, and the temples of his gods."*

Thomas Babington Macaulay, The Lays of Ancient Rome

The authors are indebted to Daniela Kruger for her relentless diligence in creating many of the photographs of arms and marks that appear in this book

TABLE OF CONTENTS

PREFACE	**ix**
GLOSSARY	**xiii**
CHAPTER 1: Beginnings	**1**
The Hunter and the Rifle	2
Tirol	5
Grenzer Troops: The Military Frontier as a Source of Austrian Light Troops and its Consequences	8
CHAPTER 2: Emergence of the Feld-Jäger	**11**
The Seven years' War	11
The *Freikorps* Jäger of the Late 18th Century Austrian Wars	15
CHAPTER 3: Jäger in the Wars against Revolutionary and Napoleonic France	**21**
The Wars of the First Coalitions	21
The Tiroler Jäger Regiment	32
Archduke Karl and Jäger Expansion 1806-1809	36
Defeat and Glory: 1809-1815	42
CHAPTER 4: Jäger in the Age of Metternich, 1815-1848	**47**
1815: Italian Harbinger	47
The "Kaiser-Jäger" Regiment	52
Jäger Organization, Training and Uniform	54

CHAPTER 5: Jäger in the Italian Wars, 1848-1859	**81**
Radetzky's Jäger: 1848-49	81
Debacle in 1859	100
CHAPTER 6: The Seven Weeks' War, 1866,	**109**
Bohemia	112
The Quadrilateral Again	115
Defense of the South Tirol	118
CHAPTER 7: Jäger Firearms	**123**
CHAPTER 8: *"If only he had become an Unterjäger"* A Jäger Story	**163**
APPENDIX 1: Jäger Edged Weapons: What We Know and Don't Know	**173**
APPENDIX 2: The Vienna Arsenal	**195**
APPENDIX 3: Marks on Jäger Firearms	**199**
ENDNOTES	**205**
BIBLIOGRAPHY	**257**
INDEX	**269**
ABOUT THE AUTHORS	**279**

PREFACE

We came to this subject as collectors and shooters of historical arms with more than a passing acquaintance with European military history. Like many Americans we knew "Jägers," along with "Garibaldis" as the short Austrian rifles, M 1854 and 1849 respectively, grabbed up in some numbers by Union and Confederate agents during the War Between the States to supplement domestically-produced arms. As collectors we learned quickly that in Austria, The Czech Republic, Hungary and Italy, Jäger arms and equipment are valued highly. In the same way as the tag *"Confederate???"* guarantees eBay hits in the US, on the German and Italian eBays *"Kaiser Jäger"* is promiscuously employed for the same reason. European auction sales of Jäger-related items of collector quality are competitive and bargains are, accordingly, rare.

As our interest in the subject deepened it became clear that while there is much information in English and German on the Jäger troops of Austria and the German States in the 18th and 19th centuries, it is scattered widely in books and articles (see bibliography) on Austro-Hungarian military history, the Seven Years,' Revolutionary and Napoleonic Wars, the Risorgimento and the 1866 campaigns in Bohemia and Northern Italy to name the most obvious. A surprising amount of key primary and out-of-print or rare secondary material in German is accessible online. There are also some excellent European military history sites on the Internet, many catering to military miniaturists, re-enactors and war gamers. While we are well aware of the unfiltered nature of much Internet material, and have accordingly exercised extreme caution in using it, we have found that the best web popular history is assayed effectively for quality by some remarkably informed peer commentary, from which we have benefitted. While we do not base controversial assertions on Internet information alone, we do credit valuable work we have found there. In fact, our research experience has convinced us that putting this book together in any kind of reasonable time frame, and without prohibitive cost, would probably not have been possible before the Internet. This may in part, at least, explain the absence of a comprehensive treatment of the Austrian Jäger before now. As is true with Jäger troops, so also information on their arms is scattered, fragmentary, and occasionally downright inaccurate.

Our very different training, careers and experiences provided complementary comparative advantages as we have tried to extend our understanding of Jäger history and master the subtleties required for discriminating collecting by non-hedge fund magnates like us. With this has come admiration for those who designed, manufactured and put these arms into the hands of the troops in the face of often unique constraints specific to the Austro-Hungarian Empire, as well as for those who carried them.

As we have attempted to untangle the detail to tell both an accurate and a coherent story, certain realities have been inescapable. First, it was the cultural and human capital of the Habsburg lands, when properly accommodated by military policy, which formed the foundation of the formidable military tradition that remains a source of pride in an Austrian Army that even today regards each soldier as a Jäger. Second, though the details, terms and uniforms may differ, the issues, big and small, that armies grapple with do not change much over time.

As collectors, our errors, missed opportunities, false assumptions, and sometimes painfully misplaced confidence in experts has proven the wisdom of Mark Twain's observation that *"It's not what you don't know that kills you; it's what you know for sure that ain't true."*

What follows is an attempt to present a decidedly non-lethal, but comprehensive, well-illustrated introduction in English to Austrian Jäger arms, equipment, training and tactics, as well as their role in the Habsburg Empire's conflicts. In our treatment of Jäger arms we dispel some confusion and provide examples not heretofore seen in print. With respect to Jäger training, tactics and war-fighting role, our account of Austrian light infantry doctrine and practice in the late eighteenth and early nineteenth centuries differs from what is commonly encountered elsewhere. Far from not appreciating the value of light infantry, the Austrians, after much trial and error, chose a form of functional specialization. Rather than demand what they believed was an unattainable degree of flexibility from their line infantry, the Austrians created instead a dedicated corps--the Jäger-- to pursue a variety of assignments falling outside the capabilities and the mission of their line troops. It is for this reason that we identify the Jäger as precursors of special operations-type forces. Our narrative of the Jäger story from the mid- eighteenth century through the Austro-Prussian War traces a trajectory of organizational expedients and doctrinal development, gradual accommodation, remarkable tactical effectiveness and, finally, misuse bordering on waste.

For those new to the subject we have tried to provide sufficient historical context to make this book a useful introduction. For those who already share our fascination, we hope this book presents enough detail and illustrative material to make it a reliable single-volume reference to what is known and not known about those 18th and 19th century soldiers in pike gray.

The Austro-Hungarian Empire post-1866, following the loss of Lombardy and the Veneto. From Shepard's Historical Atlas, 1911, digitized version courtesy of University of Texas Libraries

GLOSSARY

A

Achselschnur: A green cord loop with tassels that Jäger wore under the arm and over the shoulder, to which the powder horn was attached. The later Austrian and German cord awarded for marksmanship (*Schutzenschnur*) is a vestige of the Achselschnur, as is the Bersagliere cordello.

Adjustierung: Officially published changes to military organization, equipment and armaments from the Hofkriegsrat and later Ministry of War.

Altjäger: A Jäger who has extended beyond his first term of service; a mark of status and not rank.

Attaqueband: Chin strap.

Augustin, Freiherr Vincenz: 1780-1859; Chief of the Vienna Arsenal, Principle Inspector of small arms and artillery and mid nineteenth-century innovator in Austrian weapons design. He was the developer of the Augustin Lock and the machine-made lock.

Augustinschloss: Lock developed by General Augustin to replace the Console lock.

B

Bajonetfechten: bayonet fighting.

Büchsenmacher: Gunsmith/Gun maker.

C

Consolschloss: Lock developed by Austrian financial bureaucrat Giuseppe Console as an expedient to replace the flintlock cheaply by only replacing three parts from the original locks.

Corsehut: Corsican hat, a kind of black felt flat-topped hat with upturned brim worn by various Austrian forces in the eighteenth century, but adopted and retained by the Jäger from 1806.

D

Delvigne: Captain Henri-Gustave; 1799-1876; Hamburg-born designer of various types of improved breeches for military shoulder arms aimed at increasing accuracy and enhancing ease of loading; advocate of the cylindrical bullet.

Diener: Batman/Striker/Servant.

Dienstzeit: Initial period of service.

Donau-Flotilla (K.u.K): The armed river fleet of the Austro-Hungarian Empire which operated on the Danube, Sava and other navigable tributaries.

Doppelstutzen: Double barreled weapon with an upper rifled and lower smoothbore barrel, intended to combine accurate aimed rifle fire with the more rapid fire of a smoothbore.

Dornstutzen: A rifle with a so-called "pillar" breech incorporating a small projection on the face of the breech (*"Dorn"* or *"Tige"*) as a design feature intended to improve accuracy.

E

Ex-propriis Cadet: Literally, from one's own resources, sometimes translated as a "paying cadet." Thus, a cadet accepted for training and service, but who was self-financing, as opposed to an *"ordinare"* or *"Kaiserliche"* cadet enjoying a paid, official appointment. This was often a path for less well-heeled or connected young men to enter the ranks of the officer corps. Radetzky began his army career as an ex-propriis cadet.

Extra-Corps: A type of short shoulder arm issued primarily to Medics, Engineers, Baggage Train, Signal personnel and other support units.

F

Federbusch: Bundle of black ostrich feathers worn on the left side of the Jäger Corsehut.

Feldjäger: Member of one of the Jäger Battalions as differentiated from the Kaiser-Jäger.

Ferdinand I: Emperor of Austria – 2 March 1835 to 2 December 1848.

Flintenjäger: Same as Karabinerjäger.

FM: *Feldmarschall*.

FML: *Feldmarschalleutnant*.

Fourier: Quartermaster.

Fourierschutzen: Quartermaster Clerk.

Franz I: Emperor of Austria. From 1792 until 1835 ruler of the Habsburg lands. From 1792 until 1806 he was, as Franz II, also the last Holy Roman Emperor before it was abolished.

Franz-Josef I: Emperor of Austria – 2 December 1848 to 21 November 1916.

Freikorps: A volunteer military organization that augmented regular troops, sometimes mixing horse and foot. Freikorps units varied significantly in quality from excellent to virtual brigands.

FZM: *Feldzeugmeister*: Rank between Feldmarschall and Feldmarschalleutnant, roughly equivalent to full general.

G

Gaiter: A type of legging that fastened over a soldier's ankle and calf to protect shoes socks and trousers.

Garibaldi, Giuseppe; 1807-1882; Italian nationalist hero. In the USA the name was attached to the Model 1849 Kammerbüchse based on its supposed use by Garibaldi in his Italian campaigns.

GLOSSARY

Girandoni, Bartholomäus: the Tirolian inventor of the Air Rifle (*Windbüchse*) used by Austrian troops briefly at the end of the 18th century, and carried by Lewis and Clark in their American explorations.

Geschichlichkeit: Skill, cleverness, dexterity.

Glied: Literally rank as in the first, second or third lines of a unit in formation. But Glied, like its English equivalent, has two meaning—in addition to referring to one of the lines of a formed unit, it also can refer to a title denoting one's place or category in a military hierarchy, i.e. a Corporal or a Major. In modern German usage, *gliedern* as a verb can mean to subdivide. Other Austrian military terms from the time under consideration here tend to mix meanings in the same way. For example, *Prima Plana* embodies elements of social status, position in a formation and even type of weapon carried. So while "rank" in the sense of a line in a formation can be used as a shorthand equivalent, Glied is more accurately understood as a subset of soldiers in a unit as defined by certain characteristics, including mission-related skill levels and arming. Hence the first and second Glied in Jäger battalions were armed with short muskets (*Karabiner*, first smoothbore, later rifled) while the third Glied, because they were the better marksmen, were armed with the rifled Stutzen, whether they actually lined up that way in formation or not. (One common practice when *line* units sent out skirmishers was to use the third rank for this purpose. Thus in Jäger units designating those armed with the most accurate rifles and most adept at open-order fighting as the *third* Glied is understandable.)

Grenzer: Part-time soldiers in Austrian service from designated military border areas (*Militär-Grenze*) adjoining the Ottoman Empire. Initially commonly employed as irregular horse and foot, but later organized as regular line infantry regiments and even boatman for the Danube Flotilla.

H

Haselstock: A type of heavy (literally hazel wood) cane carried by certain NCO's used in discipline and in directing troops.

Haubajonet: A long broad-bladed bayonet; designed to provide a double-edged, sharp cutting end for both thrusting and to prevent an enemy grasping it.

Hauptmann: Captain.

Hirschfänger: A type of straight or slightly curved short sword or bayonet modeled on those carried by civilian hunters.

Hofkriegsrat: The central military administrative authority of the Habsburg Monarchy from the sixteenth century; replaced after 1848 by a Ministry of War.

I

Inhaber: Literally regimental "Proprietor"; similar to the British Colonel-in-Chief, but who often gave his name to the regiment. In the Austrian Army some served a largely ceremonial role, while others were intimately involved to the point of personally buying and/or approving equipment, arms and uniforms.

J

Jagdhorn: Germanic hunting horn used to signal movement and actions in enemy contact; by the nineteenth century the horn had become a common European insignia for light troops, including Jäger.

Jäger: Literally "hunter"; refers to specialized light, special operations type troops in the German-speaking states; often translated into English as Rifleman, French as *Chasseur* and Italian as *Cacciatore*.

Jägerkarabiner: Shoulder arm shorter than the line infantry musket issued to members of the 1st and 2nd Glied; initially smoothbore, later rifled. Sometimes called in other armies a musketoon. Succeeded by the Kammerbüchse.

Jägerstutzen: Short rifle carried by Jäger troops of the 3rd Glied and various other Austrian soldiers designated as sharpshooters in Freikorps or Grenzer units.

Josef II: Austrian Emperor from 29 November 1780 to 20 February 1790.

K

Kaiser: Emperor.

Kaiser-Jäger: Popular name of a soldier of the Tiroler Jäger-Regiment after 1815.

Kammerbüchse: Shoulder arm with a powder "chamber" at the base of the breech smaller than the bore, allowing the black powder load to act as a "shaped charge" for a consistent burn and increased accuracy.

Kapselschloss: Percussion lock.

Karabinerjäger: Jäger of the 1st or 2nd Glied who carried a *"Karabiner"* or *"Musqueten,"* and later Kammerbüchse, instead of a Stutzen. (In early formations, this was a smoothbore short musket, later rifled.)

Kaskett: Simple stiff leather cap (Casquet) with large brim turned up in front worn by early Jäger troops and other Austrian infantry in the 18th Century.

Kavallet: An iron bed used in barracks.

Kette: Literally "Chain"; a group of 3 Jäger; basic unit for maneuver in a Jäger Company.

Kettenglied: A rank/group of chains; also called a "*Rotte.*"

Kittel: Literally a cotton "smock" or light jacket worn for fatigue duty or in the field in warm climates such as Italy.

Kleiner Krieg: Literally "small war"; the German version of the Spanish *Guerilla* or French *Petit Guerre*-- actions for which Jäger troops were well-suited.

Klumpen: Tactical massing of infantry in dangerous situation, as when threatened by enemy cavalry.

Korn: Literally a "grain" (of wheat for example); name for small bead front sight found on many Jäger weapons.

Krückenmesser: Short knife with which Jäger were equipped in the 18th Century intended to be stuck into an upright or tree to provide support for accurate rifle fire.

L

Laukart Catch: Device for mounting a bayonet to a musket utilizing a large, stiff spring on the underside of the barrel.

Landwehr: In Austria a popular militia, with both compulsory and volunteer components, authorized by imperial patent in 1808.

Leopold VII: Emperor of Austria from 20 February 1790- 1 March 1792.

Lorenz: Josef; 1814-1879; Innovator in weapons design; developer of the first widely adopted series of Austrian percussion weapons.

M

Machine Lock: Refers to the later Augustin locks made entirely by machine at the Vienna Arsenal.

Maria Theresa: Empress of Austria from 20 October 1740 to 29 November 1780.

O

Oberjäger: Rank equivalent to Feldwebel in the regular Austrian Army; Roughly equivalent to the US Army First Sergeant or Sergeant Major.

Oberleib: "Upper Body" or torso; term used in marksmanship training.

Oberleutnant: Senior or First Lieutenant.

P

Patrouillenführer: "Patrol Leader"; Gefreiter in the regular Austrian Army; Lance Corporal/Private First Class.

Porte-Epee: A cord or leather, bullion, woolen or silken band with tassel or knot hanging from an edged weapon. Design/material/color depended upon rank and/or unit.

Piquet: A sub unit in a Jäger Company. A Piquet consisted of 3 men, with 4 Piquets per Platoon.

Profossen: Provost.

Proviantmeister: Commissary.

R

Rashheit: Quickness.

Risorgimento: The nineteen-century movement for Italian independence and unification.

Rotte: Derived from the terminology of Germanic hunters – literally, a herd of wild boar, and thus tough, fast, strong and dangerous; refers to a rank of "Ketten" or groups of three Jäger.

S

Scheibenschiessen: Competition in target shooting. The "Scheibe" refers to the target itself.

Schösselklnopf: A button with which the oak leaves worn by Austrian troops were attached to the headgear.

Spanisches Rohr: A long lightweight cane carried by senior NCO's and officers generally, including Jäger.

Stabsoffizier: Field Grade Officer (Major through Colonel in the US Army).

Stabstrompeter: "Staff trumpeter"; a Jäger who blew horn and later bugle signals to control the movement and actions of Jäger troops.

GLOSSARY

Steinschloss: Flint lock.

Stichbajonet: A socket bayonet designed for thrusting with no cutting edge; narrow in profile, generally for line infantry.

Stutzen: Short rifle carried by Jäger troops of the third Glied and NCO's.

Stutzenjäger: A Jäger armed with the stutzen.

Stutzensack: A leather bag used primarily by Grenzer troops to carry their stutzen or more often their Doppelstutzen.

Schwalbennest: A semicircular device worn on the shoulders of Germanic military musicians.

Scharfschützen: A sharpshooter usually equipped with a stutzen rifle in a Grenzer or line or Freikorps unit.

T

Tirol: A province of German Austria; largely mountainous, with a tradition of cultivating marksmanship and the home of the Tiroler Jäger-Regiment or "Kaiser-Jäger."

Tiroler Hut: A round, large brimmed hat worn by as part of the traditional costume in Tirol. Used by early Jäger usually with back brim folded up.

Tirailleurs: French skirmishers of the revolutionary and Napoleonic periods. Though the term is sometimes translated as sharpshooter, they were almost entirely smoothbore-armed light infantrymen, best known for their open-order, aggressive tactics.

Tornister: Backpack worn by Austrian infantry; cover flap was generally "pony leather" with the hair side out.

U

Unterjäger: A Jäger of low seniority.

Unterleutnant: A junior Lieutenant; "Second Lieutenant".

Unteroffizier: A Jäger non-commissioned officer.

V

Vorposten: A general term referring to pickets, listening posts, observation posts, etc.

Z

Zerstreute Fechtart: A mode of fighting which is decentralized and "strewn" across the battlefield; a Jäger specialty.

Zeughaus: Arsenal building.

Zimmermann: Carpenter.

Zugstift: A long, thin bar on the combination tool which, when inserted into the hole on the ramrod, allows for more torque in removing balls, patches, etc.

CHAPTER 1
BEGINNINGS

Denn Kunst erhöht uns Kraft und Muth,
Wir zielen scharf, wir treffen gut,
Und was wir treffen fällt.

Gewöhnt sind wir von Jugend auf
An Feld- und Waldbeschwer.
Wir klimmen Wald und Fels empor,
Wir waten tief durch Sumpf und Moor,
Durch Schilf und Dorn einher.

Nicht Sturm, nicht Regen achten wir,
Nicht Hagel, Reif und Schnee;
In Hitz' und Frost, bei Tag und Nacht
Sind wir bereit zu Marsch und Wacht,
Als galt' es Hirsch und Reh...

Wo wackre Jäger Helfer sind,
Da ist es wohl bestellt;

Und färbet gleich auch unser Blut
Das Feld des Krieges roth.
So wandelt Furcht uns doch nicht an;
Denn nimmer scheut ein braver Mann
Für's Vaterland den Tod.

Erliegt doch rechts, erliegt doch links
So mancher tapfre Held;
Die guten wandeln Hand in Hand

The Hunter and the Rifle

Feld-Jäger Lied, By Gottfried August Bürger[1] (1748-1794), invokes the cultural underpinnings of the unique military units that are our subject. Accustomed to the forest and its creatures, inured to its hardships, and confident in his ability to defend hearth and Fatherland, the hunter has been a central element in Germanic military traditions since an alliance of warriors led by Arminius destroyed three Roman legions in the Teutoburg Forest in 9 AD.

Key to this confidence was skill with firearms, borne of another Germanic inheritance--the ability to craft rifled arms. In fact, rifling pre-dates firearms; it began as an innovation applied to bolts shot from crossbows. The principle of spinning a projectile in flight to increase accuracy was applied to firearms by Gaspard Kollner, a gun maker in Vienna in the 15th century, and by Augustus Kotter in Nuremberg around 1520.[2] By the Seventeenth century the hunter/forester had become a respected vocation and the sharpshooter who proved himself in spirited

Engraving by C. H. Jeens after P. von Foltz

competitions was an object of his neighbors' admiration. The fusion of these two in the waging of war led to the establishment of nothing less than the first European special operations forces.

Landgrave Wilhelm V. of Hesse[3] was the first German ruler to bring the rifled firearm into military use resulting in some of the earliest references to military Jäger. At the storming of the town of Fritzlar in 1631 during the Thirty Years' War, Wilhelm used three Jäger companies in the assault. These formations were made up of hunters and foresters carrying their own weapons.

Wilhelm's success was noted throughout the Holy Roman Empire. Within a relatively short period Bavaria, Prussia, Austria, Saxony and Hannover pulled skilled marksmen, hunters and target shooters into the ranks with some success in achieving specific, if limited, combat goals.

Militarization of the rifle was achieved often against the advice of officers unconvinced that it was a weapon appropriate for warfare, a prejudice later shared even by Napoleon.[4] A rifle was more difficult and time-consuming to load than a smoothbore musket and a poor platform for a bayonet, thus leaving the rifleman exposed and defenseless –this concern would recur in military debate for decades.

Furthermore, riflemen were problematic soldiers. They made their civilian living as professional individualists at a time when most thought the essence of war was the skillful movement of disciplined masses across an easily comprehensible battlefield under strict fire control. Cocky hunters and foresters, accustomed to operating independently in broken, obstructed terrain, often as invisible to their commanders as to their enemies, promised challenges to the tight discipline and closely-circumscribed movement of soldier and formations that was the essence of armies.

Instead, riflemen shot their weapons according to their own rules and in their own time. For 200 years rifleman volunteers were even granted "special rights"[5] a subversive concept alien to stiff military hierarchies in the German states. Jäger carried their rifles slung over the shoulder, like the hunters they were. They kept their rifles clean and in good repair, but did not burnish them as was the custom in line units. They positioned themselves where their own judgment told them they needed to be to fire effectively. It is no wonder that, for many military leaders, Jäger or sharpshooter units were nothing more than troublesome "clots of uniformed civilians,"[6] and their unique capabilities, accordingly, discounted and overlooked. For the most part, the example of the early Hessian Jäger under Landgrave Wilhelm was obscured by conventional military wisdom and went largely unutilized until the second half of the 18th century.

Of course when Britain found herself at war in North America against colonial rebels, Hessian Jäger were among the troops contracted for with Landgrave Frederich II for American service.[7] Over 1,500 of them served in America in most theaters with great distinction. The hunters and sharpshooters were an obvious choice for conflict in the American forests, but the future would see Jäger troops equally effective much closer to home.

Tirol

The Austro-Hungarian Empire was an agglomeration of rights and authorities amassed over centuries by the Habsburg dynasty in conjunction with their territorial acquisitions, and not a unitary entity like that of Prussia under Frederick the Great or France under Napoleon. Mutual obligations deriving from feudal compacts limited executive authority and protected local rights, or at least provided the basis for negotiating with Vienna. Charismatic figures like Maria Theresa charmed, rationalizers influenced by Enlightenment Reason and Absolutist theory like Joseph II pushed, but there was always a degree of give and take, meaning that the resulting arrangements were rarely optimal from the standpoint of economic or military efficiency. That being said, there was at least one element of the Tirolian social/political order that was a positive enhancement to its becoming the Austro-Hungarian Empire's nursery of independent-minded Jäger troops. As one historian[8] observes, "Tyrol's constitutional and social composition differed greatly not only from those of the five duchies that formed the rest of the territory generally known as the Habsburgs' German hereditary lands, but also from much of Europe. In Tyrol the peasantry formed a separate Estate with voting deputies in all the land's assemblies."

The compact governing military arrangements and obligations in Tirol was the *Landlibell* of 1511,[9] which continued to exert some influence over the military arrangements of Tirol until the fall of the Habsburg dynasty in 1918. By the end of the seventeenth century, Tirol was more or less incorporated into the broader Habsburg scheme, with the monarchs' authority technically deriving from his status as Count of Tirol. But the Landlibell remained as at least a theoretical limit on Tirolian military obligations to the Crown. It provided for Sharpshooter companies (*Scharfschützen*) and a larger reserve militia called the *Landsturm* both of whose duties technically were to be confined to local defense and not service with the Habsburg armies outside Tirol. One source[10] explains that for practical purposes the distinctions between the two were not always maintained, and by the time period of interest here, these could be combined in local battalions comprising a Sharpshooter company and several Landsturm companies. Sharpshooter companies were armed with their own rifles, (Tirol was blessed with high-quality iron ore for barrel-making) with which they also engaged in frequent and spirited target competitions. The Landsturm got whatever else was available to be supplied by the County arsenal established at Innsbruck in the sixteenth century, as augmented with whatever pole arms and edged weapons came to hand. Part of the old arsenal (*Zeughaus*) is still there, incorporated into the Tirolian state museum. Tirolian sharpshooter[11] companies were already formidable defenders of their homeland by 1703 and in that year took a heavy toll of invading French and Bavarian troops during the War of the Spanish Succession with their long- range shooting (one account claims, at ranges up to 500 paces).

By the early 18th century then, the foundations were established for a tradition of Tirolian sharpshooters. They cultivated good shooting and were better armed than their Landsturm comrades. With some likely resulting enhanced status to match, they can even be called elite. Their reputation resulted in high demand for their voluntary service when the Austrian army came to understand the need for such specialized soldiers, and the County eventually gave its name to the only Jäger regiment, as opposed to the independent Feld-Jäger battalions, in the Austrian army.

18th Century Tirolian Sharpshooters

Courtesy of the Palais Mamming Museum, Meran

Grenzer Troops: The Military Frontier as a Source of Austrian Light Troops and its Consequences

Like Tirol, the lands comprising the eastern and southern borders of the Austro-Hungarian Empire were subject to unique military arrangements. After the Ottoman threat began subsiding at the end of the 17th century, these often disorderly areas, sparsely-populated and subject to intermittent migratory flows, were economically marginal, supporting mostly subsistence agriculture and underdeveloped with respect to trade or crafts. Yet these same problematic areas along the Sava and the Danube adjoined a declining Ottoman Empire whose restive western provinces were a source of the kinds of threats, sectarian and ethnic conflict and chaos we are familiar with in failing states in our own time.

Landlords in these areas wanted peasants to till their fields; officers responsible for protecting and extending Imperial borders and keeping order wanted soldiers available locally; waves of Christian refugees from Ottoman-held territory wanted land; the Habsburg army needed men and the vacant eastern lands offered a way to get them without pay, at least part-time.[12] The result, by the mid 18th century, was a Military Frontier system (*Militärgrenze*) the basic element of which was land tenure (military fiefs) generally granted by the Crown to extended family groups (*Zadruga*) with common holdings in return for part-time military service with locally-based Border regiments (*Grenzer*), horse, foot and even military boatmen for service on the Danube. Able-bodied men were available for service as Grenzer with the army where needed and augmented in exigent circumstances by a militia or Landwehr composed of all males up to the age of 60 for local defense.

Well before the Wars of the French Revolution, for all the conflicting interests, off and on reforms and continuing local grievances, the Military Border was providing significant[13] numbers of badly-needed troops, many of high quality despite the generally spotty training to be expected of part-time soldiers, who served Austria-

Hungary well[14] at a very reasonable cost. While over time Grenzer infantry units would be progressively regularized, from at least the 1740's forward they were also used to harass, scout, raid and generally create confusion and alarm in enemy rear areas, what in the 18th century was known as *Petit Guerre*. This kind of activity could sometimes be expanded to include the more disciplined skirmishing, screening, sharpshooting and advance, flank and rear-guard duties later associated with regular light infantry.[15]

To some degree the availability of the Grenzer frontiersmen and their suitability and aptitude for *Petit Guerre* may have complicated development of a true light infantry doctrine and mission in the Austrian army. These half-trained frontier wild men and their skills were hardly universally valued by army professionals. By the middle of the 18th century Vienna was trying to make Grenzer regiments conform more closely in uniform and training to line units. For instance, when consecutive unit numbers[16] were established for the infantry, Grenzer Regiments were included in the system. Generally, though, the Grenzer did not make very good line troops when they were used in that capacity in Austria's 18th century conflicts, but because there was no consensus among Austria's generals regarding the value or proper role of light infantry beyond *Petit Guerre*, there was likewise little inclination to exploit the Grenzer's natural affinity for light tactics to transform them instead into light infantry proper until the turn of the century, and then the effort was halfhearted[17] at best. The Grenzer were an established component of the army capable of performing their limited functions extremely well, but they did not provide the foundation for developing a true light infantry capability for the Austrian army and may actually have obscured the need for one.[18]

JÄGER

Grenzer: Typical frontier Irregulars and a sharpshooter with his characteristing pike/shooting rest and leather bag for carrying the over-and-under double rifle/smoothbore Doppelstutzen.

New York Public Library

CHAPTER 2
EMERGENCE OF THE *FELD-JÄGER*

The Seven Years' War

The *Feld-Jäger* Battalions, which became the basic organizational unit of the Austrian Jäger troops throughout the period of this study, were born in the Seven Years' War, evolved during the wars of the late 18th century and First Coalition and firmly established in the subsequent wars against Napoleonic France and her allies. Like other military innovations, the Feld-Jäger were the children of necessity, and like most successful reforms responded to the enemy's challenge by drawing upon existing societal and cultural assets. The human capital and the tools were there, but it took nearly fifty years for the Austrian generals and military bureaucracy to fashion them into an effective force.

If the Austrian Jäger troops can be said to have had a father it would be Franz Moritz Graf von Lacy, scion of an Irish Catholic family that had followed James II of England into exile after the Glorious Revolution. After commanding a brigade at the Battle of Prague in 1757, Lacy was staff chief (*Generalquartiermeister*) to the overall Austrian Commanders in the Seven Years' War, Prince Charles of Lorraine (Maria Theresa's notably unsuccessful brother-in-law) and Field Marshal Count Leopold Joseph von Daun, who in 1757 dealt Frederick the Great his first serious defeat at Kolin.

Detail of a portrait of FM Franz Moritz Graf von Lacy
Heeresgeschichtliches Museum, Vienna

Among the innovations credited to Lacy in his role as what Christopher Duffy[1] calls "Austria's first Chief of Staff "was the establishment of a *Pionnier-Corps* in 1758 of around a thousand men, which was attached to the Staff (*Generalquartiermeister Stab*). The Pioneers worked in advance of the main body clearing obstacles, repairing and marking roads, bridging and generally facilitating movement of the army. They were men recruited from skilled trades like miners, carpenters and boatmen, who did not need to be trained in the specialized tasks they were to perform in uniform. By 1759 Lacy incorporated another contingent of men who also came to the army already skilled in their essential duties to support the Pioneers. These were two Jäger companies[2], whose primary function was to protect the Pioneers as they went about their work, often in close proximity to the enemy. Of course Jäger contingents had appeared and disappeared earlier in the Austrian army[3] proper, or as Freikorps units. In fact, Christopher Duffy suggests that Lacy's *Deutsches Feld-Jäger Corps*, as it was known, may have drawn for some of its men upon a volunteer Jäger unit already operating in the area of the army's operations: "In the early summer of 1758, a battalion of Tyrolean sharpshooters did much execution during the Prussian retreat (after Kolin) through the tangled hills on the borders of Moravia and Bohemia, and this unit probably furnished the recruiting base for the *Deutsches Feld- Jäger Corps*."[4] Unlike previous ephemeral Jäger units, though, Lacy's make a distinct mark on the records and organization of the Austrian army.

In 1760 Lacy was impressed enough by his Jäger-Corps' performance that he, supported by Field Marshal Daun, petitioned to add four new companies to their numbers, and even procure the very expensive *Doppelstutzen* to arm them[5] (See Chapter 7.) The over-and-under rifle/muskets did not receive bureaucratic approval—the Jäger would instead get the new M 1759 rifle -- the first issue Austrian *Jägerstutzen* (See Chapter 7.) But Maria Theresa herself[6] overruled her coordinating secretariat's decision to also deny the request for an increase in strength, and instead mandated that the Deutsches Feld-Jäger Corps complement be authorized at 1,000 men in ten companies, and the Jäger-Corps would be independent of the Pioneers, though both remained attached to the Staff, and with Pioneer officers commanding the Jäger companies.[7]

Much here sets the pattern for the future Austrian Feld-Jäger Battalions, from recruitment of volunteer hunters and foresters from Bohemia, Moravia and Tirol, to the first issue Jägerstutzen, to operating as detachments in the field, and even down to the pike gray basic uniform shared with their companion Pioneer corps.[8]

Austrian Jäger and Pioneer of the Seven Years' War. Note the green facings black accoutrements and Hirschfänger of the Jäger.

New York Public Library.

In action during the Seven Year's War the Jäger do not seem to have been tied for very long to the Pioneers' apron strings. As early as July of 1758[9], Prussians retreating from Olmutz lost five officers to pursuing Jäger sharpshooters in a skirmish in mountainous terrain. Lacy led this advance force, and as Chief of Staff, would have had Jäger companies with him. Regardless, the lesson does not appear to have been overlooked, and from this point on in the war Jäger detachments are seen accompanying significant independent commands—sharpshooting from cover, driving in pickets, fighting on obstructed ground like an old abattis or towns, covering retreats and supporting advances. By the end of the Seven Years' War the Feld-Jäger Corps are fighting as we know Jäger will fight in the nineteenth century. It remained for the Austrian generals to devise a tactical doctrine to govern their use, and training and command regimes to exploit their natural advantages.

The *Freikorps* Jäger of the Late 18th Century Austrian Wars

Sorting out the history of Austrian Jäger units between the end of the Seven Years' War and the French Revolutionary Wars is a challenge and yields at best a sketchy picture, as the most ambitious modern efforts[10] demonstrate. What emerges in these accounts is a succession of volunteer units raised in the Austrians' characteristically ad hoc fashion that appear and disappear through reorganization, consolidation or demobilization leaving little trace, except for a few recurring exceptions. All are *Freikorps* (volunteer) units, of battalion size, drawing their personnel from line infantry units, sharpshooters from Grenzer formations and individual volunteers, some, like those from Tirol, but not all, from areas exempt from standard military service, as well as foreigners from adventurers to deserters, and commanded generally by professional officers/Inhabers. Mostly we have the names of the units or their commanders and the geographic recruiting area, the theaters of war in which they operated, with little or nothing about their mission. The frequency of usage of the terms *Jäger* and *Scharfschützen* in their titles suggests something closer to the role of Lacy's Feld-Jäger than simply the raiding and harassing functions of *Petit Guerre*, though this certainly varied based on the quality of the individual units. We have found no evidence of the revival of Lacy's staff regiment's Feld-Jäger after 1763, despite the 1769 Generals Reglement calling for their reactivation upon the outbreak of new hostilities and their principal author FM Lacy taking the field in 1778 in the War of the Bavarian Succession. Instead Freikorps Jäger performed functions analogous to those of the Seven Years' War Feld-Jäger Corps. At the end of 1777, two Tiroler Scharfschützen battalions are described as serving as the staff infantry regiment, while six months later the vanguard of FM Lacy's army includes 400 Scharfschützen[11].

After the close of the Seven Years' War Austria mobilized three times-- in 1778 for the War of the Bavarian Succession, in 1787 for the last Ottoman War, and in 1789-90, while still engaged with the Turks in the east, in response to renewed tensions with Prussia. For all of these conflicts the Austrian army depended upon Freikorps volunteer units[12] to provide Jäger troops. In 1778 a *Tiroler Scharfschützen-Corps* was raised from volunteers from the Tirol willing to serve outside their home province, Grenzer sharpshooters from border regiments and line infantrymen who were demonstrably skilled marksmen. Unlike most of these Freikorps Jäger units, the Tirolians persist into the Napoleonic period, eventually evolving, with the addition of other volunteer cadres, into the first regular Austrian Jäger regiment in 1801.[13] More typical is the Moravian-Silesian *Gebirgsjäger*, formed at the same time, disappearing otherwise from the records, except for a Moravian-Silesian Jäger battalion, which may or may not be a successor, noted after 1805.[14]

The War of the Bavarian Succession, in which the Prussians unsuccessfully invaded Bohemia from east and west, furnished a sad coda to the career of Prussia's great warrior king. Avoiding large pitched battles, Frederick's old opponents Austrian Marshals Lacy and Laudon, both well acquainted with the value of

Freikorps Jäger of the late 18th Century. Figure on the left represents a Jäger in a mixed Freikorps formation known as the Green Laudons, originally formed by FM Ernst Gideon Freiherr von Laudon, which saw service in various conflicts up to the War of the First Coalition. Elements of the Green Laudons were incorporated in nos. 3 and 4 Light Infantry Battalions of 1798-1801. The Loudon Jäger seems to be carrying a hanger reminiscent of the standard Austrian grenadier saber, while the Jäger on the right carries a straight-bladed Hirschfänger with its typical shell motif guard.

N.Y. Public Library.

effective light troops[15], managed, through a war of defensive positions based on interior lines, augmented by skillful raiding and effective disruption of Prussian logistical arrangements, to make life miserable for their opponents, thus giving the conflict its sobriquet "The Potato War." Jäger units were admirably suited for this war of raids and skirmishes, with their old patron and advocate Franz Moritz Graf von Lacy combining small-unit offensive operations against enemy supply lines with an overall static defense to checkmate the Prussians. Eventually Austrian financial woes and a Russian-French mediation forced a negotiated peace which yielded the Hapsburgs little, but the expansion of Jäger volunteer units in subsequent conflicts suggests they had, once again, demonstrated their value in Bohemia in 1778-9.

Ten years later, as what was to be the final major conflict with the Ottoman Empire loomed, Austria attempted to raise a volunteer Jäger force of 2,500 to 3,000 men. In an unusual move, volunteers were permitted from all 37 districts from which the regular German Infantry regiments were normally drawn, as well as the County recruiting area normally restricted to Tirol's *Land-und-Feld Regiment*.[16] But the ambitious goal of 20-25 companies was not attained, and the recruits raised were distributed among regular infantry regiments and pioneers, as well as the Danube flotilla. On a smaller scale, a regular infantry lieutenant, Andreas Boer,[17] was permitted in 1789 to recruit 500 volunteers in the eastern Hungarian counties of Arad and Bihar, which became known as the *Boer'sche Scharfschützen-Corps*. This unit had the dubious distinction of numbering an unusually large proportion of poachers and other n'er do wells in its ranks. Nevertheless, it was later permitted to absorb Bosnian veterans of another volunteer unit, and saw service in the Banat during the war. At least some companies of the Tiroler Scharfschützen-Corps also served in the Turkish theater, before being transferred west as another conflict with Prussia threatened at the end of 1789.

By early 1790 a Corps of Observation was being assembled in Bohemia and Moravia in anticipation of hostilities resuming with Prussia. The principal volunteer

Jäger formations deployed there were the Tiroler sharpshooters and a so-called *Deutsches Jäger-Corps*, a consolidation of the smaller Sinzendorff and Dandini Freikorps units. As extended talks began following the accession of Leopold II in 1790, Austria saw fit to demobilize the Freikorps Jäger by the end of the year. Peace agreements with the Ottomans and the Prussians were concluded in 1791, not least because what the Austrian Chancellor Kaunitz had been calling "the French nonsense"[18] was looking less like a fortuitous weakening of a major rival, and more like a serious threat, both strategic and tactical.

CHAPTER 3
JÄGER IN THE WARS AGAINST REVOLUTIONARY AND NAPOLEONIC FRANCE

The Wars of the First Coalitions

Austrian *Schadenfreude* at the discomfiture of a traditional enemy and illusions of limited interventions in collaboration with counter-revolutionaries was shaken by aggressive French moves along the Rhine and in the Habsburg's Belgian provinces, followed by a French declaration of war in the spring of 1792. Within a year, in addition to Austria, Prussia, the Dutch Republic, Hesse, Hanover, Spain and the Holy Roman Empire were at war with revolutionary France.

Faced with conducting far-flung offensive as well as defensive operations principally with masses of recruits distinguished more by their revolutionary ardour than rigorous training, often commanded by former noncoms and junior officers, the French were forced to improvise tactics that made do with these limitations while exploiting what advantages they had. Necessity and experimentation bred adaption and adaption bred intelligent design. What eventually developed was streamlined organization and looser tactics whose success depended less upon drill than mobility. Relatively large numbers of French skirmishers in extended order acting in cooperation with simplified masses of infantry and well-handled artillery delivered French successes in the 1790's.

Oversimplifications and exaggerations abound about the capabilities and impact of French Revolutionary infantry. For example, as Rory Muir points out, it was not "untrained recruits fired by revolutionary doctrines and adept at using their initiative," who made the most effective skirmishers, but rather experienced solders from specialized light units.[1] Nevertheless, French mobility, heavy use of skirmishers to screen advances, disrupt the opposing lines and cover retreats, paired with effective artillery, whose largely bourgeoisie officer corps spared it the revolutionary dislocations of the other branches, needed to be countered. Masses of French skirmishers could not be allowed to approach the formed lines of their opponents unopposed. The same was true of mobile artillery adept at operating in close support of French infantry. Without an opposing screen of skirmishers to discomfit and drive off the French gunners, unacceptable damage would have been done before the formed bodies of troops could close, while skirmish screens by their nature would suffer less from this same artillery than their closed-up comrades.

Austrian generals resorted to a variety of ad hoc alternatives to confront the French tactical challenge. In this case necessity was not so much the mother of invention, as merely of making do until something better turned up. Despite the successful record of Lacy's Feld-Jäger companies in the Seven Years' War, and the effectiveness of the volunteer Jäger in later conflicts, there was no attempt to create regular army Jäger units. Once again, the only Austrian Jäger deployed in the 1790's were with Freikorps units. In addition to the by now familiar Tiroler Scharfschützen-

Corps there were three others—the German Jäger-Corps (also known by the names of a succession of commanders, including Geppert, Dandini, Mahony, Plank and D'Aspre,) The Dutch Jäger-Corps, also known as the Le Loup Feld-Jäger-Corps after their commander, Lt. Colonel Johann Le Loup, and the Lombard Jäger-Corps, sometimes known by the name of its first Inhaber as the Würmserische-Freikorps, and sometimes as the Lombardisches Jäger-Corps Corti after Colonel Antonio Corti, a subsequent commander.[2] Generally speaking these units were composed of two battalions, with the battalions numbering about 500 men each, though often operating tactically as independent companies.[3]

An early-war example of an experienced Jäger detachment's tactical effectiveness comes from fighting at Aldenhoven during the Austrian advance on Aachen in 1793[4]:

"Several [frontal attacks against] the French positions were in vain, and all were repulsed with heavy Austrian loss. French fire was so effective that the Austrians abandoned Röthgener Castle and Oberröthgen again, pulling back behind the Patternhof and taking cover in a huge orchard east of this farmstead. The stalemate lasted until about 13.30 pm. Around that time two locals reported to the Austrians that they knew a way to reach the French positions unseen and were willing to guide them.

"[1 ½ companies of Tyroler Jäger were detached] these locals led them through a deeply cut hollow road into the Eschweiler Forest, from here following a path hidden by trees and thick bushes, right behind the French positions on the Stich Hill. Arriving there, the Tyroleans at once opened fire at the surprised French gunners and the infantry covering them. The French limbered up their guns, and retreated hastily along the road to Stolberg, crossing the Inde Brook, and following the road through the village Eilendorf to Aachen. They were pursued for a while by part of the Jäger. On the Stich Hill the French had abandoned much of their baggage and ammunition."

This was Jäger operating in their classic fashion: in detachment, independent of the formed main body, and out of sight of anyone but their immediate commanders, utilizing their skills at concealment and sharpshooting.

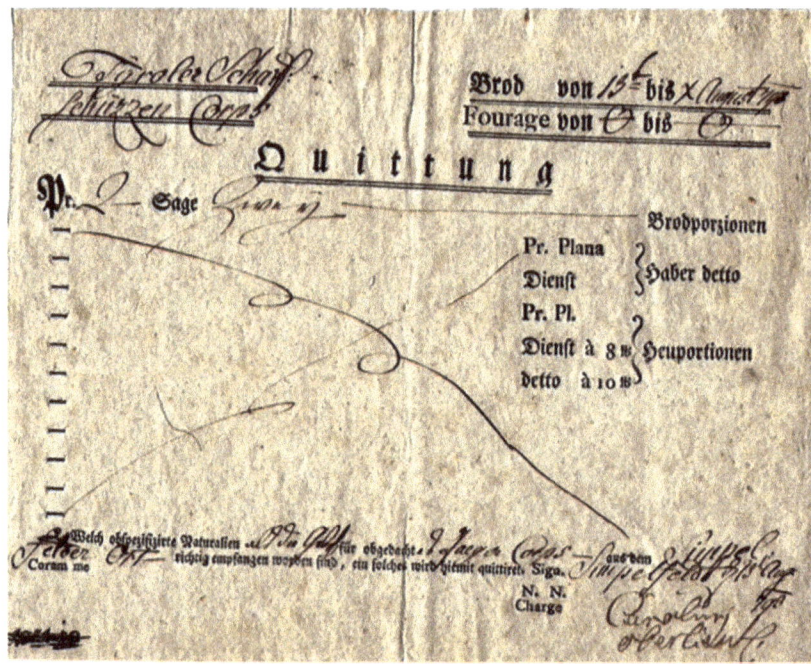

A Tiroler Scharfschützen-Corps rations receipt of 1793.

Authors' Photo

Jäger also were employed to screen in advance of the main formed body, counteracting the enemy's skirmishers by turning the tables on them. Colonel, later Brigadier, Guillaume Philibert Count Duhesme[5] who served in Flanders, observed:

"The Austrians came on with more, and more skilful and seasoned, light troops; their Tirolians and Le Loup Jäger were known and dreaded in the early engagements. The fear, panic and collapse of the advancing columns of troops from Valenciennes and Lille must be attributed to the enemy slipping along the flanks of these columns. Their riflemen, hidden in brush, in ditches, punished our formed battalions, which, bravely in line, were decimated without seeing their enemy. Many fine officers fell victim in this way to sharpshooters in these early skirmishes."

In addition to the Freikorps Jäger, Austrian commanders drew on Grenzer and regular line infantry units as well mixed Freikorps formations, like the Green Laudons to counter the new French light tactics.

Authorities like Rothenberg and Hollins[6] regard the Grenzers' effectiveness as light troops as having diminished overall since the Seven Years' War because of their postwar incorporation (Generals-Reglement of 1769) into the army as regular line units, while maintaining their strictly part-time military obligations. While it may be true that this "hybrid" condition, as well as significant losses in the Turkish War, could have made Grenz Regiments generally less effective as light troops, the Grenzers who took the field in 1792-97 did not do so in the formations prescribed in the 1769 regulations. Instead two combined (*componierte*) six-company Grenz infantry battalions culled from several regimental districts and two combined 4-company battalions of Grenz-Scharfschützen were mobilized.[7] The skirmishing value of detached companies of picked men armed either with Doppelstutzen or Jägerstutzen[8], and, as such, subject to more extensive training and a larger allocation of practice ammunition than the line, cannot have been entirely negligible[9].

The final Austrian expedient was to order some regular infantry out of the line to serve as skirmishers, sometimes in combination with Freikorps and Grenzer, sometimes when no other light troops were available. As early as 1793 Prince Josias of Saxe-Coberg, Austrian commander on the Lower Rhine and Flanders, prescribed deploying the third rank[10] of formed infantry forward in independently-operating platoons (*Zug*) combined with light cavalry to clear French skirmishers.

Various commentators refer to the third rank of line infantry being detached for flank, screening or "reserve" duty in the War of the First Coalition, some attributing it to provisions in the 1769 Regulations which allows for such an expedient, with others pointing to the generally broken terrain of Flanders necessitating alternatives to fighting in linear close order.[11] Contemporary anecdotes seem to suggest some Austrian success in discomfiting the French on these occasions. Duhesme describes how:

> "[The Austrian skirmishers,] well commanded, disputed ground just long enough to make us waste time and our own *Tirailleurs*. They enticed us from one position to another till they reached that which they really intended to defend. There they let us use up and scatter our last battalions, whose ardour shattered itself against their prepared positions. Fresh [Austrian] troops would then counterattack in the most perfect order, in turn throwing out skirmishers upon our flanks, and thus attacking at advantage troops dispersed and fatigued, our units in disorder and unable to rally most of their men."[12]

The Austrians managed, by turning to whatever happened to be at hand on a particular battlefield, whether Freikorps Jäger, Grenzer, line troops, or a combination thereof, to respond to the tactical challenges they encountered. In his study of the work of Prussian military reformer Johann Yorck, count von Wartenburg, Peter Paret credits the Austrians with greater adaptability: "Austrian commanders ... with their strong and well-integrated complements of light troops, were sometimes tempted to adapt to the new conditions, [while for their Prussian counterparts] tactical formations were not modified during the war against France. Change, for the time being, was a topic for discussion, to be advocated or condemned rather than carried out."[13] It is always easy to classify some commanders as flexible and visionary and others as rigid and pedestrian in their tactical thinking, but, instead, Paret makes a more valuable observation: "The problem of innovation was partly one of timing. At first, any change, regardless how necessary, could lead only to confusion and reduced effectiveness." Transitions are always difficult, as the transitional situation, by definition, incorporates new and old imperatives, allowing neither to be ignored, but instead requires striking a balance between them.

The Austrian attempt to strike such a balance is illustrated in tactical instructions, *Observationspunkte*,[14] for general officers campaigning in Germany in 1796. These, while conceding grudgingly that there may occasionally be no alternative to employing skirmish tactics for some offensive movements, insist that tight, linear formations are preferable. Drawing on Austrian experiences in Flanders, the instructions concede that the conditions made it difficult to attack in tightly-ordered lines with the "unfortunate consequence for the army of upsetting the ideas on the true method of attacking the enemy…Even by the line infantry attack *en tirailleurs* [was] almost the only method [feasible]." Yet the instructions go on to lament the "misuse [that]…weakens the impetus of the attack," cautioning commanders against losing time either by skirmishing or by the fire of small groups, and encouraging instead doing everything possible to maintain cohesion and close order, insisting that well-trained infantry advancing rapidly in closed ranks is what wins battles. Even if "when attacking a village or wood it be considered useful to employ a few companies or scattered *tirailleurs* which would be supported by companies or battalions in close order, it should be impressed on the men that as soon as the company commander has the drummer beat alarm, they must gather by him without the least waste of time, and reform." Rothenberg notes[15] that the lesson drawn from the campaigns of the 1790's as embodied in the *Observationspunkte* as well as subsequent regulations, was that only a small portion of the troops available be employed as skirmishers, and that "skirmishing was conceived basically as defensive, screening the closed formation against hostile skirmishers" and therefore that skirmishers only be employed close to the main body, easily recallable.

The challenge of balancing tight linear order and close tactical control with the messy realities of war against Revolutionary France produced mixed, not to say conflicting, Austrian tactical doctrine in the last years of the eighteenth century. Moreover, none of the instruments for applying this doctrine on the battlefield—Freikorps Jäger, Grenzer, or regular line infantry—combined the skills and discipline required to maintain the delicate balance Austrian commanders sought. In the brief 18-month respite after the Peace of Camp Formio in 1798, the Austrians began a series of reforms including introducing new arms (see Chapter 7), and augmenting the cavalry and artillery. The reforming impulse also extended to creating fifteen battalions of light infantry. If skirmishing was to be tightly-controlled and closely coordinated with the main body, what better way to insure it than to introduce to light tactics on the battlefield all of the discipline and professional incentives of the regular line infantry?

A "Peculiar Ephemeral Creation: "The Light Infantry Battalions 1798-1801

"A peculiar ephemeral creation halfway between Jäger and regular German Infantry"[16] is how Ottenfeld describes the fifteen battalions of regular Austrian light infantry established in 1798. These were built around existing individual Freikorps formations, augmented by new recruits from various Habsburg-ruled areas including Italy, Hungary, Galicia, Croatia and Slavonia. Some of the better Freikorps units, such as the Green Laudons, Würmser, elements of the Erzog Carl, and others were included in this reorganization.[17] The Tiroler Scharfschützen-Corps, Le Loup, The Deutsche Jäger-Corps (aka Mahoney, D'Aspre, et. al.), however, retained their Freikorps status. The new light infantry battalions were designated by a number 1-15, but were also known, as was the Austrian practice, by the name of their commander. Unlike regular line units, they had no Inhaber, perhaps suggesting something of a stepchild status. These battalions only existed for three years and were dissolved, the troops being then incorporated into line infantry regiments at the end of the

War of the Second Coalition in 1801.

Light Infantry in the "Roman" or "classical" leather helmet authorized in 1798 and worn by Austrian line infantry through the 1809 war. Note the Jägerkarabiner-type shorter musket and the officer's Spanisches Rohr cane. Presumably the officer's sword is the M 1798 for light infantry officers Ottenfeld notes in his table on p.830.

Print after Rudolf von Ottenfeld

We know very little about the light infantry battalions and why they did not survive after the Peace of Luneville. Austrian Major Wrede,[18] writing at the end of the nineteenth century, provides a thumbnail sketch of the history of each battalion. While there is little basis to form a judgment about their effectiveness, there is also not enough, in our view, to support the harsh general condemnations of supposed Austrian lack of appreciation for, and facility at, light infantry tactics found in accounts by modern historians, most notably Rothenberg.[19] What little we can glean from Wrede suggests a mixed bag, with a few units involved in big battles like Stockach and Marengo, as well as smaller engagements in the Alpine passes, while others seem to have been dispersed in occupying towns, and, finally, one Italian unit that *"kam nicht vor dem Feind"* [20] at all. August Gräffer, writing around 1800, provides more detail in his still curt accounts of each battalion's history through 1799[21] and the picture that emerges remains mixed, but Gräffer identifies more successful assaults, skirmishes and river crossings, than does Wrede, while also noting reverses.[22]

At the Battle of Stockach, 20 March, 1799, Corporal Jacob Fleischer of Light Infantry Battalion Nº. 12 (Rubenitz) leads a detachment of volunteers to wooded high ground to deliver flanking fire against French cavalry attacking a smaller force of Austrian Uhlans. The 12th Battalion had been established in 1798 primarily comprising veterans of the O'Donnell Freikorps.

From a print by T. Mollo

Based on admittedly limited information, we suspect that this Austrian compromise proved a bad bargain all around. Subjecting Freikorps veterans to regular discipline and drill, while attaching them to a variety of commands, under conventional commanders who may or may not have known how to manage or use them to advantage is not likely to have been a prescription for spectacular success. In all, this short-lived light battalion expedient most likely fell victim to a failure at the doctrinal and command levels, rather than as a consequence of the quality or capacity of the troops or their immediate commanders.

The next effort at enhancing Austria's light infantry capability, in contrast, was built on the experience of the best Freikorps Jäger formations—those very units that had remained independent of the light battalions of 1798. It suggests not so much a lack of appreciation for light tactics as a conscious prioritization and preference for functional specialization.

Finally, there is in an 1859 popular account of the life of Marshal Radetzky, an anecdote and accompanying engraving depicting an unconventional/combined arms episode involving Freikorps Jäger at the Battle of Marengo.[23] Radetzky, then a Colonel, was Adjutant-General on the Austrian commander Melas' staff, but had previously in the campaign commanded an Italian Pioneer battalion. He was with a detachment of Pioneers and Jäger reconnoitering for a spot to build a short bridge over a flooded, muddy-bottomed ditch to permit Austrian troops to attack into a gap that had opened in the French lines north of Marengo village. The bridging work had begun, but time was short. Radetzky is said to have suggested to the commander of the Pioneers that he have some of his men form several human bridges (*lebendige Brücken*) to permit Jäger and infantry to cross so that he could lead them in a surprise assault on the village. The authors, in addition to his ingenuity and courage, credit Radetzky's generosity for giving the Pioneer commander, a friend, full credit for the human bridge expedient.

Jäger and Hussar officer (Radetzky) crossing human bridge of Pioneers at Marengo. Note that Jäger are portrayed accurately with black cross belts and Jägerstutzen while Pioneers' belts are white.

Engraving by Leutmann, Kuhn, Raffet, et. al.

The Tiroler Jäger Regiment

The demise of the Light Infantry battalions notwithstanding, the need for an Austrian capability for disciplined skirmishing, screening, sharpshooting and advance, flank and rear-guard duties remained. The short interval between the Peace of Luneville and the disasters of 1805 saw a second attempt at regularizing Freikorps light infantry. This time men from the best volunteer units would be gathered together in Austria's first Jäger regiment, followed over the next decade by a succession of Feld-Jäger battalions. If the light battalions had been square pegs crammed into round holes, the new Jäger formations were an organic creation, exploiting existing Austrian cultural and human capital in much the same manner that the new French light tactics had done.

Like most Austrian military reforms, those that created regular Jäger formations were nothing radical, and they looked back as much as forward. The objective since 1792 had been to meet the French *Tirailleurs* and mixed order with controllable, ordered skirmishing and sharpshooting-- that did not change. Instead there seems to have been recognition that the desired results were more likely obtainable by building the new light formations around skilled independent fighters "*Einzelkämpfer*," leaving the work to those who had already acquired the skills to do it,[24] and then constructing a military organization around them that army traditionalists could tolerate, if not always wholly embrace. For the traditionalist, training line troops to operate independently could never have been an attractive alternative—success bred as many concerns as failure, after all. Better to respond to harsh tactical necessity by employing a relatively small number of anomalous troops, already because of their backgrounds inclined to independence of thought and action, segregated in their own small units, and circumscribed by a command structure at least theoretically capable of enforcing orthodox incentives and promotion rules. This kind of wary integration of unconventional specialist units into armies has not been confined either to the early nineteenth century or to Austria.

The Tiroler Jäger Regiment was authorized by an order of 22 September, 1801.[25] Originally comprising three battalions of six companies, this regiment was formed with troops from the Tiroler Scharfschützen-Corps, the Deutsche Jäger-Corps (also known at the time by the name of their commander, Kurz) and the Le Loup (*Niederländischen*), Jäger-Corps. Additional men were drawn from Infantry Regiment Number 46, whose recruitment areas was Tirol, but was then stationed in the Veneto. The regiment's Inhaber was Field Marshal Gabriel Marquis de Chasteler de Courcelles. Lt. Colonel, later Field Marshal, Philipp Ritter Fenner von Fennerberg was commander. Fenner led the Tiroler Scharfschützen-Corps in the Turkish War and the Wars of the First and Second Coalitions. In 1809 he would be assigned to a command in his native Tirol, but would rejoin the Jäger after 1815.

Philipp Ritter Fenner von Fennerberg, 1759-1824, first commander of the Jäger Regiment. Here he is pictured later in life wearing the Order of Maria Theresa he was awarded at the end of the wars against Napoleonic France.

From a portrait by Wilhelm Hecht

The outbreak of the War of the Third Coalition in 1805 found the Tiroler Jäger Regiment battalions dispersed, as would continue to be the norm in the future, attached to various larger commands. The First and Second Battalions found themselves with General Mack's main army in Germany, while the Third Battalion was assigned to Archduke Johann's corps in the Tirol. In the confused marching and counter-marching and various, sometimes inexplicable, detachments that characterized the self-styled "Unfortunate Mack's" erratic handling of the army in October of 1805, the First Battalion made its mark[26] before the final disaster. As part of a brigade under General Konstantin Ghilian Karl D'Aspre (an experienced light infantryman who had earlier commanded a Jäger Freikorps unit) assigned to guard the Danube crossing northeast of Ulm at Gunzberg and locate the approaching French on the north bank of the Danube, the First Battalion made contact with Marshal Ney's advance guard on 9 October. The Jäger held the French long enough for Austrian infantry and guns to come up to defend the crossing, but two companies of the Jäger, two guns, and General D'Aspre himself were captured by the French on the north bank.

The two battalions were reunited on 15 October when both found themselves defending the last hill before Ulm, the Michaels-Berg. Ney stormed the heights, placed his artillery and Mack's fate was sealed.

The Second Battalion, commanded by Fenner himself, successfully evaded the initial French net at Ulm because in the confusion that prevailed in Mack's doomed army after the Michaels-Berg skirmish, General Franz Jelačić's Corps, to which they were assigned, decamped[27] south—whether on Mack's order or not is unclear. The battalion distinguished itself during the retreat to Vorarlberg, according to Wrede,[28] but eventually was surrendered with the rest of Jelačić's infantry to Marshal Augereau in November. The troops were paroled with a promise not to serve against France for one year and allowed to march to Bohemia.

Following the disaster of Austerlitz Austria was forced to accept the Treaty of

Pressburg (26 December, 1805). Among Pressburg's punishing terms was Austria's surrendering Tirol and Vorarlberg to Napoleon's ally Bavaria. As a result the Tiroler Jäger Regiment was redesignated in 1806[29] as the Jäger Regiment Number 64, with its new recruitment area extended to any German-speaking Austrian districts.

Archduke Karl and Jäger Expansion 1806-1809

Archduke Karl (Charles) of Austria, Duke of Teschen, younger brother of Emperor Franz I, is the most complex of the key characters in Jäger history. Arguably Karl was Austria's most successful battlefield commander against revolutionary France and Napoleon—an inspiring leader with the capacity to manage large bodies of troops as successfully as any of Napoleon's opponents. He also applied himself diligently over many years to preparing the Austrian army to confront each phase of the Napoleonic onslaught. As such, it was necessary for Karl to operate within the most rarified circles of court and bureaucracy, and his influence varied accordingly, depending on the ebb and flow of imperial whim and ministerial politics.

Karl is not a favorite of modern historians, who regard him as a well-intentioned, but cautious, sometimes defeatist[30] figure who just could not confront the real challenges that Austria faced:

> "Before military reform could become effective, a thorough reform of Austrian society and state was required and neither the archduke nor his opponents were willing to go that far…As a recent historian observed: 'A service whose most influential reformer was a conservative contending against soundly entrenched reactionaries, could never become fully reconciled to the techniques and to the energy and activity demanded of modern war.' In the end, though much was accomplished, much was left undone." [31]

Certainly the Archduke was no radical and he probably would have concurred with Disraeli's sentiment that: "Toryism is worn out and I cannot condescend to be

The Archduke Karl in 1812, by Isabey.

The Albertina Museum, Vienna

a Whig." His prime objective always was preserving the dynasty and therefore its principal support—the army. Whatever caution he exhibited, on the battlefield or in the counsels of state reflected this fundamental principle.

By the beginning of 1806 Austria's preeminent general had pressed his claim as the indispensable man successfully, and at least for a while the shaken Emperor concurred, appointing the Archduke as *Generalissimus* to command all forces in wartime and to "supervise and direct" the entire military establishment in peacetime,[32] including controlling the *Hofkriegsrat*, the central military administrative authority of the empire. But whatever paper authority conferred at this or any other time, evaluations of the Archduke Karl's reform efforts between 1806 and 1809 can never overlook the simple fact of Austrian life: "Charles was not Napoleon, and Francis was not the Directory."[33]

The 1806-9 reforms concentrated on improving the regular forces' ability to carry out their conventional missions in the traditional manner. Occasionally novel elements appear, including expanded treatment of open-order tactics and skirmishing in the 1807 regulations, but on closer examination these apparent novelties defer to the traditional verities—closely-controlled, rigorously-disciplined movement, well within sight of the regimental and even brigade commanders. Karl was no close-minded conservative; he was a realist whose ambitions for a revived Austrian army reflected priorities derived from his experience in the field. For the Archduke, it was steady, well-drilled and motivated line regiments that won battles for Austria, regardless of the tactical value of light troops. As far as light tactics were concerned, the 1807 regulations seem informed by the proverb *"Wer zwei Hasen auf einmal jagt bekommt keinen."* (He who chases two rabbits at once will catch none.) The new regulations effectively de-emphasized anything but the most limited and controlled[34] skirmishing and other open-order fighting by line infantry.[35] For less conventional work something else was needed.

By early August of 1808,[36] the Archduke was making the case to the Kaiser for an expanded specialized Jäger force to fulfill Austria's future need for effective light infantry-- insisting the Jäger Regiment Number 64, was only an essential first step. In deference to the budgetary constraints of the time, Archduke Karl recommended a cadre system be adopted,[37] dividing the existing Jäger regiment into nine "divisions" (2 companies) with these scattered in likely recruiting areas throughout the German-speaking portion of the Empire (four in Bohemia, two in Moravia, two in Austria, and one in "inner" Austria). Each of these divisions could serve as a core for a future battalion. Comprising these core divisions would be *"Waldjungen"*-- professional hunters and proven sharpshooters who met all army standards. Additional reserve

Limited and controlled skirmishing for line infantry as envisioned in the 1807 Regulations. Watercolor by M. Yung, from Album de 16 Battailles de la Revolution et de l'Empire, Paris, Henri Plom, 1860.

personnel needed to bring the battalion up to strength would be enrolled from the division's district and train with their division for three weeks in the first year, and two weeks in subsequent years.[38] Divisions would consist of 270 active Jäger during peace time. With two reservists to be recruited per active duty Jäger, each division could be expanded rapidly into a battalion of six companies in wartime.[39]

On 18 August 1808, the Kaiser ordered adoption of all of the Archduke's recommendations, placing Karl personally in charge of the new Jäger organization. Indicative of the army's strained circumstances, it was stipulated that recruits should bring their own rifles until the imperial system could provide appropriate arms.[40]

Even with an Archduke heading the effort, the expansion of the Jäger corps did not always go smoothly. Among Karl's requests approved by the Kaiser was the power to appoint commanders for the new Jäger divisions. These were to be men selected for their special qualities, both leading and training Jäger, and managing the reserve component—neither quality necessarily found in the average line infantry officer. Even a distinct professional career track for Jäger officers was envisioned.[41] But within a month of the Archduke's appointment, some putative subordinate of the Archduke's in the Hofkriegsrat instructed all line infantry regiments to transfer any "excess" officers immediately to the Jäger. This was naturally an opportunity for alert regimental commanders to jettison their dead wood. Accordingly, plenty of the "sick, lame and lazy" officers from line regiments were sent to the Jäger, even one who had already been medically discharged.[42] After it was brought to his attention, in late September the Kaiser called a halt to this dumping of unsuitable officers on Jäger units, and the Jäger officer billets were for the most part satisfactorily filled.[43]

By November of 1808 larger events seem to have overtaken the original plan. Sentiment for renewed hostilities with France was growing. Already Austria was discussing forming a new alliance against Napoleon.[44] In the Jäger case divisions were to be expanded immediately to their full six-company battalion strength of 860 under the command of the current officers.[45] It is worth noting that with this change of plan a hard-pressed military administration which had to count every Kreuzer, led by a supreme commander a modern observer dismissed as "still mired in the eighteenth century,"[46] chose nevertheless to bring the Jäger battalions to full strength on the brink of a new war. It is difficult to reconcile this decision with a hidebound Austrian devaluation of light troops.

The Austrian regular army of 1809 consisted of sixty-one line infantry regiments of three battalions each, a Grenadier division, seventeen Grenz infantry regiments of two battalions each, thirty-five cavalry regiments, five field artillery regiments, a five-company Bombardier Corps, small contingents of technical troops like

Pioneers, Sappers, Miners and Pontonniers as well as the just over 9,700 men of the nine Feld-Jäger battalions. Total paper strength was about 470,600.[47] This number was theoretically augmented by the compulsory Landwehr and some volunteer Landwehr units.

The Feld-Jäger Battalions were commanded by Majors, Lieutenant Colonels, or Colonels. These "staff" officers (comparable to our current concept of "field grade") were appointed directly by the Kaiser. Companies were commanded by Captains or Captain-Lieutenants.[48] There was no official tactical handbook provided for Jäger battalions, beyond a short tract of 1810 which Rothenberg describes as consisting "merely of instructions for the individual manual of arms." [49]

One of the great benefits of the Jäger units in the cash-strapped Austrian Army was their relatively lean logistical requirements. For the most part they supplied/resupplied themselves with pack horses, unlike the line infantry that required large baggage trains. Besides being less expensive, this light mode of logistical support also enhanced the mobility of the Jäger in all types of terrain.

Minimum height requirements for a Jäger were "5' 2" or 5' 3" ", with 5' 1" being acceptable in "serious cases." These men, after a four-week trial period, were to serve for the new term of ten years, as had been adopted for all infantry in Archduke Karl's reforms. At the end of their *Dienstzeit*, they had the option to reenlist for periods of six to ten years. These reenlistees were referred to as *Kapitulants* and were allowed to marry. Their male children had the opportunity to be educated in the Kaiser's *Knaben – Erziehungsheim*, a sort of boarding school system provided for the sons of the Kapitulants.[50]

While Jäger uniforms and equipment are dealt with in detail in Chapter 4, what was to become their iconic black, tall flat-topped, turned-up Corsican Hat (*Corsehut*) appears in its familiar form during this period before the outbreak of war in 1809. Earlier Jäger had worn a leather casquet, low hat with upturned brim at the back or the "classical" or "Roman" helmet. The Corsehut certainly was not exclusive to them after Austerlitz. Pioneers, some artillerymen, sappers, miners and other auxiliary branches, as well as many Landwehr and volunteer units also were issued forms of the Corsehut, but the Jäger tenaciously retained it, if in somewhat altered form, throughout the nineteenth century.

Evolution of Jäger headgear, Print after Rudolf von Ottenfeld

Defeat and Glory: 1809-1815

The War of 1809 (War of the Fifth Coalition) ended in a crushing defeat for Austria, resulting in loss of about 20% of her pre-war population in the harsh territorial settlement imposed by Napoleon and his Bavarian allies in the Treaty of Schönbrunn in October 1809. But Austrian skill in nearly bagging Davout's exposed corps around Regensburg (Ratisbon) and sheer tenacity in the big battles around

Vienna at Aspern, Essling and Wagram, stunned the French, to the point that Napoleon would later silence disparagement of the Austrian army with the retort:" It is obvious that you were not at Wagram." [51]

The Jäger battalions were distributed among three Austrian corps[52] at the beginning of hostilities in the spring, often deployed in mixed detachments with light cavalry screening advances. The 7th and a company of the 8th Feld-Jäger Battalions, attached to the II Austrian Corps as part of the northern arm of the drive into Bavaria, on 13 April encountered French cavalry probing east towards Amberg. After the accompanying Uhlan picket was driven in, the Jäger posted themselves skillfully in a long wooded defile at Ursensollen and drove the French back, with both sides suffering significant casualties in the skirmish. The next day an advance element of I Corps, including the 1st 2nd and 3rd Feld-Jäger Battalions, was ordered to replace the II corps units and continue to probe westward in the area. The Jäger annoyed the Austrian cavalry general commanding the detachment with their persistent sniping at the French light infantry and battery they encountered near Allmansfeld and were ordered to cease fire and merely observe the enemy.[53]

Austrian efforts on the south bank of the Danube came to a bloody end in the Battle of Eggmühl and subsequent French storming of Regensburg (Ratisbon). The 7th Feld-Jäger Battalion was part of the small Austrian garrison holding the town, losing more than 50 % of its strength in the battle.[54] During the retreat from Regensburg we encounter the first reference to a name later esteemed in Jäger history. Unterleutnant Karl Kopal,[55] of the 6th Feld-Jäger Battalion was wounded leading his half-company in a rear-guard action on the town's outskirts keeping the retreat route open, and was promoted to Oberleutnant. Colonel Kopal would lead his 10th Feld-Jäger Battalion (Chapter 5) in their defense of the cemetery at Santa Lucia outside Verona in May, 1848, and died after losing an arm in the successful assault on Madonna del Monte at the Battle of Vicenza the following month.

In the remaining big battles of 1809 the Jäger battalions are not uncommonly seen employed like line infantry, proving themselves equal to the best. At Aspern the 2nd Battalion was with Winzingerode's Brigade in their frontal attack on the village and its subsequent tenacious defense. Three Jäger officers of the 2nd were mentioned in dispatches for their heroism at Aspern.[56]

The 1st, 2nd, 3rd and 8th Battalions fought in the tremendous two-day battle at Wagram in July. With over 300,000 troops engaged it was the largest battle in history up to that time. The 8th Feld-Jäger performed both light and conventional tactical roles on the first day. Along with a battalion of the volunteer Archduke Karl Legion, the 8th initially delivered effective flanking fire from concealed positions against advancing Saxon troops.[57] They later withdrew to the village of Baumersdorf, which protected a key crossing of the Russbach stream, initially neglected by the French. Baumersdorf's two bridges were finally attacked by a famous French line infantry regiment nicknamed The Terrible 57th. "[T]he Austrian Jäger could not be budged. Mostly recruited from the Alps or the hills of northern Bohemia, the defenders were physically some of the strongest soldiers in the Habsburg army, and more than a match for the 'Terrible 57th' who for the first time in their regimental history, fell back in disorder." The Archduke Karl was on hand to witness these events since he had ridden up to lead a light cavalry thrust against the stalled French advance. At the end of the first day, Baumersdorf was still in Austrian hands.[58] Nonetheless; the second day of Wagram handed Napoleon an expensive victory and the effective end of the war along the Danube.

In the Tirol, the 9th Feld-Jäger Battalion served under the former Inhaber of the original Jäger regiment of 1806. General Johann Gabriel Chasteler de Courcelles, with a 10,000-man detachment from Archduke Johann's Army of Inner Austria, was sent to upper Tirol to assist an indigenous Tiroler revolt against their newly-installed Bavarian rulers and protect the right of the Archduke's main army operating further south between the Adige and the Piave. Small detachments of Jäger accompanied by a few light cavalry were used to bolster the spirited, but often disorganized Tirolian rebels at key locations.⁵⁹ The difficult terrain also required posting detachments in the mountains to secure lines of communication.⁶⁰ By May Chasteler was forced to retreat north while Johann was pushed back beyond the Isonzo and into the Inner Austria from which his army drew its name. During Chasteler's retreat a Division (two companies) of the 9th Feld-Jäger and five Tirolian volunteer companies were credited with a stubborn defense of Strub Pass, just southwest of Salzburg, against a Bavarian brigade of 3,000 with 12 pounder and howitzer batteries.⁶¹

The War of 1809 (War of the Fifth Coalition) ended with an armistice in July and subsequent harsh peace settlement (the Treaty of Schönbrunn) in October. In a political shift the Kaiser dismissed Archduke Karl under the guise of taking personal command. As one historian observes: "So ended the military career of the best general Austria then had, and probably the best she ever had." ⁶² Karl died in 1847, but never served in the field again.

When Napoleon invaded Russia in 1812 Austria was obliged under the terms of Schönbrunn to send a corps in support of the Grande Armee. While there was supposed to have been an understanding between St. Petersburg and Vienna that neither would engage the other traditional ally any more vigorously than appearances required, the Austrians fought well enough for the Russians to deliver a protest citing their secret agreement.⁶³ The 5th and the 7th Feld-Jäger Battalions, in company detachments, raided Russian supply lines, took a Russian field gun and routed a battalion of Russian Jäger at the point of their bayonets.⁶⁴

For the remainder of the wars against Napoleon Jäger battalions continued to be employed tactically in a mix of light and line-infantry functions. They were represented at the big battles of Dresden⁶⁵ and Leipzig and in the invasion of France. Occasionally, as in the case of the 1st, 2nd and 6th Feld-Jäger Battalions, there is a degree of functional specialization reflected organizationally by their assignment in 1813⁶⁶ and later to the so-called "Light Division," commanded by an aggressive cavalryman, Prince Moritz von Liechtenstein. The frequent pairing of light cavalry with Jäger, often in small advance detachments, gave rise to the Austrian Hussar's axiom "The right stirrup belongs to the Jäger," referring to the practice in situations of "necessity or sudden danger [whereby] the Jäger winds his left arm round leg and stirrup together, keeping his rifle ready under his right arm, and is carried off by the Hussar as fast as the horse can be made to go under the double burden."[67]

Taking the Napoleonic Wars as a whole, as we have seen, Jäger units were called upon to serve multiple tactical functions. From that of conventional line infantry, to the kind of flanking, advance and rear-guard skirmishing, sniping, harassment and disruption of formed units, operations against enemy rear areas, in broken terrain and villages and even supporting indigenous rebels against a common enemy, Jäger roles frequently corresponded what in later armies becomes the domain of Special Operations Forces.

A Jäger outpost with Hussars,

From a painting by Franz Habermann

CHAPTER 4
JÄGER IN THE AGE OF METTERNICH, 1815-1848

1815: Italian Harbinger

Joachim Murat, King of Naples and Marshal of France, abandoned Napoleon his patron and brother-in-law following the Battle of Leipzig, signing a treaty with Austria, and joining the Sixth Coalition against France in early 1814. The son of a bourgeois farmer and innkeeper, Murat began to fear that the Congress of Vienna would restore his Neapolitan crown to the Bourbons, and so when Napoleon returned to France from exile in The Hundred Days, the flamboyant cavalryman embraced his old comrade in arms once again and declared war on Austria. The Austrians mistrusted Murat and had assembled a force in Lombardy in anticipation of such a move. The resulting short campaign of 1815 foreshadowed Jäger campaigning in Italy over the next fifty years, and also saw the first operations by what came to be known popularly as the "Kaiser-Jäger."

At the end of Austria's long struggle against Napoleon the Austrian army fielded a dozen independent Feld-Jäger battalions. December of 1813 saw the initial step in reviving the old Tiroler Jäger Regiment --in a new form, but with an old commander, Lt. Field Marshal Philip Freiherr Fenner von Fennerberg as Inhaber. Fenner in 1813,[1] operating on the right flank of the Army of Inner Austria, was pushing back with raids into his native Tirol and received both a wound and the cross of the Order of Maria Theresa for his efforts. At the end of 1813,[2] an imperial order created the *Fenner-Jäger-Corps*, initially as one battalion, which was to be recruited from the restored county. The battalion commander would be Karl von Call, who had been Lt. Colonel of an infantry regiment, born a Tiroler in Bozen (Bolzano). The Fenner-Jäger were to be organized along the lines of the Austrian Feld-Jäger battalions, but after the re-establishment of Austrian control of Tirol in 1814, volunteers were sufficient to permit expansion to three battalions of four companies each. Major Peter Freiherr Pirquet von Merdaga, another holder of the Order of Maria Theresa, formerly of the 8th Feld-Jäger Battalion, was initially appointed to command of the Second Battalion (he would subsequently take command of the First). By July of 1814[3] the Fenner-Jäger, effectively now of regimental size, under a new overall commander, Colonel Karl Schneider, Freiherr von Arno, along with elements of Nº. 9 and Nº. 11 Feld-Jäger Battalions, became part of the Austrian buildup in Lombardy against Murat. Schneider, seven times wounded in his previous service, had also been awarded the Maria Theresa Order, and commanded the 2nd Feld-Jäger Battalion at Dresden where he led their assault on the Machzinsky Redoubt and suffered a severe leg wound. At the upper levels, at least, standards for Fenner-Jäger officers seem to have been high.

Although often dismissed as a vainglorious attempt to maintain a comic-opera kingdom,[4] with little support from his putative "subjects," Murat managed to move north swiftly in the spring of 1815 with a force of about 50,000. At Rimini on 31 March he issued a proclamation full of liberal and nationalist sentiments calling upon all Italians to unite against the Austrian interlopers in Lombardy and the Veneto: "Italians! The hour has come to engage in your highest destiny." He took Modena, Florence and Bologna, initially pushing the scattered Austrians north of the Po. Murat's objective was Milan, capital of Austrian Lombardy, where he anticipated large numbers of Napoleonic veterans would join him. The reorganized and reinforced Austrians stopped Murat's forces at the Po, and after two days of fighting at Occhiobello, the campaign turned in Austria's favor. Murat was forced to retreat and was brought to battle by converging Austrian forces in early May at Tolentino in the Marche. At the end of three days' fighting Murat's fate was sealed. His army broke apart and by the end of the month, abandoned by his generals who signed a peace with Austria, he fled to Corsica. Murat was captured by Neapolitan troops in October and executed by firing squad. Vain to the end, he asked his executioners not to aim at his face.

The Fenner-Jäger were assigned in late March to the II Corps of Frimont's Army of Italy commanded by Feldmarschalleutnant (FML) Bianchi. By April, however, they were serving with FML Neipperg's I Corps. Adam Albert, Freiherr von Neipperg, a diplomat as well as a soldier, was a figure of some eminence, if for nothing else becoming the lover, and later husband, of Napoleon's second Empress, Marie-Louise of Austria. An energetic and aggressive light cavalryman, Neipperg seems to have had the wit to use the Jäger effectively, but also kept them on a tight leash, sometimes restraining their aggressive instincts. Neipperg employed the Jäger as an advance guard and in raiding across the Po after the Battle of Occhiobello, as well as in the relief of Ferrara. (See map, Chapter 5.) Neipperg ordered several descents by Major Peter Martin Pirquet's First Battalion, Fenner-Jäger on the coastal area south of Ravenna, sometimes in company of a half-squadron of dragoons,[5] progressively pressing on Murat's right flank. On 21 April Pirquet's battalion took a bridge over the Savio River, north of Cervia, by direct assault, at the cost of twelve dead and twenty-six wounded. Continuing south, on 23 April at Cesenatico, on the Adriatic coast just north of Rimini, Pirquet, despite the relatively open surrounding countryside, infiltrated the town unseen and led 200 of his Jäger and 26 dragoons over the town's bridge, and overwhelmed the unsuspecting Neapolitan infantry, numbering around 1,800, before they could fire a shot. Pirquet estimated that initially more than 1,500 laid down their arms, but because so many of his Jäger were occupied in plundering, many Italians retrieved their arms, some began firing and most eventually were able to flee. The final tally was about 300 prisoners.[6]

Fenner- Jäger and Austrian dragoons at Cesenatico.

Detail of a painting by Franz Habermann

The loss of his position on the Savio and skirmish at Cesenatico with its threat of continued Austrian movement south along the Adriatic coast endangered Murat's right, contributing to his decision to give battle at Tolentino. The 9th Feld-Jäger Battalion[7] fought with FML Mohr, commanding Bianchi's left and center, at Tolentino and afterwards in combination with Austrian cavalry rounded up fleeing Neapolitans. R. M. Johnston in his account of the battle observes that the Austrian commander at a critical point shifted the Jäger to his left "to strengthen his line. He relied greatly on their good rifle practice, for he was very weak in artillery...When within firing distance the Jäger and Austrian field-pieces sent a plunging fire down the hillside on the Neapolitans, and nearly immediately they broke."[8]

After taking Cesenatico Pirquet had hoped to move further south continuing to discomfit the retreating Neapolitans, but instead he received from Neipperg what was in fact a second order recalling him to his base at Adria,[9] north east of Ferrara, to reunite the Fenner–Jäger battalions (the first instruction having been countermanded after the Savio River crossing when Neipperg ordered Pirquet instead to continue south.) Once back at Adria Pirquet was lionized. He reflected in his diary: "I have not given up a single prisoner, and have earned the confidence of my soldiers"[10] On 4 May Pirquet led two battalions of Fenner-Jäger toward Mantua, eventually rejoining the main army destined for the occupation of France.

In the spring of 1815 along the Adriatic coast between Cervia and Cesenatico the Fenner-Jäger were operating 123 km (76 miles) from their base, in an "inhospitable landscape"—open, largely uncultivated, crossed by many drainage ditches, with "precarious visibility,"[11] despite this they managed to move quickly and stealthily enough to surprise the large garrison in Cesenatico, and by the next day their commander was ready to resume the move south. The Jäger practice of operating without a baggage train but only pack mules certainly contributed to this mobility and stealth. It may also help explain the lapses Pirquet noted[12] in which his Jäger are occupied with plundering the prisoners in hand rather than securing others. As the local historian Ferretti[13] notes, the bleak area the Jäger had just traversed, in which the few inhabitants subsisted on frogs, eels, carp and whatever little could be cultivated in the arid soil, likely made the temptation of the Neapolitans' haversacks impossible to resist.

With Murat's army broken the bulk of the Austrian force in Italy turned to France. While Austria was not involved directly in the Waterloo campaign, Frimont's Army of Italy crossed the Alps via Susa and Mt. Cenis, before Napoleon's second abdication, eventually occupying the great French arms manufacturing center of St. Etienne.[14] We can only speculate about how arms stocks that eventually were inventoried in Austrian arsenals as captured French weapons, including what became the barrels for the Model 1842 Kammerbüchse, came from new arms from St. Etienne. This would certainly account for their condition being good enough for Ferdinand Früwurth to utilize in the '42's. (See Chapter 7) The Fenner-Jäger served as the Austrian advance guard in crossing the Ticino into Piedmont (the Kingdom of Sardinia) and the Second Battalion continued to lead the advance over the Alps. The 9th Feld-Jäger Battalion, too eventually was ordered north and served in the Austrian occupation force in France[15].

The "Kaiser-Jäger" Regiment

An imperial order issued from Paris on 14 August, 1815 authorized expansion of the Fenner-Jäger-Corps to form the "Tiroler Jäger-Regiment" of four battalions, with the necessary additional troops to be recruited from Tirol and Vorarlberg. Returning Napoleonic veterans were a source of additional men.[16] The order was effective 1 January, 1816,[17] with Kaiser Francis himself as Inhaber, (origin of the regiment's unofficial but ubiquitous appellation *Kaiser-Jäger*) seconded (*Zweite Inhaber*) by Field Marshal Fenner. The date for inception of the Tiroler Jäger-Regiment is commonly acknowledged in Austria as 16 January, 1816[18] which is when

Officers and men of the Tiroler Jäger-Regiment (left) and Feld-Jäger Battalion Nº. 4. Note the initially-prescribed tight "Hungarian" trousers.

From: Abbildung der k.k. Österreichischen Armee durch alle Waffengattungen, engravings by W.W. Waniek, 1820

Heeresgeschichtliches Museum, Vienna

the Regiment's depot and staff headquarters were opened in Innsbruck, to which the unit had returned from France in late 1815. Innsbruck thereafter embraced the Regiment as its own and is the site today of the *Kaiserjägermuseum*. The Regiment was armed as follows: ⅓ with Stutzen and Haubajonet, and ⅔ with smoothbore, Stichbajonet, and some form of infantry saber, consistent with the practice in Feld-Jäger battalions.[19]

First deployments of the Regiment were against local insurgencies in Italy[20]--initially the First and Fourth Battalions to Naples in 1821 in support of the restored Bourbons, who along with the Piedmontese monarchy faced constitutionalist agitation by the liberal secret societies known as the *Carbonari*. In 1831 the first three battalions were dispatched to various central Italian cities as the Holy Alliance tried to sustain the postwar order created there by the Congress of Vienna. The Third Battalion remained garrisoned in Parma for four years while the 10th and 11th Feld-Jäger Battalions were deployed in various restive Italian cities and towns.[21] While Murat's Proclamation of Rimini had been largely a loud noise from an empty vessel, Italian nationalism was indeed smoldering and would blaze up along with other revolutionary movements across Europe in 1848.

Jäger Organization, Training and Uniform

With the Tiroler Jäger-Regiment in 1816 joining the twelve Feld-Jäger battalions, Austria's Jäger force assumed the form it would retain until 1849. Likewise by the Age of Metternich, the organization, training and uniform of the Austrian Jäger had also more or less taken the shape they would retain for most of the period covered by this account. It is therefore appropriate at this point to turn to these distinguishing features of the Austrian Jäger forces.

Organization

Like Lacy's original Deutsches Feld-Jäger Corps, the Tiroler Jäger Regiment of 1801 and the Jäger battalions proposed by Archduke Karl in 1808, a Jäger battalion of 1848 consisted of six companies.[22] With each company numbering 231 men, peacetime Field Battalion strength was 1,402. In wartime a seventh Depot Company was formed by requiring each field company to give up 40 men resulting in wartime battalion strength of 1,257.

The Battalion staff consisted of one "Staff Officer as Commander," one Adjutant, one Senior and five Junior Medical Officers, one Paymaster (*Rechnungsführer*), three *Fourieren* (Quartermasters), one *Fourierschützen*, one staff trumpeter, and two "Strikers" (batmen or servants). During hostilities, a Commissary Officer (*Proviantmeister*), a Wagon master/*Profossen* (Provost), a Gunsmith and an additional Striker were added to the table of authorizations.

Each Company was commanded by a Captain or *Captainleutnant*, consisted of one *Oberleutnant*, two *Unterleutnants*, two *Oberjäger* and eight *Unterjäger*, ten *Patrouilleführer*, one Quartermaster clerk, two Trumpeters, one Carpenter, 200 Troopers and 3 Strikers (batmen –*Diener*) for a total of 231 Men. In wartime, this number grew to 247 men with the addition of 4 Unterjäger, 10 Patrouillenführer, one Quartermaster, and one carpenter. Companies carried a number as well as the name of their commanders. A Division, a common tactical unit, was two companies. They were designated as Right, Left and Middle Division.[23] The six-company organization would be reduced in February, 1849 for most Feld-Jäger battalions to four companies.[24] Battalions number 8, 11, 23, 24, and 25 retained six companies. In 1861, the organization reverted to six companies per battalion.[25]

In light of the effectiveness of the Feld-Jäger battalions in 1848, the Austrian army augmented the original 12 in 1849 with 13 more (numbers 13-25) and another seven in 1859 (26-32). With the 1849 expansion, the first non-Tirolian Jäger Battalions were raised in Transylvania (numbers 23 and 28). In 1860, two Hungarian Jäger Battalions were raised (31 and 32). Five composite Feld-Jäger Battalions were formed from the 2nd Depot Companies raised for the 1866 campaign by each regular battalion, becoming numbers 33-37.

Training

In 1802, then Major Max Sigismund Armand Josef von Paumgartten, (1767-1827) a soldier with significant experience with Jäger units in multiple campaigns, wrote a manual, the *Abhandlung über den Dienst der Feldjäger zu Fuss*. Paumgartten's treatise is comparable to a combination of the US Army Ranger Handbook and the Infantry Small Unit Leader's Guide.[27]

Paumgartten describes the missions, formations and techniques of Jäger forces in the Austrian army providing a complete guide for the young officer and NCO. His book, if not directly, then at least by implication, provides the criteria for training Jäger to accomplish their missions in the manner prescribed.[28] The emphasis in Paumgartten was on the Jäger mission in the "*kleiner Krieg*" or small war,[29] and in this respect remarkably prescient.

In addition to Paumgartten, Leopold Freiherrn von Unterberger (1734-1818) published in 1807 branch-specific guidelines for the training in, use of and care of firearms and equipment in the Austrian army, *Wesentliche Kentnisse der Infanterie-Cavallerie Feuergewehre zum Gebrauch der Offiziere der k.k. österreichischen Armee*.[30] It includes sections dedicated to Jäger weapons and training.

Unterberger provided detailed guidance[31] for officers regarding the proper use of the bayonet including not permitting troops to dig with the bayonet or stick it into the ground. For Unterberger, the bayonet, if misused, would diminish the primarily defensive effectiveness for which it had been designed. He also provided practical advice on caring for shoulder arms (for example, don't allow troops to bang butt plates on the ground during drill, as this can cause damage to the stock and contribute to the loosening of all components).[32] He provided precise instruction on how to pack weapons for wagon transport to avoid damage, and practical advice such as "pick up lead after firing on the range; this can be added to the lead from Infantry muskets and reused."[33]

More generally, Unterberger understood the proper function and real value of the Jäger. Because they did not shoot in ranks or in controlled volleys, but individually, the Stutzen (*Kugelstutzen* or *Bürschtrohr*), up until then reserved largely for hunting and target shooting was an appropriate arm for them.[34] He noted the advantage was accuracy, the drawbacks slowness of loading and the need for greater care to be taken when cleaning the rifle.

A third unofficial source of guidance for the conscientious junior officer appeared in 1812, written by a Jäger Oberleutnant, August von Constant Villars.[35] He had served with one of the nine short-lived Jäger Divisions, (N°. 3,) established by the Archduke Karl in 1808. Since these two-company cadres were to form the core of a wartime expansion into full Feld-Jäger battalions, it is not surprising that an officer assigned to one would have undertaken a guide of this sort. The *Handbuch ueber des Vorposten-Dienst zum Gebrauche des Jäger-Officiers im Felde* seems to have been completed in 1810 after the end of the War of the Fifth Coalition, and was published in 1812 in Linz,[36] where the 3rd Feld-Jäger Battalion was stationed, as new hostilities loomed.

Constant Villars' 164-page handbook is an operations manual for Jäger officers and cadets with emphasis on the range of possible detached and unconventional missions and situations readers might encounter. These include combined Jäger/light cavalry patrols, covert and/or night patrols and other detached duties, advance, rear and flank guard, uses and perils of various natural and man-made terrain features, ambush, foraging, attacking pickets and small detachments, villages or walled positions, even the various difficulties potentially encountered in carrying off captured cannon. A representative excerpt[37] in translation here—is a scenario in which a mixed Jäger and light cavalry detachment on patrol meets and engages enemy cavalry.

> "*On encountering the enemy*: If the (cavalry) advance guard discovers a not very formidable enemy in the distance, the Jäger lie down in concealment, and some

of the cavalry—the best horses only-- go forward, skirmish with the hostile patrol, and push forward if the enemy flees. The remainder of the cavalry will hold back, concealing themselves.

If the advancing cavalry are pursued rashly by the enemy, the concealed Jäger spring up and give them a salvo at 10 paces, on which signal the hidden cavalry breaks out of cover, the retreating cavalry reforming behind them, and the now blown enemy, diminished by the unexpected attack by the Jäger, will be easily taken or cut down."

Jäger and light cavalry advance guard

From a lithograph by Matthias Trentsensky

Heeresgeschichtliches Museum, Vienna

As far as official Army publications go, a substantive guide appeared in January of 1841, when the *Hofkriegsrat* published detailed regulations on the training of Jäger forces including descriptions of their assigned missions and how they were to be accomplished.[38] While the only earlier official publication was the thin volume of 1810, noted above as having been of little value,[39] its inadequacies were, as we have shown, more than compensated for by unofficial works, whose content is largely echoed in the succeeding official guidance.

The 1841 regulations specify that Patrouillenführer and Unteroffiziere were required to be good shots and effective instructors. Instruction in marksmanship (*Scheibenschiessen*) and bayonet fighting (*Bajonetfechten*) were designated the responsibility of these relatively junior NCO's.[40]

Officers were to be well-trained in placing listening/observations posts or detachments to the front of main bodies (*Vorposten*), to provide early warning and to force the enemy to deploy prematurely into combat formations, as well as patrolling, reconnaissance of an area, leading an advanced or rear guard action, the attack, the defense, and also as secondary instructors in marksmanship and bayonet fighting.[41]

Marksmanship training was designed to product excellent shots at long range. The Stutzenjäger were required to engage consistently the target's upper center of mass (*Oberleib*) at maximum effective ranges. Karabiner-Jäger, the less-accomplished shots, less well-armed, were only required at maximum effective range to hit the target. Stutzenjäger were trained only to shoot when assured of a hit while the Karabiner-Jäger were to maintain a constant volume of fire.[42]

The 1841 regulations prescribed that loading and shooting be taught and practiced in the kneeling, sitting, and prone positions. Jäger were to be taught to shoot moving targets as well as to shoot with a fixed bayonet.[43] Of the annual ammunition allowance for training, the regulations required that 50% would be used for targets at 300 paces or less. 25% was to be used at distances of 300-600 paces, and 25% at 600-1200 paces. The high value placed on good shooting is demonstrated by the approval of a marksmanship cord (in subsequent form called the *Schutzenschnur*) and cockade in 1851 for wear by Jäger who had achieved high levels of shooting proficiency. Further evidence is that an Austrian army always short of cash, nevertheless awarded monetary prizes to outstanding marksmen.[44]

Essentially Jäger training was aimed at equipping them not to decide battles, but to direct the action. Jäger troops were to strike the enemy well in advance of the army and act as a potent security screen. Defined missions included advance and rear guard, and the attack and defense on broken ground unsuitable for line units including gorges/ravines, mountain passes, forests and villages.[45]

Jäger with a civilian guide on reconnaissance

Detail from an engraving by A. von Jochen

New York Public Library

They were to train to fix enemy skirmishers well forward of friendly positions to keep enemy forces confused as to the nature of friendly defensive dispositions or axes of advance and well away from them. Jäger were to be capable of securing the flanks of large columns on the march and were taught to seize and occupy houses, bridges, and forests, protecting and clearing the main axis of advance.[46]

Training incorporated the principle that only one quarter to one third of the Jäger Company would be deployed at a time. The remaining force was located 150-200 paces to the rear, providing tactical support as well as a source of reinforcement and resupply. Divisions forward were rotated to allow for rest, weapons maintenance and redistribution of supplies and ammunition.[47]

Jäger defending against Light Cavalry. Note the Klumpen of Jäger at the left.

Engraving by Franz Habermann.

Jäger units were trained in conventional line infantry formations as well as some unique to their units. While they may have been required to learn the line evolutions of the day, the 1841 regulations specifically require that the Jäger be distinguished by skill and competence (*Geschichtlichkeit*) as well as speed and quickness (*Raschheit*).[48] To this latter end, Jäger also underwent an intense program of physical training, including long distance running, sprinting, and running backwards.[49]

The Jäger learned a *"zerstreute Fechtart"* meaning a "strewn" or scattered- type of fighting – not centralized, but rather spread out over the terrain. This included training in the effective utilization of terrain for the "standing fight", the attack, the retrograde movement and the defense against cavalry.[50]

Jäger were taught to fight in "chains" (Ketten) of three men. A "rank" of these chains (*Kettenglied*) was called a *"Rotte"* (term translated as "horde" and used, in hunter's language, to describe a herd of wild boar). There were three steps between men in a chain, with the Stutzen-Jäger in the middle. Depending on terrain, eight steps separated chains. Terrain was used for cover and concealment and chains were trained to provide mutual fire support.[51] Unterberger showed great concerns about the survivability of the Jäger *"im Voposten."* He was, like many European senior officers of the day, worried that the slowness of rifle loading in an exposed position left the Jäger vulnerable to cavalry and infantry attack. He believed the short sword he carried was useless to the Jäger after he fired his rifle in the face of the enemy. The Jäger in this scenario had the choice of running away or of being captured,[52] which accounted for Unterberger's championing of the *Haubajonet*, which he regarded as serving primarily a defensive function. The sharp partially double-edged socket bayonet, when fixed, would not interfere with shooting or loading and could not be easily grasped and removed by the enemy. With the Haubajonet the Jäger could better defend himself against infantry and cavalry and, in the right circumstances, attack with it.

The 1841 regulations required that Unteroffiziere be trained to control the fight and were therefore to be located behind the Ketten. They were taught to observe enemy movement and to react quickly to either counter enemy successes or exploit observed weaknesses. To do this, they utilized no less than 19 horn signals, all of which the Jäger had to be trained to recognize.[53]

After 1849, much of the Jäger training dictated by the 1841 regulation remained the standard, though the new *Stosstaktik* prompted much additional training in the bayonet attack in the 1850's and 60's.

The relatively complicated, decentralized and independent missions assigned to the Jäger troops would be difficult today even with modern communications equipment and GPS technology. The tactical competence of the Jäger in all of these assigned tasks in all theaters in which Austrian troops campaigned, is a tribute to the professionalism of the officer and NCO corps in the Jäger units and is the best measure of an intense, focused and ultimately highly successful collective training philosophy.

The effectiveness of all of the Jäger training, both individual and collective, is borne out by the competence, discipline and record of these Jäger units in every campaign conducted by Austrian ground forces. As to marksmanship, a kill shot at 600-1200 paces (about 500 -800 yards) is something that eludes most of today's soldiers even with high tech modern weaponry. The degree of skill attained then by the Jäger is the domain now of Special Operations.

Jäger Uniform and Equipment

Little is written about the uniform and equipment of Jäger troops prior to the mid 18th century. Jäger serving at that time likely wore the civilian forest green clothing dictated by their profession.

In the 18th century, Lacy's Feld-Jäger were assigned to Pioneer units and wore the "pike grey" uniform jacket of that arm, but trimmed in green rather than the

Pioneers' black.[54] "Hungarian" cut (relatively tight) grey trousers with dark green trim, and Hungarian boots were issued to these Jäger troops. A grass green waistcoat was also worn. Most representations of Jäger of the Seven Years War period show the casquet—a plain low leather cap with turned up front brim. By the 1770's Ottenfeld/Teuber indicates a "Corsican" hat, with turned up rear brim was worn, with a white/green feather holder and a white/green tassel.

Jäger uniforms of the Seven Years' War period

New York Public Library

The frog for the saber as well as the saber belt was of black leather, thus establishing the pattern of black accoutrements for Austrian Jäger troops. A raw calfskin *Tornister*, (rucksack) a cartridge box with black shoulder strap, and a rifle sling of black *Juchtenleder* ("Muscovy leather") were also issued.[55] NCO's received a pair of leather gloves, and a porte-epee.[56]

For the earlier period we don't know a lot about Jäger officer's uniforms. In Lacy's day, since the Jäger were attached to the Staff Infantry Pioneers, a staff infantry officer uniform or a pioneer officer uniform would both be plausible. By the early 19th century,[57] officers of Jäger troops wore the pike grey tail coat with grass green trim, narrow fitting pike grey (Hungarian) trousers with gold braid on the seams and knee length boots. A black and grey sash was worn, silk for field grade and camel hair for company grade officers. A pair of light yellow gauntlets and a gold port epée with fringe was also issued. Doctors wore the pike grey jacket with black trim.[58]

The bicorn hat was akin to that worn by infantry field grade officers-- black with gold border lace trim, a loop of gold over the top to secure the black cockade and a golden rosette in the right and left corners.[59]

Enlisted uniform was similar to the officers. A pike grey coat and trousers were complemented by knee length boots (replaced by shoes and low-cut black cloth gaiters with 6 buttons in 1818).[60]

In the late 18th century Jäger and other related units like the Tirolian Sharpshooters wore a regulation casquet. This was a simple low leather cap with the brim folded up in front. It had a green pom-pom and the national yellow and black cockade on the left side and a brass plate with the imperial cipher in the front. Similar versions of both of these were worn by Austrian forces of various types.[61] Freikorps Jäger in the 18th century seem to have preferred the Hessian or Prussian style of Jäger uniform, including a tricorn hat.

The Tiroler Jäger and Scharfschützen in the late 18th-century in many instances adopted the native round, wide brimmed Tirolian hat (*Tiroler Hut*) with the brim turned up in the back or on one side.[62]

"Chasseur Tyroliens, 1793" A Tiroler Sharpshooter of the early French Revolutionary wars period. He wears the Tirolian hat turned up at the back.

Albert Grégorius

Jager did for a short period adopt the impractical "classical" 1798 leather helmet with the imperial cipher and their own green crest, rather than the usual yellow and black.[63]

Jager circa 1798, print after Rudolf von Ottenfeld

The enlisted hat after 1806 was the *Corsehut* (Corsican hat) with a bundle of black feathers (*Federbusch*) with *Attaquebändern* (chinstraps) fastened under the chin with leather buttons. A heart-shaped brass hat badge, with three points up and one down, was engraved with the battalion number[64] was prescribed, but may not always have been worn.

Also issued were a cotton *Kittel* or smock for fatigue duty, neck scarves that sensibly do not seem to have been rigid stocks, a small hammer to assist in loading, a *Holzmütze* (tompion) to keep the bore dry in wet weather, and variegated short grey gaiters with six buttons.[65]

Hair was to be cut short.[66]

Company trumpeters were distinguished by their grass green *Schwalbennester* (swallows' nests) with white arched border often worn on each shoulder by Germanic military musicians.[67]

Unterjäger (Corporals) and *Stabstrompeter* (staff buglers) carried the *Haselstock* a long hazel cane. This was carried on a black sling suspended from three buttons on the jacket, perpendicular to the strap for bayonet and saber and under it. In garrison, the Haselstock was carried in the right hand. An alternative was the *Spanisches Rohr* a similar, but much lighter cane, made from the reed-like Spanish Pipe plant, which was carried by senior NCO's.[68]

As is often the case with unconventional units, the Jäger of the early nineteenth century didn't feel bound by many of the dictates of uniform regulations. Local commanders looked the other way as Jäger wore the epaulets and *Achselschnur* (shoulder cords) though expressly forbidden. The Federbusch was often worn by enlisted Jäger – also not prescribed in the rules.[69]

The "Adjustiriung" (literally, Adjustment, i.e. Uniform and Equipment Modification) of 1811

In 1811, a number of modifications were made to Austrian uniform and equipment regulations. Officers were no longer required to have a mustache. Officers' trousers were changed to a more comfortable, grey design. Epaulets were forbidden.[70]

Much else remained the same—including the Pike grey jacket "grass green" trim and collar with a row of yellow buttons, which had already become "recognized and feared."[71] In the Feld-Jäger battalions, jacket buttons were marked with a hunting horn and the battalion number.[72]

Officers kept the same style bicorn as Infantry officers.[73] Field Grades added a

Jäger circa 1809: Detail of a plate from T. Goddard & J. Booth, The Military Costume of Europe, 1812. Showing a typical mix of regulation and non-regulation elements.

gold lace border. The enlisted Jäger retained the Corsehut but most significantly were finally formally authorized to wear the Federbusch. A *Schösselklnopf* (sprig button) was placed on the hat to hold the sprig of oak leaves (*Feld Abzeichen*) traditionally worn by all Austrian troops.[74]

The Tornister was made from raw calf leather like that of the infantry, but with black straps. A powder horn was issued only to the Stutzenjäger and was hung from a double length of grass green lamb's wool cords (*Achselschnur*). This rather complicated arrangement was fastened directly to the jacket at the back and had a tassel on each end.[75]

Jäger shoulder cords, on the left a detail from a Napoleonic-era watercolor by A. Mollo shows the powder horn tucked behind jacket flap. The detail on the right, from a circa 1819 depiction, shows the powder horn/cord arrangement. After the Napoleonic Wars the tassels were replaced by woolen balls and as such they survived in the later Schutzenschnur.

Heeresgeschichtliches Museum, Vienna

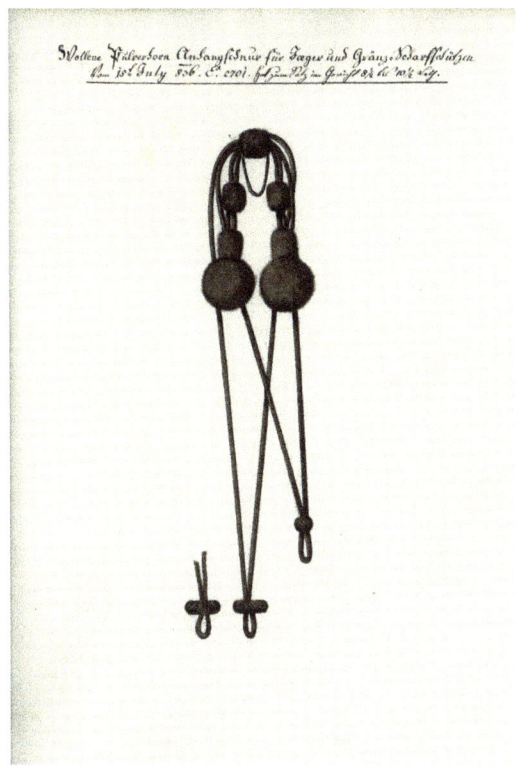

Powder horn cords (Achselschnur) of 1836, from a series of drawings by Anton Schmideder.

Heeresgeschichtliches Museum, Vienna

There were two types of cartridge box. For the Stutzenjäger, the box was of black leather and divided into three compartments. The right-most compartment carried 29 or more lead balls. The other two carried 5 flints, a screwdriver, and an oil bottle. In the cover was a compartment which carried cleaning patches and other necessities.[76] The box for the Karabiner or Flintenjäger Jäger was slightly smaller.

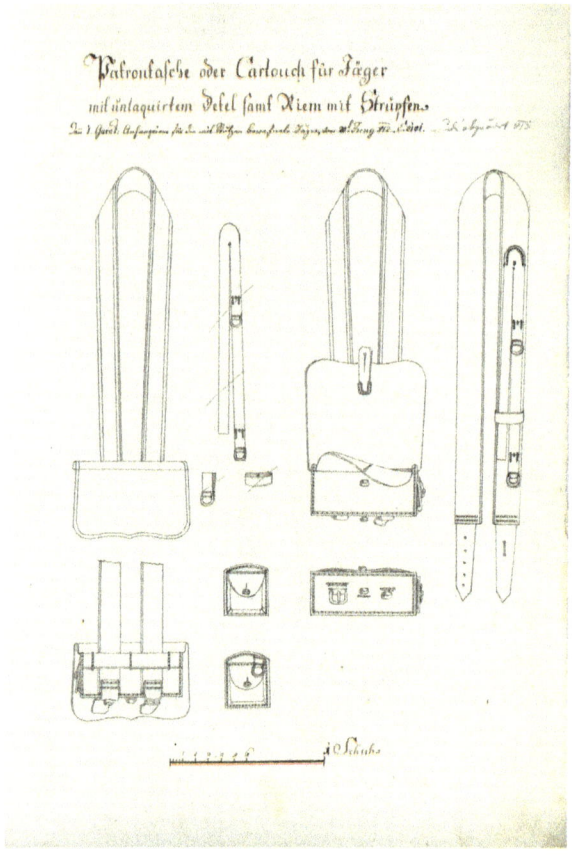

Napoleonic period cartridge box for Stutzen-armed Jäger. This design, with minor changes, continued in use until after the Second Italian War in 1859. The ramrod-carriage straps attached to the sling are shown on the right. From a series of drawings by Anton Schmideder.

Heeresgeschichtliches Museum, Vienna

Mannschaftsvorschrift of 16 July 1828

This document was the most draconian attempt yet to impose uniform regulations on the Jäger, prompted by their continuing tendency to treat the uniform largely as a matter of personal interpretation. It followed a less than fully-effective imperial decree requiring all formations immediately to cease wearing items proscribed by regulation.[77]

It provided specifications for the form of the Corsehut, calling for a 7 1/8 inch side brim to be turned up and approved the wearing of the Federbusch.[78]

A brass hat device to be affixed to the taller left side of the hat consisted of a large brass Jäger horn was prescribed. The middle of the horn contained the Tirol's single-headed eagle for the Tiroler Jäger Regiment, and the battalion number for those assigned to Feld-Jäger battalions.[79]

The fusiliers' overcoat with yellow brass buttons, a pike grey jacket and trousers like the fusiliers were prescribed. "Wings," a small roll of cloth, were added to the shoulders of the Jäger jacket to prevent the rifle sling from slipping off of the shoulder. A vest, shirt, gaiters, shoes, Kittel and bread bag like those of the German infantry were also issued to Jäger.[80]

Sideburns were authorized for all Jäger. Mustaches were allowed for everyone excepting "*Regimentscadets*" and "*Ex propriis-Gemeiner*".[81]

The Adjustierung of 1836

The Corsehut was slightly altered by the addition of a reinforcing bottom leather band on the underside of the brim and extending slightly up the upturned sides as well as a chinstrap of black patent leather. The brass horn with either Tirolian eagle or battalion number and Federbusch, tucked behind the left brim were retained. A Forage cap, the same as that of the Line infantry, but in pike grey with grass green facings, was authorized.[82]

Corsehut with Tiroler-Jäger insignia showing leather reinforced brim edges only. These antedated the 1836 alterations which extended leather reinforcement to the full underside, and partially extending up the outer sides of the brim.

Detail from one of a series of later drawings by Vincenz Lychdorff

Heeresgeschichtliches Museum, Vienna

The jacket of pike grey was to be cut like that of the German infantry officer's "campaign blouse"[83] and identical for both officers and enlisted men. Facings were grass green and buttons were yellow brass for all Jäger. Shoulder wings were now specified to be grass green. Tiroler Jäger Regiment brass buttons were to be plain while the Feld-Jäger buttons had their battalion number. Remainder of uniform items resembled German infantry except for the trousers which were pike grey with grass green piping. All Jäger leather was black.[84]

The officers received the general officers' bicorn but without the generals' braid. This was worn with a Federbusch. Edge braid was like that of infantry officers. At the ends of the loop were two uniform buttons now with Jäger horn decoration.[85]

Jäger uniform circa 1837

Heeresgeschichtliches Museum, Vienna

Uniform and Equipment after 1850

The Corsehut remained unchanged until 1861 when the brim was reduced in size. It was made, as before, of waterproof felt and had a chinstrap and brim trim of black patent leather. A wide grass green cord now encircled the hat and ended in woven acorn slides at the back. The Federbusch was now fastened to the left side of the hat by a leather "shoe". This shoe was held in place by a brass horn with the Tirolian eagle or battalion number.[86]

The forage hat lost its grass green piping in 1860. The off-duty Jäger cap did have a grass green cord, and was usually decorated on the left with a feather similar to those worn by hunters in alpine regions. The NCO cap had a small brass horn with either Tirolian eagle or battalion number. The remainder of uniform items was to be similar to the German infantry with previously noted variants.[87]

Officers continued to wear the bicorn hat until 1861. It had remained largely unchanged since early in the century, with the Jäger horn on the loop with either the Tirolian eagle or a battalion number. In 1861 the altered Jäger Corsehut was adopted by all ranks with the only distinction being gold cord, acorns, and slide flecked with black for officers. The officers' Federbusch shoe was covered with a loop of gold stripe fastened with a gilded horn. The officer's black forage cap had a small gold horn with silver battalion number or Tirolian eagle and was worn with a feather like the enlisted off-duty cap. Remaining uniform corresponded to that of the German infantry officers with previously noted differences.[88]

With the adoption of the Lorenz system of percussion cap rifles, a cap pouch made of black leather and lined with lambs' wool was adopted. (No separate cap box had been needed for the Augustin-lock armed Jäger because the fulminate primer "tubes" were packaged with the cartridges.) This cap pouch was affixed to the cartridge box strap in the middle of the Jäger's chest.[89]

Detail of Jäger equipment, 1840's, from the 1851 Abrichtungs-Regelement für die k. k. Jäger. The powder horn and the powder measure, hanging from its short strap, are shown.

Through the 1840's and the beginning of the Lorenz era the cartridge box was carried on a heavy 2 ½ inch wide strap worn over the left shoulder. Sewn to the front of this cartridge box sling was another strap of more pliable leather, split in two below the stitching. Attached to one side of the split strap were two iron rings. These were used along with an additional ring sewn to the right side of the cartridge box to receive the stutzen-armed Jäger's ramrod.[90] The simple cylindrical powder measure was also suspended from this strap. The other side of the split strap served as a lanyard to be tied at the knob end of the ramrod. The leather lanyard is pictured in use in the illustration below, which also shows the earlier-type of ramrod carriage, though the Corsehut pattern is clearly that of the 1860's.

The arrangement for carrying the stutzen ramrod persisted at least through 1859. By the 1860's photographs show that a change has been made, with the ramrod moved to the Jäger's left hip, housed in a leather tube attached to the frog supporting the bayonet and its scabbard, similar to the arrangement adopted much earlier for Bavarian Jäger troops.[91]

Lorenz-armed Jäger showing old style ramrod carriage (left and middle figures). Rod, with its leather retaining strap, is flipped over kneeling Jäger's shoulder as he reaches for a percussion cap from his pouch. In the photo detail on the right of a Jäger of the 1860's, the new tube for housing the ramrod on the bayonet frog is shown clearly.

NY Public Library; Authors' Photo

The conversion to Augustin tube and percussion cap ignition along with prepared paper cartridges had made the powder horn and measure functionally obsolete. Despite that fact, these were retained by Jäger troopers for many years after the adoption of the new system. Jäger were after all Jäger and clung to such distinctions.

A powder horn of the 3rd Feld-Jäger Battalion with part of its post-Napoleonic period Achselschnur

Courtesy of the Dorotheum, Vienna, Auction 08.09.2016

CHAPTER 5
JÄGER IN THE ITALIAN WARS, 1848-1859

Radetzky's Jäger: 1848-49

The upheavals that broke out across Europe in 1848 directly challenged governments in France, the German states, the Habsburg Empire and the Italian states, but indirectly at least, shook the post-1815 settlements across Europe. Outside France, what began as demands for broader political participation soon merged with nationalist aspirations. This was certainly the case in the Kingdom of the Two Sicilies, which saw the first outbreak of the 1848 revolutions against the unsavory Bourbon monarchy that had been reinstalled in southern Italy after the defeat of Murat in 1815. Unrest and eventually rebellion soon broke out in Rome and Austrian-held Lombardy and Venetia, and in March of 1848 Milan, capital of Austrian Lombardy, rose in rebellion against the Austrian forces.

Jäger in action during the "Five Days of Milan," March, 1848

Adam Brothers

After five days of street fighting, and with the threat of imminent intervention from the army of the Kingdom of Sardinia (Piedmont)[1] in support of the rebels, the Austrian commander-in-chief in Italy, Field Marshal Radetzky, on 22 March ordered an evacuation of Milan that took his army east over the Mincio River and into the so-called "Quadrilateral," comprised of the four fortress cities of Peschiera, Mantua, Verona and Legnano. On the same day as the Austrian withdrawal, Venice rose in revolt against the Austrian authorities.

The ensuing Italian war of 1848-49 (generally called the First War of Italian Independence) would be fought, except for the final big battle at Novara, in a theater of operations bordered by the Ticino in the west (the boundary between Austrian Lombardy and the Piedmontese kingdom), the Rivoli plateau on the eastern side of Lake Garda and the South Tirol in the north, the Po, which separated Lombardy and the Veneto from Parma, Modena and the Papal States in the south, and the Piave in the east. The geography presented real logistical concerns for Radetzky, since with the Veneto in revolt, resupply and reinforcement from Austria-- itself in revolutionary turmoil-- could be restricted to the difficult routes through the mountainous South Tirol, which itself was threatened.

The Italian theater of operations with battles and locations referenced in the text.

Johann Josef Wenzel Anton Franz Karl, Graf Radetzky von Radetz was 82 years old in 1848. During the Napoleonic wars Radetzky compiled a distinguished battlefield record, and after Wagram became Austria's organizer of victory over Napoleon as Imperial staff chief and in 1813 Chief of Staff to the allied Supreme Commander, Prince Schwarzenberg. He was an innovator and army reformer, but with a common touch and a concern for their physical well-being that endeared him to his troops,[2] who called him "Father." Radetzky commanded Austria's forces in Lombardy and the Veneto from 1831 to 1857, when he retired after more than 70 years' service to the Habsburg dynasty.

Marshal Radetzky greeted by a Jäger during the retreat from Milan.
Detail of a painting by Albrecht Adam. Alamy stock photo.

Radetzky's mission on taking command in Italy in 1831 was made clear by Kaiser Franz: "I am commissioning you to wake up the army in Italy and prepare it for war."[3] This preparation included everything from assembling an excellent staff and inculcating its officers in his methods, bringing cavalry training respecting weapons and maneuver up-to-date, and a thorough mapping of the anticipated theater of operations.[4]

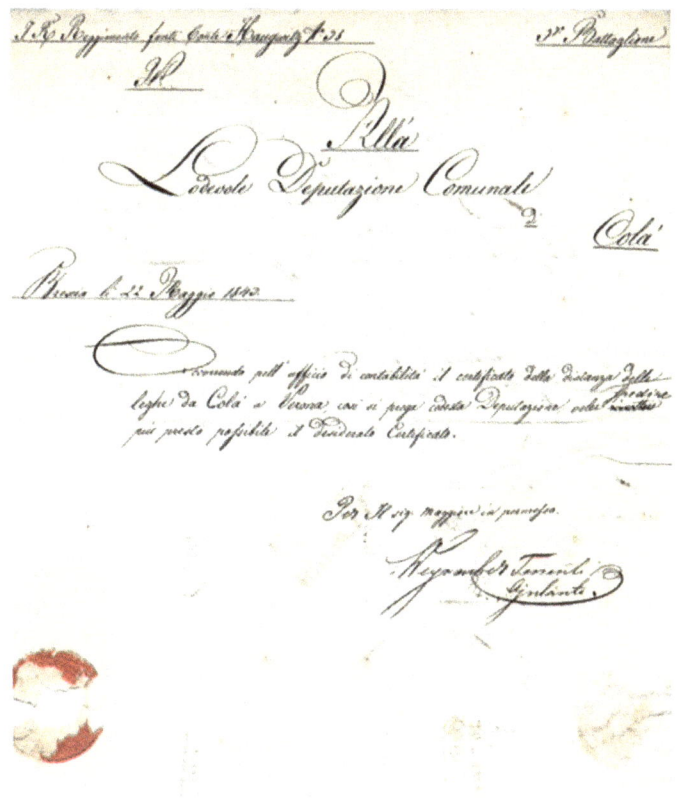

Preparations: The Adjutant of Austrian Infantry Regiment #38 requests officials of the Commune of Cola (within the Quadrilateral) to verify the distance between Cola and Verona, 22 May 1843.

Authors' Photo

The campaign that ensued would be over difficult terrain. In the north, east-west movement was usually from mountain peak to mountain peak, alternating with deep valleys, gorges and gullies requiring numerous river and stream crossings. In the south the country was heavily cultivated, crisscrossed by many rivers and intersecting irrigation canals and ditches, with the raised road surfaces often bordered by marshland or trees, inhibiting off-road movement. The human geography was equally problematic. In Lombardy and the Veneto anti-Austrian sentiment was for the most part an urban and a noble/bourgeois phenomenon, while the country people (*contadini*) of Lombardy and the Veneto generally stood aside from the conflict, not particularly sympathetic to the local Italian nationalists or to the Piedmontese interlopers. Thus, the Austrians could expect that the populations of the cities and large towns they needed to hold would generally be hostile, while those operating in the open countryside did not generally face open enmity unless it was provoked.[5]

The movements and battles of 1848-1849 in northern Italy have been admirably and exhaustively chronicled by Michael Embree in his Radetzky's Marches.[6] For our account of the role of Jäger troops in this conflict we have relied extensively on Embree as well as a contemporary compilation of official accounts.[7] With respect to Jäger troops, the paramount impression derived from these histories is that the conditions prevailing in northern Italy in 1848-49, from the character of the Austrian leadership to the physical and human realities of the campaign, created an ideal environment for Austrian Jäger, officers and men, to utilize their unique skills. These conditions produced what was often a war of detachments—small, sometimes ad hoc combined infantry/cavalry/artillery groupings-- dependant for success upon being well-led by junior officers accustomed to operating independently some distance from their main bodies. Hard stand-up fighting by solid line infantry, capable and well-lead cavalry and effective artillery notwithstanding, Custoza and Novara would not have been possible without the dozens of small-unit actions that, taken together, justify designating the war of 1848-1849 as the high point of Austrian Jäger history.

Jäger of 1848-49

New York Public Library

At the outbreak of hostilities in March, 1848 Radetzky's field army included seven battalions of Jäger-- three from the Tiroler Jäger-Regiment (aka Kaiser-Jäger) as well as the 8th, 9th (four companies), 10th and 11th Feld-Jäger. When Field Marshal Nugent crossed the Piave with his Reserve Corps in May to reinforce Radetzky he brought with him three companies of Jäger—a division from the 9th Feld-Jäger and a company of Tiroler Jäger.[8] By April, with a threat in the north to be dealt with, Jäger were also operating in the South Tirol to the west of Trento.

After the retreat into the Quadrilateral in late March, as Radetzky was reorganizing his army and consolidating his positions, a threat emerged to his lines of communication to the north in the form of an attempted rebel invasion of Southern Tirol. The threat was from a hodge-podge of Lombard volunteer units-- students, local "civic guards" and other largely disorganized, undisciplined, poorly-equipped and often insubordinate gaggles of townsmen, whose enthusiasm vastly surpassed their military effectiveness,[9] but could not be ignored. Against them were eventually deployed elements of three battalions of Jäger (two from the Tiroler-Jäger as well as the 3rd Feld-Jäger Battalion) and two battalions each from two line infantry regiments, along with four squadrons of light cavalry and five guns. A third, largely-Italian, infantry regiment, showed itself so unreliable that Austrian Lt. Field Marshal Ludwig Welden, commanding in the South Tirol, found himself with only about 5,000 effectives.[10]

The Lombard volunteers' invasion of South Tirol in the end was a failure, but its chaotic amateurism-- a largely uncoordinated series of locally-initiated, opportunistic spasms of mayhem, as opposed to an organized campaign, presented its own challenges for Welden. As Embree describes the situation, "Partly due to the nature of the terrain and the mixed nature of the populace, constant patrolling and probing by both sides was perhaps more frequent than in some other areas. There were almost constant unrecorded minor skirmishes."[11]

As soon as news of the March revolts in Vienna and Milan reached Trento agitation began. On 19 March three companies of the 3rd Feld-Jäger, paired with a squadron of light cavalry suppressed mobs in Trento, with the Austrians facing more-or-less constant trouble in the South Tirol throughout April and May. As Lombard volunteers drifted east from the frontier towards Trento, Jäger divisions or companies found themselves engaged initially in rear-guard actions as the Austrians consolidated their positions and brought up support. In this *"kleiner Krieg"* the

Jäger skills bore fruit as isolated detachments were able to avoid being cut off, moving rapidly from valley river crossing to hilltop town towards reinforcements and defensible positions. Very quickly the tables were turned as volunteer forward movement was halted then reversed by tenacious Austrian defense and effective flanking movements. In skirmishes at Toblino and Varrone facing the Tiroler Jäger and 3rd Feld-Jäger as well as the very solid Infantry Regiment Schwarzenberg (Nº. 19 IR), the Italian volunteers suffered disproportionate losses, and on 17 April were ordered by the Lombard Provisional Government to abandon the invasion of Tirol. In the cold and rain volunteer morale plummeted; units broke apart, and many deserted. Welden soon counterattacked and restored the South Tirol front to relative calm by the end of May. As had been the case during the Napoleonic wars, Jäger were sometimes employed during mopping up in the South Tirol to support, if not stiffen, local militia (*Landsschützen*) and volunteer formations.[12]

In the South Tirol in 1848 the Jäger capacity for swift movement in difficult weather and terrain proved as valuable as their fighting abilities.[13] On one occasion Italian volunteers called the *Cacciatori della Morte* (lit. Hunters, more appropriately, Riflemen of Death) fell short of their fierce appellation when four and a half companies of the 3rd Feld-Jäger, after being roused at 5 am, were transported on boats along the north end of Lake Garda to the western shore and force marched west for 12 hours to disrupt an intended Italian attack[14] and compel their retreat.

The Piedmontese King and his generals were encouraged by Radetzky's retreat into the Quadrilateral and crossed the Mincio to follow him. The Jäger of Wohlgemuth's and Strassoldo's I Corps brigades were heavily engaged during the month of April and early May, often in exposed positions, in various actions contesting the Piedmontese river crossings, the Austrian defeat at Pastrengo, and the pyrrhic Austrian defensive victory at Santa Lucia. Embree provides complete accounts of all of these engagements, but details of three deserve some attention here.

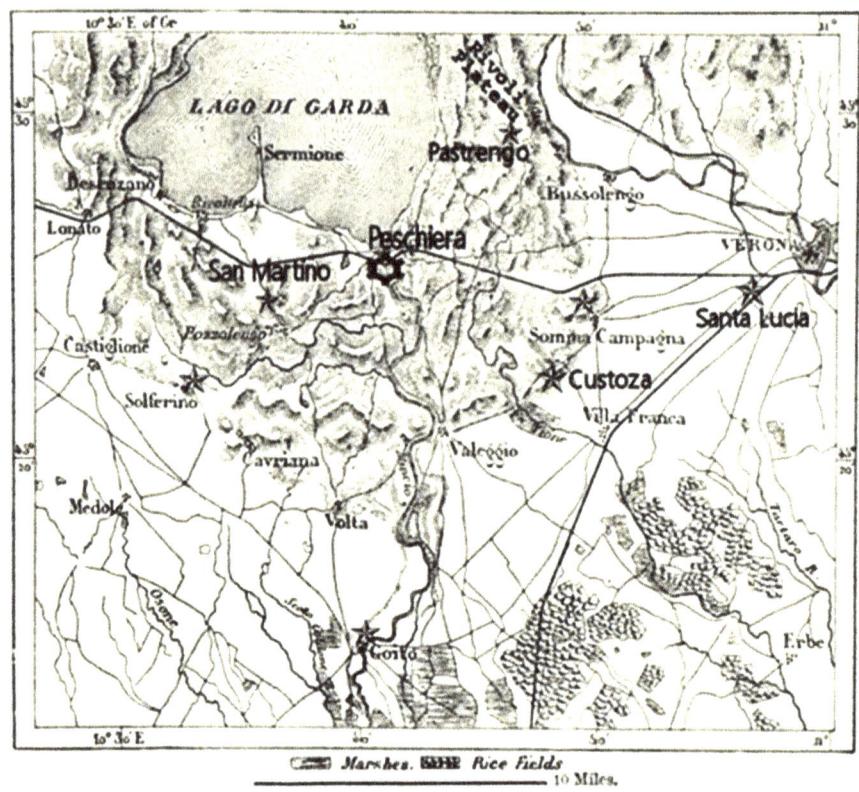

Battlefields of 1848-1866 in the vicinity of Lake Garda referenced in the text.

From E. Reculus, The Earth and its Inhabitants, Vol. 1, Europe, New York, Appleton & Co., 1883. Fig. 74, Mouth of the Adige Valley, augmented by the authors.

When the outnumbered Austrians were forced from Pastrengo on April 30, a company from the 4th Battalion of the Tiroler Jäger, commanded by Captain Anton Freiherr Pirquet von Merdaga, son of Peter Martin Pirquet of Cesenatico fame,[15] formed the rearguard on the Austrian left. Captain Pirquet deployed his company around an inn, protecting the approaches to a pontoon bridge over the Adige from the approaching Piedmontese right wing. An 1853[16] account of the 1848-49 war describes the company holding off a number of attacks, but eventually being encircled and forced to abandon the inn buildings due to the danger of falling debris. Taking positions in ditches and depressions in the ground and behind trees, the Jäger continued fighting, despite calls from the Piedmontese for them to surrender. Eventually Pirquet was forced to order a bayonet charge to break what had become an encirclement, and in running fights through rough terrain the Jäger held off the Piedmontese long enough to allow most of the company to reach the pontoon bridge. A contemporary periodical[17] placed Pirquet's losses at 30 men. Embree, following contemporary opinion, credits the Jäger action with "undoubtedly[18] allow[ing] other units to withdraw safely."

Captain Pirquet continued to lead his company in the ensuing months, including skillfully covering another retreat at Goito on 30 May and an assault at Vicenza on 10 June. On 10 or 19 July, sources differ on this point, Pirquet assumed command of a company of the 3rd Battalion, Tiroler Jäger serving with the newly- reorganized IV Army Corps east of Lake Garda on the Rivoli Plateau.[19] On 22 July on the old Napoleonic battlefield of Rivoli, Pirquet's company was the advance guard for a small combined arms column, including three more companies from 3rd Battalion, Tiroler Jäger, approaching Rivoli from the northeast. These troops were supposed to converge with a larger Austrian column from the northwest to push a smaller Piedmontese force south, flank and destroy them as part of a broader plan of Radetzky's to split the approaching Italian forces in advance of his July general offensive. In his account of the engagement at Rivoli, Embree[20] characterizes the Austrian commanders' movements as "ponderous," "sluggish" and "ill-coordinated." Pirquet's advance guard was caught unsupported in a strong, swift Piedmontese counter-attack, and driven back on their main body. The 23 year-old Captain was killed, as was one of the Austrian brigade commanders, and in the ensuing confusion the northeast column withdrew. The northwest column also encountered strong resistance, and with no converging left-wing in evidence, pulled back, leaving the Piedmontese in possession of Rivoli and in a position to reinforce Piedmontese moves towards Verona.

Austrian infantry holds off the Piedmontese to permit evacuation of the wounded following the debacle at Rivoli. A wounded Jäger leans on the wagon wheel at left.

From an early twentieth-century Italian patriotic postcard

Loss of the promising son of the Tiroler Jäger's Second Inhaber, himself a hero of the Regiment, was a blow at the time, no doubt, but it also is an indication of the elite status the Tiroler Jäger, and by extension, Austrian Jäger troops generally, had attained by 1848. As the aristocratic son of a Field Marshal and holder of the Order of Maria Theresa, the younger Pirquet could have had his pick of regiments, and yet chose to serve with the Jäger. Pirquet's career with the Jäger also illustrates their tactical role and limitations. They were expected to operate in advance of the main body and as a rear guard, on their own, in rough terrain, and to be able to extricate themselves through their superior skills from tight spots on the battlefield. When called upon to do so, they were effective storm troops, and as we shall see, their good shooting and steadiness in isolation permitted them to hold a fixed position tenaciously. But the most effective employment of Jäger was not as battle-winners, but rather, with proper support, they excelled as creators of the conditions for victory.

Propelled more by enthusiasm than deliberation, the Piedmontese wave rolling east from Pastrengo finally was dashed against the stone walls of the small villages immediately to the west of Radetzky's stronghold of Verona. On 6 May the 10th Feld-Jäger Battalion of Strassoldo's Brigade held one of these villages, Santa Lucia, for four hours against attacks from four good Piedmontese Brigades, capably supported by artillery.

While the 10th Feld-Jäger's defense of Santa Lucia is rightly heralded as heroic, earning the battalion and their commander, Colonel Karl Kopal, well-deserved glory, on reading contemporary accounts there is also plenty of evidence of simple, solid professionalism. Kopal and his officers left nothing to chance. With several days to prepare their positions and well-informed about the approach of the enemy, the 10th was ready.[21] The walls of the cemetery were crenellated and a shooting platform was built. The church tower was used as an observation post and the schoolhouse was manned. Signal fires were prepared to warn Verona of the approaching enemy and forward observation posts were established on the roads leading to Santa Lucia. Every bit of useful cover was exploited from rubble piles to gardens. Embree notes the result: "although Kopal's men were heavily outnumbered, they were well-positioned and, together with the guns, caused many more casualties to the brave Piedmontese than they themselves suffered."[22]

The 10th Feld-Jäger Battalion in the church yard at Santa Lucia, 6 May, 1848. Note the Stutzenjäger using his powder measure and horn--perhaps for a long shot.

Adam Brothers

By all accounts the Piedmontese troops performed well. One of Radetzky's aides was "especially astonished to see how the Piedmontese boldly brought their guns right up into the midst of our skirmish line, and the speed which, despite our fire, their sappers cut down the poplar trees alongside the road to protect the pieces from attack by our cavalry."[23] The flanking fire of this artillery helped finally drive the battalion out of the village. Strassoldo's Brigade and that to its left pulled back successfully about a mile, but not without having to resort to their bayonets,[24] establishing a new perimeter around 1 pm. The action shifted predominantly to the Austrian right until mid-afternoon when Radetzky ordered Santa Lucia to be retaken. By this point the 10th Feld-Jäger had been placed in reserve and did not participate in the attacks.

View of the 10th Feld-Jäger's defense of the village of Santa Lucia, with Piedmontese artillery in the foreground.

Detail from an early 20th-century Italian patriotic postcard.

After first being stalled by continued Piedmontese resistance, the attempt to retake Santa Lucia finally succeeded, but no pursuit of the retreating Piedmontese could be attempted. The 10th Feld-Jäger suffered the greatest number of casualties of any unit engaged at Santa Lucia, with two officers and 16 men killed, 50 wounded and 30 missing.[25]

In early June, 1848 under serious logistical pressures, Radetzky gambled that he could strip Verona of most of his troops while turning east on Vicenza to take the place and open his lines of communication in preparation for a decisive offensive operation against the main Piedmontese army. While the 3rd Feld-Jäger and 3rd Battalion of the Tiroler Jäger remained to protect the ever-troublesome South Tirol and Rivoli Plateau, the Jäger with Radetzky's main force were assigned to a brigade in each of the two Divisions of I and II Corps,[26] while the III Corps got none. Brigade commanders with Jäger units could continue the practice, if the necessity arose, to combine detachments of Jäger, light cavalry and artillery, since two squadrons and one battery were assigned to each of them. Rocket batteries, which proved useful for unsettling and even panicking the kind of inexperienced troops often being encountered,[27] were also available in each corps' artillery reserve.

The 10th Feld-Jäger Battalion remained with Strassoldo's Brigade following the reorganization. Their part in the assault on Vicenza began at 8 am on 10 June on the key objective, the Berico Hills, to the south, which dominated the city. The two most prominent architectural features of this area were the *Villa Rotonda*[28] and the church and cloister of Madonna del Monte. Both were heavily defended. The 10th Feld-Jäger's objective was the church and its appendages, which they took by storm.

The 10th Jäger and Austrian line infantry attack Maria del Monte.

Lithograph after V. J. Lancedelli by Paterno's, Vienna, 1849

Colonel Kopal, who had specifically been urged by Radetzky[29] not to lead the attack after his exertions at Santa Lucia, was wounded in the right arm by a musket ball as he led the battalion in what became vicious hand-to-hand fighting among the buildings.[30] The church complex was taken at a cost of two officers and 21 men dead and Kopal and four other officers and 90 men wounded or missing. Embree[31] quotes a staff officer:

> "Nothing held the jubilant spirit of the Tenth back, and in the twinkling of an eye, the most key points of the enemy were taken with the bayonet...[S]ome Jäger were dispatching (men) out of hand. I must confess that we all hoped for an example! 'Let them run away!' rang out Radetzky's command alone, since he was always magnanimous; more so, though, when luck was on his side."

Marshal Radetzky dismounts to attend the wounded Colonel Kopal being carried off the field at Vicenza.

Lithograph after B. Bachmann-Hohmann, by L. T. Neumann, Vienna, 1849

Kopal lost his arm and died from complications of the amputation on 16 June. He was buried with full honors in Vicenza two days later.[32] A monument to Kopal was unveiled in 1853 in Znaim (Znojmo), not far from the small town in Moravia where he was born[33].

Oberst Von Kopal of the 10th Feld-Jäger Battalion: "Ein Mann von eminentem militärischem Talente, Bravour und Feldtüchtigkeit."[34]

From Strack, Das Kopal-Denkmal in Znaim und das k.k. 10. Feld-Jäger Batallion

Lichtenstein's Brigade, attacking Vicenza from the east, stormed the Padua Gate district. The 8th Feld-Jäger, which in March had lost four companies of Italians to desertion, was the spearhead of a storming column led personally by General Lichtenstein over barricades and against heavy small-arms fire from the surrounding houses at the cost of 65 casualties. Notwithstanding these exertions it finally took a mortar battery[35] to clear out the stubborn defenders. With the Berico Hills in Austrian hands, and the city's eastern perimeter penetrated, holding Vicenza became untenable for the Piedmontese and the city was surrendered on 11 June. Radetzky's communications through the Veneto back to Austria were now secure and he could turn his attention to destruction of the Piedmontese army.

Back in Verona, with his army of about 47,000 reorganized, Radetzky began operations in late July and, despite setbacks, from that point forward the Austrians were on the offensive. Notwithstanding the inevitable exceptions, for the Jäger battalions the battle at Vicenza was a turning point. Before, with the Austrians reeling, supply lines threatened and not enough line troops to meet every challenge, the Jäger filled the gaps, with their special skills and capacity to operate remotely and independently, multiplying what Austrian force was available through small operations-- from disrupting enemy supply lines to securing lines of retreat and communications and skillfully-placed sharpshooters holding critical bridgeheads. Before Vicenza one is more likely to encounter terms like, *Vorposten*, *Scharfschützen*, *Streifzug*, and *Streifcommando*, or at least *Spitze der Avantgarde* in accounts of Jäger actions, or to read of small units of Jäger operating in tandem with a few guns or rocket tubes and some light cavalry in delaying or disrupting the enemy. Certainly because of the nature of the terrain and the inadequate number of troops available, operations in the South Tirol were more likely to maintain this character for the entire war. But in the main theater, from the Quadrilateral to the Ticino, after June 1848, including the battles of Custoza and Novara and their preliminaries, there is much more emphasis in the original accounts of Jäger leading attack columns, taking guns, in bayonet charges, and as skirmishers covering assaults "*als Tirailleurs.*"[37] While it is perfectly reasonable for Austrian commanders to have used the best troops at hand for the jobs changing military circumstances required, it also may have introduced for some "lessons," which as future wars suggest, might have been best left unlearned about how best to employ Austria's Jäger troops.

DEBACLE IN 1859

Austria's War of 1859 (Second War of Italian Unification) was an unmitigated disaster. The contrast with 1848-49 could not have been more marked. When hostilities commenced the Commander-in Chief, FZM Franz Graf Gyulai, tried to resign for lack of confidence in his own abilities, which was entirely justified as events would demonstrate. Staff and command adjustments to help prop him up resulted in a divided command structure that if anything made the situation worse.[38] Further complicating the command situation was the presence of the Kaiser through most of the conflict, accompanied by FML Karl Graf Grünne, a senior military advisor (Adjutant General) who had despised Radetzky and schemed for years to get him retired. Also in the Kaiser's entourage was Radetzky's brilliant and devoted staff chief Heinrich von Hess, who as Quartermaster-General had sent a respected protégé to Gyulai to head his staff. Gyulai refused even to speak to this new Chief of Staff in the weeks preceding the war.[39] While many units had served in 1848-49, the leadership had changed: most Corps commanders had important commands under Radetzky a decade earlier, but none of the Division commanders had led a brigade or more in the previous war.[40]

Throughout the campaign logistics were a nightmare, and at times the troops fought without having been fed.[41] Troop deployments were inhibited by concerns about their political reliability. After a decade of nationalist propaganda that continued after suppression of the 1848 upheavals, the high command in Italy was concerned about disaffection among Hungarians, Croats and Italians in the ranks and were reluctant to utilize them in critical front-line positions.[42] Finally, in contrast to 1848-49, on far too many occasions the Austrians found themselves outmaneuvered and surprised, suggesting a curious failure[43] to tap the light cavalry and Jäger effectiveness in reconnaissance under Radetzky. Overall in 1859 the Austrians seem to have been out-generaled rather than out-fought.

Materially, the only French advantage was excellent rifled artillery. This advantage could have been diminished had the new Austrian Lorenz rifles' long-range potential been exploited effectively against gun crews. By 1859 most Austrian infantry had been issued a superior shoulder arm, the Model 1854 infantry rifle. With an accurate relatively-small caliber compression bullet (.54) and good sights, they certainly had an edge over the new big-bore French rifles of dubious accuracy. Unfortunately many of the Austrian troops had limited experience with their Lorenz's, and Austrian parsimony with respect to training ammunition limited time on the practice range for line troops, effectively negating what should have been an asset.[44]

The successful Austrian tactics of 1848-49, later codified by Radetzky and Hess in the regulations of 1849, emphasized speedy and flexible movement and exploiting the new speed and accuracy of firepower through troops deployed in line or in loose, mobile skirmish formations.[45] If the Austrian army had been able to apply this doctrine effectively, the War of 1859 would have turned out quite differently.

After the war, the Austrians adopted a wholly different tactical doctrine, embracing *Stosstaktik*, their version of the French "cult of the bayonet," which many believed had beaten them. Radetzky's success from maneuvering rapidly to permit bringing enhanced firepower to bear was neglected in favor of maneuvering to get the infantry in a position to charge with the bayonet. The ultimate consequence was Austrian commanders in 1866 obligingly leading their troops into the effective range of the rapid-fire Prussian Needle Rifle. In the case of the Jäger, this was a far cry from Unterberger's conception of the Haubajonet as a purely defensive weapon. The War of 1859 was thus not only a defeat, but became the source of the wrong lessons, contributing to future losses.

More Jäger battalions were present in the army in Italy in 1859 than had served under Radetzky. Five battalions of the Tiroler Jäger Regiment (Kaiser-Jäger), Nos. 2, 3, 4, 5 and 6 were with the main army, while the rest remained in Tirol.[46] Fourteen Battalions of Feld-Jäger were with the main army.[47] Of the 31 Austrian brigades in the order of battle at the time of Magenta in early June, 17 included at least one Jäger battalion. For the others Grenzer battalions performed the functions of light troops.

In 1859 Austria's Jäger troops justified their reputation for good shooting and hard, stand-up fighting when called upon to do so. The trend noted from the offensive phase of the 1848-49 war continued and was extended. In Austria's meandering and reactive defensive war of 1859 Jäger troops were used predominantly either for conventional infantry functions, like bayonet charges or holding fixed positions, or even when in light infantry roles proper like skirmish screens or flankers, it tended to be in very close proximity to the main body.

Jäger in action in 1859. The cooler lightweight cotton Kittel and oilcloth covers for Corsehut are depicted.

Lithograph by Reinhart, after Noltsch

The first significant action of the war, at Montebello on 20 May, is illustrative of the Jäger experience in the entire conflict. It was a meeting engagement. Three converging Austrian division-sized columns on a reconnaissance in force on the Piedmontese side of the Ticino ran into a French infantry division and some Piedmontese light cavalry who knew they were coming.[48] Initially the French were hard pressed, but they brought up support and the Austrians were checked, falling back to positions around the little village of Montebello, taking defensive advantage of the heavily-cultivated countryside, stone houses and walled cemetery typical of the region.

The 3rd Feld-Jäger Battalion[49] had been watching the left flank of the lead brigade, advancing past Montebello to the hamlet of Genestrello, driving off Italian light cavalry with "a well-directed hail of rifle bullets."[50] According to a generally anti-Austrian contemporary British account, "It was … the energy of the sharpshooters, who had successfully stormed the heights and farm-yards of Genestrello and who here displayed a bold intrepidity that overcame the courageous resistance of the French troops." Eventually French reinforcements forced them back to Montebello, where they subsequently took up defensive positions. A modern historian describes the Jäger concealed in the tall wheat, "springing out of the earth at every step the French took."[51] From Montebello's walled cemetery:

> "[T]he rifles of the 3rd battalion of sharpshooters did deadly execution on the attacking foe. The French were repeatedly led to the storm. "*En avant, mes enfants!*" cried General Beuret, putting himself at the head of the storming column-"*Je vais vous montrer le chemin!*" But at this moment the brave officer reeled in his saddle and fell, bearing in his forehead the bloody mark of a rifle-bullet. In spite of their wild cries of Vive l'Empereur!" the French were unable to take the grave-yard by storm."[52]

Eventually French batteries had to be brought up to clear the Austrians out of Montebello.

Leading the Austrian probe through Montebello had been the so-called "Flying Division" of General Karl von Urban, a larger version of the kind of mixed "task force" familiar in the 1848-49 war, but less common in 1859. Division Urban's primary mission was to rove through the Austrian rear areas, securing communications and eradicating guerilla bands. After Montebello, in keeping with Gyulai's kaleidoscopic pattern of unit-juggling, Urban was reinforced with an additional brigade, including the 19th Feld-Jäger Battalion.[53] He rushed north with this brigade to respond to an incursion by Garibaldi and his *Cacciatori delle Alpi* (Alpine Hunters or Riflemen) Italian volunteers across the Ticino into the area between Lakes Maggiore and Como on the Austrian right flank. Urban would spend the next weeks chasing the *Cacciatori* and local recruits, eventually diverting about 11,000 Austrians from the big battles of Magenta and Solferino. In a series of engagements Urban failed to defeat Garibaldi's volunteers decisively, and the 19th Feld-Jäger were called upon to execute a fighting withdrawal in one case and to extricate cut-off Austrian line infantry in another.[54]

The worst day for the Jäger in the 1859 War came at Palestro on 31 May. In the only strategic achievement in this dismal campaign, the French and Piedmontese in late May managed a northward move across the somnolent Gyulai's front, from the foot of the Apennines to the area between Casale and Vercelli, just east of the 1849 battlefield of Novara. On 30 May the Piedmontese had crossed the Sesia and taken the village of Palestro. French Marshal Canrobert's III Corps was moving in support, but was held up by rain-swollen rivers and streams. The next morning only the 3rd Zouave Regiment had managed to reach the vicinity of Palestro to buttress the three Piedmontese divisions. Austrian FML Baron Zobel, VII Corps, attempted an attack to retake the area. Szabo's Brigade, including the 7th Feld-Jäger, was detached from II Corps to assist in Zobel's effort. Initially Szabo made good progress, hooking around Palestro along the bank of the Sesia, but came under enfilading fire from French batteries on the west side of the river. In the ensuing

7th Feld-Jäger Battalion at Palestro in a contemporary Austrian engraving. When the French took the bridge in the right background over a canal, the battalion was trapped and lost about 500 men drowned or captured. The troops depicted, if meant to be French should be Zouaves, or if Piedmontese should not have red trousers.

© age fotostock

confusion Szabo unknowingly crossed the front of the Zouaves, who then charged the left rear of the 7th Feld-Jäger—who had been advancing on Szabo's left flank and were already facing a Piedmontese brigade in Palestro at their front. In the attack Szabo lost all his guns and the Jäger were pushed back into Szabo's line infantry. The infantry fled in confusion; the bridge to safety over a canal to the east of town was taken by the Piedmontese before the Jäger could reach it, and the result was, as Brooks[55] describes it, "[virtual] annihilation of the battalion." About 500 Jäger were either drowned or captured. Zobel's total loss on 31 May was over 2,000 troops. The Austrians retreated towards the Ticino and Magenta, where despite the heavy losses, the remainder of the 7th battalion was engaged.[56]

In the Battles of Magenta and Solferino, Jäger battalions served essentially as elite line infantry. Magenta degenerated into a street-fighting brawl in which French general officers led their men like junior officers in assaults on barricaded buildings. Jäger units were credited at Magenta with accurate shooting, tenaciousness in defense[57] and a successful rear-guard action following a forced march that contributed to a largely well-ordered Austrian withdrawal.

At Solferino on 24 June the most salient role played by Jäger troops was in the stand by FML Benedek's VIII Corps on the Austrian right flank north of Solferino, on the "hill" of San Martino-- actually a deep plateau comprising several high points, with a Church and various stone farmhouses. The countryside was heavily cultivated. As a modern Italian historian describes it "Grain crops, vines, mulberry and fruit trees…frag[mented] the battlefield in many small areas where the defenders had an undeniable advantage." [58] In all Benedek had at San Martino room to deploy his defense in considerable depth, backed by good artillery positions and plenty of area to marshal reserves and reorganize and resupply units as necessary. As Prof. Badone notes, the only defect of the position was its liability of encirclement, but the Piedmontese never attempted it. Benedek held the entire day, and after the fighting in Solferino proper had sputtered to an end in a violent rainstorm, was able to conduct a night withdrawal in the face of the enemy, with all his guns, while still covering the army's right.

Attached to Benedek's six brigades were four Jäger battalions: the 2nd and 5th Tiroler Jäger, and the 3rd and 9th Feld-Jäger and plenty of artillery for the task at hand.[59] In an unusual situation for an Austrian commander in this war, Benedek had complete control of the field without interference from other commanders. The situation was simple, hold the line and plug gaps where necessary. With the natural and man-made obstructions in the landscape reducing unimpeded firing zones to no more than 150 meters in most places[60] the Piedmontese attacks in column failed successively, in spite of attempts by their *Bersagliere* battalions to provide fire support. With the Jäger in well-covered positions on both flanks,[61] at those ranges the result is not surprising.

Italian patriotic postcard depicting the Piedmontese assault on San Martino. Austrian positions are on the heights in the background.

While Badone[62] suggests that there were opportunities during the day to do so, Benedek engaged in no large-scale counterattacks against weakened and isolated Piedmontese units, except for a last-minute foray, led by Benedek himself, at the head of newly-arrived Infantry Regiment N°. 39 to blunt Italian attacks during the Austrian withdrawal.

After Solferino both Emperors had had enough. In early July Franz Josef and Napoleon III met and concluded an armistice. By this Peace of Villafranca Lombardy was ceded to France, which subsequently transferred it to Piedmont, laying the foundation of a unified Kingdom of Italy. The Veneto remained in Austrian hands. The Kaiser resolved never again to command troops in the field.[63] Gyulai and the Radetzky-hating Grünne were dismissed and Benedek was promoted to Feldmarschalleutnant. Gyulai's neglected Chief of Staff Colonel Franz Kuhn went on to a distinguished career, as successful defender of the Tirol in the War of 1866, and an energetic advocate for mountain troops and the place of the Alps in Austrian strategy,[63] eventually becoming Austria's Minister of War.

CHAPTER 6
1866: THE SEVEN WEEKS' WAR

Austrian Jäger troops fought in three conflicts in the 1860's. In the short Schleswig-Holstein campaign against Denmark in alliance with Prussia, with *Stosstaktik* firmly enshrined in Austrian tactical doctrine, the 9th Feld-Jäger Battalion again proved at Oeversee that Jäger could charge with the bayonet every bit as well as crack line infantry, even in the cold and difficult conditions that prevailed.[1] When Austrian Archduke Maximilian was installed by Napoleon III as Emperor of Mexico an Austrian force of 10,000 men, including Jäger, was dispatched in 1864 to support him. One source claims three battalions of "Jäger," not further identified, were sent, another identifies the troops as six companies of the 1st Battalion, Tiroler Jäger (Kaiser-Jäger).[2] Thürheim is silent on the subject, which may reflect the fact that the Austrian forces were technically volunteers.[3]

Ironically, the French discomfiture in the Mexican fiasco contributed to the outbreak of the Austro-Prussian War of 1866, also called The Seven Weeks' War. The demands of the Mexican enterprise, along with some vague promises from Bismarck, kept Napoleon III neutral, freeing Prussia and her ally, the new Kingdom of Italy, each to seek their reckoning with Austria in 1866-- Prussia to settle once and for all the question of leadership of the German States, and Italy to wrest the Veneto and the Trentino from Habsburg control.

The war was fought on two fronts, in Bohemia and the old 1848-49 battlegrounds of the Quadrilateral and southern Tirol. Bohemia was judged by Vienna to be vastly more important, yet it was in the south that Austrian troops delivered a decisive military victory, although one which events in Bohemia would rob of any strategic value for Austria.

Austrian leadership on both fronts was better than that of 1859. Northern Army commander FZM Ludwig August von Benedek was Austria's most popular soldier. Brave to a fault, with a solid battlefield record, Benedek was popular and respected among the troops. On the negative side of the ledger, Benedek had never commanded more than a corps in battle, and would have preferred the command in Italy, where he said he knew every tree on the road to Milan. Unfortunately, Benedek allowed himself to be saddled with a Chief of Staff "cautious to the point of timidity"[4] as well as the presence in the field with him of the K.u.K. Army Chief of Staff, an annoyingly querulous and nasty defeatist. As comparable high level supernumeraries had in 1859, his presence muddled and slowed the command situation in Bohemia.

Benedek was soldier enough to recognize the danger of blind adherence to the *Stosstaktik* doctrine. As reports of opening engagements began coming in, he ordered[5] that bayonet charges not be attempted without having been preceded by effective small arms and artillery fire preparation. But in the middle of a campaign such a major tactical alteration was beyond the capacity of the Northern Army's staff operation to effectuate. Benedek's best corps commander, FML Ludwig von

Gablenz, was watching the frontier with Prussian Silesia as the enemy forces emerged from the mountain passes of the Reisengebirge and Lusatians, and exhibited a wise preference for deft Radetzky-like fire and maneuver[6] and flank attacks, avoiding ruinous frontal assaults.

Commander of the army in the Veneto was Archduke Albrecht, son of the great Archduke Karl of the wars against Napoleon. Albrecht was a stiff aristocrat without Radetzky's and Benedek's common touch,[7] but the officers and men had confidence in his solid, competent leadership.

General Franz Kuhn in command in the Tirol was an advocate for mountain troops[8] who understood the kind of war he was fighting there and utilized effectively the capabilities of his Jäger troops.

Jäger of the 1860's. Note the change in the Corsehut pattern and ramrod carriage now alongside the bayonet.

In material terms Austria's new rifled steel guns were much better than Prussia's shorter-range and less versatile smoothbores, but fire-support doctrine lagged technical capacity. While the superiority of the rapid-firing Prussian Needle-Rifle (*Zündnadelgewehr*) is universally accepted among historians as providing the Prussian infantry with a huge advantage, this "superiority" was dependent more upon Austrian tactical doctrine, which, by discounting the importance of aimed fire and embracing the cult of the bayonet, provided ample targets, than it was on the fragile, flinch-inducing Dreyse of dubious accuracy at longer ranges. It was the Prussian infantry who won the Six Weeks' War and not their rifles. Furthermore, if Austrian tactical doctrine compromised the effectiveness of K.u.K. Jäger troops, this was not the case with the Prussians. Prussian Commanders used Jäger units for reconnaissance, sharpshooting, screening and skirmishing. In an account[9] of the victory parade in Berlin after the cessation of hostilities an observer notes: "The… Brigade was composed of the Jäger of the Guard – riflemen recruited from all foresters and gamekeepers of Prussia, renowned marksmen, who had done much hard duty during the campaign and reaped their reward in the loud applause of the people of Berlin."[10]

Bohemia

The Austrian Northern Army of 1866 was organized as army corps without divisions; each corps comprising 4 brigades of 2 2,300-man regiments each. Attached units included one eight-gun battery of 4-pound guns and one Jäger Battalion. Average overall Corps strength was around 24,000.[11] 26 battalions of Feld-Jäger served with the Northern Army.[12]

At the onset of hostilities in June, Prussia immediately occupied several of the German states and invaded Austrian Bohemia. As Prussian troops came out of the mountain passes, they met stiff Austrian resistance in which Jäger formations played a significant part. At Wenzelberg, the 25th Feld-Jäger Battalion distinguished itself by repeated spoiling attacks that kept the Prussians from consolidating their positions and ultimately forced them back toward the passes.[13]

Approaching Königgrätz, as the Prussian patrols attempted to cross the Bistritz, well-trained and led Austrian Jäger acting as a forward screen harassed and ran them off.[14]

As the Prussian advance toward Königgrätz developed, the lead Prussian elements aligned to attack the villages of Sadowa, Dohalitz, and Bistriz. These units reached the river in good order, but then had to fight for every inch of ground.[15] The advancing Prussians were funneled into the narrow alleyways of the villages. This street fighting almost completely negated the Prussian Needle Rifle's limited advantages. Austrian Jäger fought from the cover of houses and rooftops, their accurate fire inflicting heavy losses on the attacking Prussians. Because of the smoke and the concealment of the enemy, the Prussians' ability to load quickly and without standing erect availed them little when they could find no targets.[16]

Finally, the Lorenz's toll became so great that the Prussian artillery, which had up to then been engaged in counter-battery fire against the accurate Austrian guns, shifted to the villages of Mokrovous and Dohaliltz and flattened them, causing huge fires and copious smoke. It was this that finally forced the Austrian Jäger and remaining infantry to withdraw up the hill towards their batteries.[17]

As the Prussians now streamed across the Bistritz, the size of this main effort surprised the Austrians. Faulty Austrian intelligence, due largely to the same inferior system of patrolling that had plagued them in 1859, permitted the Prussians to mass forces on the Austrian side of the river and to move on Königgrätz, where the deciding battle of the war was about to be fought.[18]

Reviewing the extensive literature of the campaign of Königgrätz, it is clear that utilization of Jäger forces varied tremendously between Brigades. Some used them exclusively as line infantry and others more correctly in their special operations roles.

Notable examples of misuse of Jäger units include III Corps General von Appiano's failure to deploy the 4th Feld-Jäger Battalion as a screen for his brigade, which permitted the Prussians to mass overwhelming strength to force the Austrians out of Chlum. More typical was the recourse, in the desperate Austrian attack to retake lost ground via Rosheritz, to throw the VI Corps' 17th Feld-Jäger Battalion into an infantry attack next to the elite Hoch und Deutschmeister Regiment of Vienna, with that regiment's bands playing.[19]

The lessons of this short war as they apply to the use and efficacy of Jäger troops reveal that the Prussians seemed to do it right and accordingly reaped the benefits, while the Austrian commanders seemed limited in their understanding and haphazard in their tactical use of Jäger formations with predictably mixed results. More importantly perhaps, the Northern Army's failures were to a degree attributable to poor intelligence, and it is not unreasonable to suggest that at least some of the intelligence failures were the result of neglecting to employ combined Jäger and light cavalry detachments for reconnaissance as had served Radetzky so well in 1848-1849. Fortunately, because of the innate quality of these troops, even when misused, Jäger performed magnificently. But, from the luxury afforded by time and distance, we cannot help but regard much of it as a lost opportunity and waste.

The Austrian Jäger at Königgrätz once again proved superb in the kind of standup infantry roles they were assigned. It may be that in the circumstances nothing else was possible, but regardless, the battle represented a sad coda for the nineteenth-century Jäger as much as it did a tragedy for the Austro-Hungarian Empire.

In 1866 on the Italian front Austria's commanders used their Jäger troops more effectively.

The 17th Feld-Jäger Battalion at Chlum

From a late 19th century Austrian patriotic postcard.

The Quadrilateral Again

The formula for Austrian success in Italy was characterized succinctly in a 1905 review of Colonel H. M. Hozier's account entitled *The Seven Weeks' War*: "Archduke Albrecht, similarly to Benedek, was opposed by two armies, the united strength of which was greatly superior to his own. But, unlike Benedek, he fell roughly upon one of them, that of the [Italian] king, with the result that [the other] shrank back from its intended passage of the Po."[20]

In 1866 the new Kingdom of Italy was allied with Prussia. After some prodding from Bismarck, King Victor Emmanuel finally declared war on Austria on 20 June. The Italian prospect was daunting, even though with over 120,000 troops they heavily outnumbered Archduke Albrecht's force of about 75,000 in the Veneto.

The hot summer weather with its threat of malaria and typhus, the difficult choice of a relatively easy crossing of the Mincio directly into the formidable mutually-supporting defenses of the Quadrilateral, as opposed to a more difficult passage of the Po and Adige to get behind that Austrian bastion, strained the capacities of Victor Emmanuel's nascent general staff and the tempers of his egoistic generals. In the end the obvious choice of a frontal attack to fix, and a swing around from the south to cut off and destroy the Austrians in the Veneto proved too much for a divided Italian command (only the King himself could issue orders to the commanders of either of his main armies) and an inadequate army organization just not yet ready for a major war.

The Austrians, on the other hand, in addition to the advantage of internal lines, were fighting on ground that they not only knew, but had been preparing since the 1830's. Most significantly, due to what one near-contemporary observer called "the strictest surveillance"[21] of the enemy, they anticipated the Italian moves, while managing to conceal their own. Well before the outbreak of hostilities Archduke Albrecht had established a screen of cavalry and Jäger to observe and harass Italian thrusts towards the Mincio, while also keeping the commanders of Pula's light cavalry brigade, the 21st Feld-Jäger and other detachments along the river line apprised of his intentions: "I wish to point out to you that it is not my intention, if the enemy attempts the passage of the Mincio, to obstinately oppose it; so your business will consist in harassing him, so as to delay his movements as much as possible, while constantly remaining in contact with his troops. In case of retreat you will fall back on Villafranca, and thence on Verona"[22] (which eventually became necessary).

Because of inhospitable terrain along much of its banks, Italian options for suitable crossing points over the Po were limited to about a 45 km stretch,[23] which was well-covered by a brigade of infantry, the 10th Feld-Jäger Battalion and a Hussar detachment.[24]

On 20 June, the Austrians were informed in writing by the Italians that hostilities would begin in three days.²⁵ Already Austrian forward observers had been noting significant enemy concentrations at crossing points on the Mincio and Po.²⁶

The bulk of Italian forces under General Marmora, accompanied by the king, crossed the Mincio on 23 June and began moving towards Verona.²⁷ The next day General Cialdini managed to get elements of his southern force across the Po, but the Archduke was positioned to engage them in detail and also prevent their getting to the Adige in his rear, "everything ...depended...on his outposts, and how well they served him was proven by the results." ²⁸

With the combined benefits of good intelligence and skilled leadership, Austrian troops were assembled under the walls of Verona and prepared to advance on 24 June against the enemy in the familiar Sommacampagna-Custoza area. Albrecht risked moving west into the jaws of a theoretical pincer, but was confident in the knowledge that the Italians were incapable of closing a trap around him.²⁹

In the "terrible, inelegant brawl" that was the Battle of Custoza hundreds of Austrian troops died in *Stosstaktik*- inspired bayonet charges.³⁰ In one assault, the 4th Battalion, Tiroler Jäger-Regiment, (Kaiser-Jäger) and 15th Feld-Jäger Battalion, despite the bravery of the enemy, eventually drove the Italians from the summit of Monte Croce, a key feature of the high ground between Custoza and Sommacampagna.³¹ As the Austrians moved through Santa Lucia, where Kopal's 10th Feld-Jäger had made its stand in 1848, they encountered 200 Italians who had laid down their arms and the bodies of two Jäger, stripped, beaten to death, and left hanging upside down by their canteen straps.³² As the day wore on, and the Italians were pushed back to their bridgeheads, the fluid, largely uncontrolled course of the battle at one point raised concerns about the Austrian right. The 36th Feld-Jäger Battalion and elements of Nº. 17 Infantry Regiment were tasked to screen the flank and accordingly occupied Pra Vecchia as a strong point. In a decisive development at 2000 hours, on the Austrian left, the village of Villafranca was taken³³ by the 23rd Feld-Jäger battalion leaving the Italians no alternative but to seek the safety of the left bank of the Mincio. By midnight, with no overall command capable of controlling the dispirited troops, the main Italian Army was in full retreat, while Cialdini's southern forced dithered astride the Po.

Custoza was the decisive battle of the campaign and a complete Austrian victory. Had an energetic Austrian pursuit followed, the utter destruction in detail of the entire Italian Army was possible, and with that, a significant strategic victory with potential far-reaching effect for the new Italian Kingdom, and Habsburg fortunes generally. But this was not to be.[34] Eventually, in response to Königgrätz, the Austrian Southern Army was called north, finally giving up the Quadrilateral, and with it the Veneto, of its own accord.

Defense of the South Tirol

As events were unfolding in the Quadrilateral, a threat from another source developed in the South Tirol, which the Austrians had expected would be a backwater, and only stationed about 15,000 regular troops there, including companies from the 1st, 2nd, 6th and Depot Battalion of the Tiroler Jäger-Regiment (Kaiser-Jäger). Austrian forces in the region were organized in a separate command from the Veneto and were supplemented by three types of militia.[35] The *Landsschützen* were a local Tirolian defense force, organized in companies with elected officers. When mobilized they were considered on a par with regular infantry companies. Their numbers totaled around 4,000. The *Volunteers* numbered around 2,700 and were poorly equipped and of little value in the campaign. The *Landsturm* were militia companies organized throughout the German-speaking areas of the Empire and were considered a last resort. In Tirol they numbered around 90,000, with only 50,000 rifles available for issue. The regulars did the bulk of the fighting while the militia and volunteer units were limited to local defense, but played a necessary role as the Austrian strategy in the Tirol was to hold only key strong points in the valleys with limited numbers of regulars, which could call upon mobile regulars in reserve when threats emerged.

Both commanders in the Tirol were notable. The legendary Giuseppe Garibaldi, in an always uneasy relationship with the Italian regulars who considered him and most of those he led as insubordinate hotheads, led a force of about 38,000, mostly volunteers, supplemented with some regular artillery units. No less formidable was Major General Freiherr Franz von Kuhn, who had been elevated to the command in Tirol at the outbreak of hostilities after having served there for several years; he was also one of the few Austrian senior officers to come out of the Italian debacle in 1859 with an enhanced reputation. Kuhn was an advocate of mountain troops, and suited by experience and disposition for this challenging command. One Austrian soldier/chronicler of 1866 wrote of Kuhn: "above all, his burning energy for his craft…shone from his eyes."[36]

Major General Freiherr Franz von Kuhn, by Ludwig Ferdinand Graf

Heeresgeschichtliches Museum, Vienna

The Italian advance into the Trentino began on 21 June, but both sides' movements were affected by the result of Custoza, with Garibaldi ordered to suspend his offensive, while Kuhn was initially ordered to move in support of an anticipated Austrian advance over the Mincio. This notion was abandoned on 3 July. The campaign was a sequence of threats and countermoves, including even small flotillas on Lake Garda, as Austrian and Italian forces engaged in the back and forth fighting, often involving on the Austrian side small, mixed-arm Austrian detachments by now familiar to readers, as well as a few larger actions as Kuhn proved himself a master at plugging holes, exploiting opportunities and overcoming significant threats.[37]

A truce was arranged on 24 July, but drawn out negotiations and extensions continued into August and eventually Garibaldi's volunteers, with much grumbling and wounded pride, were required to leave the occupied parts of South Tirol.[38]

Jäger troops played a key role in the fight for the Tirol. They were von Kuhn's "fire brigade" and were called on in many situations to screen, hold key terrain, and provide reconnaissance of enemy positions, all key and appropriate Jäger missions.

A good example is that of Captain Zephiris of the "Kaiser-Jäger," who with the 7th and 9th Companies of that regiment, was ordered on 11 July to "put out a feeler" to the Austrian front (essentially a reconnaissance in force) to find and fix the enemy somewhere southeast of the Austrian base at Spondalunga, not far from the Swiss border.[39] The Jäger encountered a superior force and eventually were compelled to break out of an enemy encirclement at the point of their Haubajonets, while reinforcing Austrian forces engaged the enemy.

The deadly accuracy of long-range Jäger fire was demonstrated on 3 July when three companies of Kaiser-Jäger on the right flank of the Austrian position on Mt. Suello, just east of the northern end of Lake Idro, turned back multiple assaults by two Italian regiments led by Garibaldi himself, who sustained a wound to the thigh.[40]

The terrain around Lake Idro

Illustrated London News, 1866

The 33rd Company of the "Kaiser-Jäger," Oberleutnant Schindl, conducted a tenacious defense in terrible conditions when they were forced from their positions observing an enemy advance on a flimsy Austrian blockhouse in the Ampola Valley north of Lake Idro, including placement of heavy Italian guns. Retreating to the blockhouse, grandly styled "Fort" Ampola, the 200 Jäger joined a few artillerymen and 33 men from Nº. 11 Infantry Regiment commanded by Oberleutnant Anton von Preu garrisoning the place. They were quickly surrounded by a large advancing Italian force. Subjected to plunging fire from the Italian guns on the heights above the valley and threatened with a new heavy battery on the valley floor, they held out for three days in a building designed for 50 before finally surrendering on 19 July, But in the time thus won, Kuhn was able to marshal a large force to counterattack and clear the area.[41]

Clearly Kuhn knew the capabilities of his Jäger troops in 1866 and utilized them effectively. As a senior officer and major postwar theorist of mountain warfare, Franz von Kuhn's insights would be critical in preparing Austria's army for the mountain fighting that would come in 1914-18. In these battles Jäger would add new military distinctions, confirming their preeminent place in Austrian military tradition.

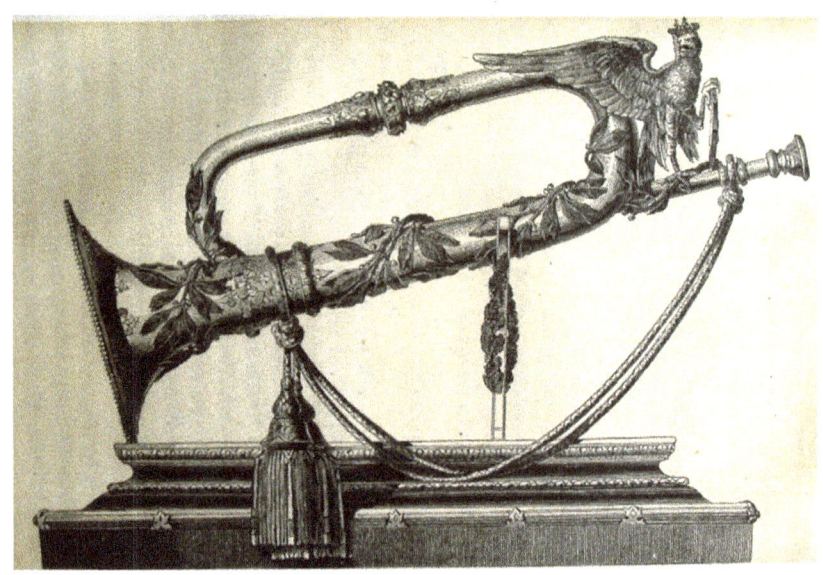

The presentation trumpet (Ehrensignalhorn) commemorating the distinguished service of the Nº. 10 Feld-Jäger Battalion in 1848-1849.

From Strack, Das Kopal-Denkmal in Znaim und das k.k. 10. Feld-Jäger Batallion

CHAPTER 7
JÄGER FIREARMS

The earliest Jäger units in Austrian service carried non-issue private weapons conforming to no official model designation.[1] From the time of the War of the Spanish Succession until the 1750's units raised for the duration and then disbanded would either bring their own hunting rifles with them into service, or else the proprietors of Freikorps Jäger units could procure suitable rifles from gun makers in centers like Suhl or Ferlach to equip their units. What the authors suspect is an example of one of the latter is pictured below. No maker's mark is discernible on the barrel flat. It resembles Jägerstützen attributed[2] to the Hessian Jäger of the 1770's in lock form, large finger-rest trigger guard, thumb piece, side plate, stock carving and cheek piece, wooden patch box cover, rear two-leaf flip sight in a dovetail, military iron ramrod, high relief brass hardware, and no bayonet bar, though the stock is definitely bulkier and now is fitted with a rear sling swivel that is likely a replacement for the original civilian-type button. The weapon is robust enough to have stood up to being used as a club when necessary. The bore has been reamed smooth, but barrel dimensions would accommodate a conventional Jägerstutzen caliber of .60-.65. The barrel is not swamped, but while a bit heavy at 10.2 lbs. (4.62 kg) the rifle is well-balanced and surprisingly handy. Supporting an Austrian connection is the thumb piece-- a Maria Theresa silver Thaler coin inletted in the stock.

Early Jägerstutzen with Maria Theresa Thaler thumb piece.

Authors' Photos

The M 1759 Jägerstutzen: A Dead End

In 1759, with a likely insufficient supply of rifled arms for an expanding Feld-Jäger corps, a "Commission Rifle" was placed in service.[3] This was the first rifled arm in the Austrian inventory but differed in important respects from those that followed. The Model 1759 was a flintlock with 6 lands and grooves and a bore of 15 mm (around .60 caliber). It shows signs of having been a stopgap weapon; put together at least in part of elements of other Austrian arms, according to Erich Gabriel,[4] in particular the M 1754 infantry rifle. Furniture was iron and the ramrod was wooden and carried in a channel under the stock. The trigger guard was a simple bow, without the finger support that became characteristic later. The stock was black-stained beech wood and without the patch box of later Jägerstutzen. The rifle was 112 cm long (44") and weighed 3 kg (6.6 lbs). There was no provision for a bayonet as Jäger at this time carried a Hirschfänger, similar to the kind of straight short sword used by hunters,[5] or another form of short infantry hanger. Nor is there in the representations we have of this rifle, any sign of sling swivels. This is odd, given Jäger practice, and may be inaccurate, or just further evidence of the "put together" stopgap nature of this arm.

The M 1759 Jägerstutzen

Print after Rudolf von Ottenfeld

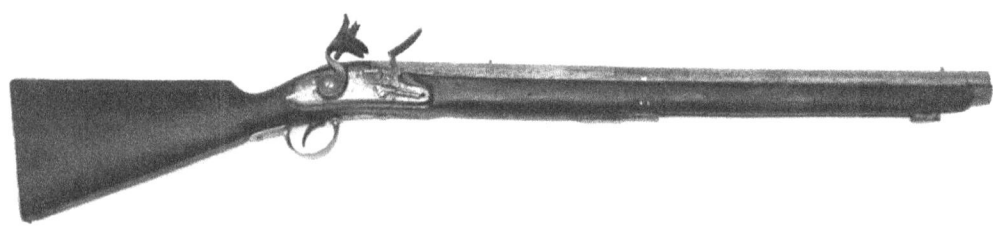

Authors' Photo

The heavily used and repaired weapon pictured above is similar in enough respects to the descriptions and images above of the M 1759 Jägerstutzen to merit noting here. The heavy 18th century barrel, which we believe is not the original rifled barrel bored out smooth, but rather a replacement, is not well-fitted to the stock. It has been cut off at the level of the brass nose cap, resulting in an overall length of 109 cm (43") which is 3 cm (1") shorter than the M 1759. The stock is black-stained beech with no sign of sling swivels ever having been present, though there is evidence of there having been at least one barrel pin. The hammer, lock plate and pan are like those of the Austrian M 1754 infantry musket. The simple bow trigger guard is brass, as are the civilian Jäger-type ramrod pipes and nose cap. (The representation of the M 1759 above by Ottenfeld also shows a brass trigger guard, butt plate and nose cap.)The 15.5 cm (6.25") left side plate is missing, but its inletting suggests a larger version of the M 1769 Jägerstutzen side plate. One characteristic this gun shares with the M 1769 and the M 1807 Jägerstützen is the distinctive completely flat area running from the butt plate up to the trigger plate of all of these arms. The wide brass Jäger-type butt plate may be original, though it has been altered to accommodate a decorative insert, now gone. No rear sight is present, but in a dovetail 13 cm (about 5") from the breech there is an iron peg, to which the sight may have been attached. In the place of the front sight is a similar dovetail-mounted peg. Weighing about 3.5 kg (8 lb.), this gun is lighter than the M 1769 Jägerstutzen, but is ungainly, with an awkward straight club-like stock with a very wide butt that does not shoulder at all well. In light of what we know of civilian Jäger rifles of the period, even assuming the original barrel was somewhat lighter, this seems like a gun designed by someone who either knew little, or because of other considerations-- like the order to use parts from other arms-- was forced to care little, about what made Jäger rifles desirable arms. If this sorry specimen is the remains of a M 1759 Jägerstutzen, later Jäger would have been well rid of it.

The Model 1769 Jägerstutzen

For our purposes, the first[6] widely issued service weapon for Jäger troops in the Austrian Army is the Model 1769 Jägerstutzen pictures below. This is a flintlock rifle of about 46 inches (1050 mm) in length that weighs 4.14 kg (a little over 9 pounds), and fires a 14.6 mm (about .60 caliber) round ball. Rifling has a right twist with 7 lands and grooves. The barrel is attached to the full length walnut stock by means of the tang screw, the front sling swivel screw, and two keys. For those accustomed to the more robust stock carving found on other weapons of the period, the M 1769's is definitely low relief and almost rudimentary. There is a cheek piece on the left side of the butt. The swamped barrel is octagonal for its full length. The top flat is marked *IOH SPÖ H I A NEUSTAT*, the Spöck family of gun makers were active in Wiener Neustadt 1765-1790.[7] A button for the sling is affixed to the stock behind the brass trigger guard finger support. In front of the button is a female-threaded plate to receive the ramrod knob when not in use. There is a wooden covered sliding patch box, a brass front blade sight and a two-leaf rear flip sight in dovetails with a long flat finial extension towards the muzzle. The lock and ramrod are both in the white, the remaining parts being blued. The heavy ramrod is iron with a simple top hat-shaped brass tip with central female-threaded opening to receive ball puller, worm, etc., and carried in a channel under the barrel, held in place by three brass pipes, the foremost one being made in one piece with the nose cap. The brass mountings of this rifle—ramrod pipes, trigger guard, side plate, nose cap and butt plate-- are similar to those on civilian Jägerstützen of the period. To assist in loading, the ramrod is equipped with a male-threaded removable turned walnut knob with a large central brass disc. When unscrewed from the rod the knob was carried behind the trigger guard. The M 1769 is an elegant, handy, well made rifle. It and the subsequent Model 1779 were the last Austrian Jägerstützen of the classic Germanic type before the advent of a distinctly Austrian design in 1795-6.

M 1769 Jägerstutzen. Note ramrod knob housed behind trigger guard.

Authors' Photo

The Jägerkarabiner: Early Types

In Rudolf von Ottenfeld's magnificent illustrated account of the Austrian army, Oskar Teuber, who wrote much of the text, goes on at some length[8] about *"heillose Confusion"* over the armament for the first and second ranks (*Glied*) of Jäger, i.e. those not armed with the *stutzen* or short rifle, at the time of the French Revolutionary Wars. To sort out the "hellish confusion" he invokes Max Sigismund Armand Josef von Paumgartten's 1802 *Abhandlung über den Dienst der Feldjäger zu Fuß*[9], a treatise on the duties of Feld-Jäger reflecting on the author's own service in the Wars of the French Revolution cited above. "Ottenfeld" here corrects a seeming omission by Anton Dolleczek, in his own contemporaneous book on Austrian weapons cited above. Whereas Dolleczek is silent[10] on any special armament for the non-stutzen-armed Jäger before the M 1807 Jägerkarabiner, Ottenfeld notes Paumgartten's description of a musket, shorter than the standard infantry model (*Musqueten*), fitted with an infantry-type socket bayonet, as the standard weapon for the first and second ranks. Ottenfeld even shows a circa 1800 Jäger so armed, alongside his third-rank comrade, in an accompanying illustration.[11]

In the photo below is such a pre-1807 Jägerkarabiner, corresponding to the one illustrated by Ottenfeld, except for the location of the rear sling swivel. It is 122.6 cm (48 ¼") long overall and weighs 3.1 kg (7 ½ pounds.) The beech stock features a cheek piece, but no patch box. The round, blued barrel has a bore of 17.6 mm (.66 caliber) that is not rifled. Furniture is in brass, with the rear sling swivel mounted in front of the trigger guard and the forward swivel on the middle barrel band. Rear and front bands are secured with springs. There is no rear sight, nor any evidence that there ever was one; the front sight is on the band. The ramrod is iron with 3 grooves under its flat head that may have been intended to also act as a jag, since the other end of the rod is not threaded. A somewhat stiff spring catch (not the refined form that is identified as Laukart) under the barrel secures the Austrian M

1799 triangular socket bayonet (*Stichbajonet*). The lock is flat, and the hammer is serpentine, rather than the Unterberger reinforced type, which could suggest a pre-1798 date.

Pre-1807 Jägerkarabiner and M 1799 bayonet

Author's Photo

The Doppelstutzen

Arming Jäger of the same unit with two different firearms was the solution the Austrians settled on to solve the problem of slow loading for rifles. A more expensive alternative was the double rifle (*Doppelstutzen*). As noted above, Grenzer sharpshooters were the only troops we can assert confidently were ever issued this weapon, since a request to arm Jäger with them was denied in 1760. In an "over-under" arrangement the Doppelstutzen had a rifled barrel on top and a smoothbore barrel underneath. This design permitted deliberate, accurate rifle fire combined with quicker, easier-loaded smooth bore defensive fire when needed (for example, against threatening cavalry).

The top barrel was rifled with a right twist of 7 lands and grooves. The bottom barrel fired a round ball of around the same caliber 14.8 mm (around .58 caliber). Two models are known, a Model 1768 and a Model 1795, though the evidence of

Lacy's 1760 requests suggests there were earlier versions. The Doppelstutzen was the same length as the Model 1769 Jägerstutzen. These were beautifully crafted weapons made by the premier gun makers in Austria, and were expensive. Sights were like the Model 1769 Jägerstutzen. The M 1768 ramrod was iron with a turned wooden grip and was carried separately, but in the later model the ramrod was carried on the side of the rifle, between the barrels. At 5.5 kg (twelve pounds) it was a heavy rifle to carry, and although equipped with sling swivels, seems to have been carried in a leather sack (*stutzen sacke*), as shown in the illustration on p. 128 above. In the case of Grenzers at least, a pike with a hook to act as a shooting rest, and as last-ditch defense against cavalry was provided. The Doppelstützen could not have been issued in great numbers. Their scarcity on the collectors' market and extremely high cost of production seems to argue that there were not many made. According to Ottenfeld 256 Grenzers in each Grenzer infantry regiment were equipped with the double guns. In the last Turkish War of 1788-1790, the serious threat always posed by Turkish cavalry may have argued for issuing Doppelstützen to the Grenzers in these kinds of numbers. Absent further information, these can be regarded as the arms Jäger did *not* get in significant numbers, though Ottenfeld[12] suggests that there were at least some Doppelstutzen-armed Jäger c. 1778.

The M 1768 Doppelstutzen

Courtesy of the Dorotheum, Vienna, Auction 12.12.2016

The Model 1779 Jägerstutzen

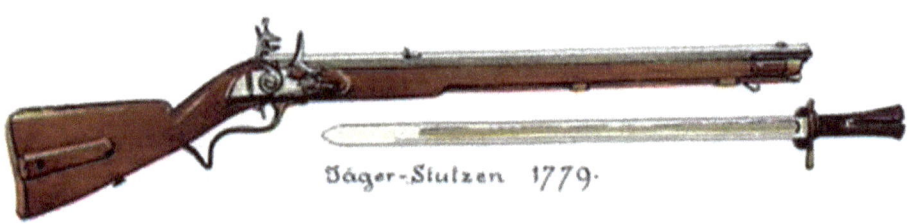

Print after Rudolf von Ottenfeld

The Model 1779 Jägerstutzen shows features that clearly point to its fabrication using parts from captured Prussian weapons, notably the trigger guard and larger caliber. At 4.8 kilograms (10.6 lbs) it was heavier than the M 1769 and was 4.5 cm (1.8 inches) shorter (shortening the weapon sped the loading process and likely provided more thickness of metal to accommodate rifling) and was bored to 17.6 mm (.69 caliber) as compared to the 14.5 mm (.58 caliber) of the Model 1769 (reflecting the larger bore of the Prussian Infantry muskets used in the Model 1779's construction). Following the Prussian model, it had a bar for mounting an Austrian version of a Hirschfänger bayonet.

The Model 1795/6 Jägerstutzen

The M 1796 Jägerstutzen and M 1796 Haubajonet

Print after Rudolf von Ottenfeld

The Model 1795/96 Jägerstutzen as originally configured was very similar to the M 1769: with a 14.5 mm (58 caliber) bore, length of 105.2 cm (41 ½ in) and weighing 4 kilograms (8.8 lbs). In a change from earlier models, the powder chamber was somewhat widened and the threads in the breech plug were made deeper (presumably for additional strength at that connection). Originally, the rifle had a full-length octagonal barrel and was fitted with a bar for a Hirschfänger bayonet.

In 1796, the rifle was reconfigured: the stock was shortened and the front 11cm (4.3 inches) of the barrel was rounded to allow for the use of a Haubajonet. It was then designated the Model 1796 Jägerstutzen and, other than a small difference in weight (the M 96 weighed 3.8 kg or 8.4 lbs) and length, (102.5 cm or 40.4 in) was the same rifle as the Model 1795.

The M 1796 is notable because, with its Haubajonet, it establishes the form Austrian Jägerstützen would essentially maintain until the end of the nineteenth century.

The Model 1807 Jägerstutzen

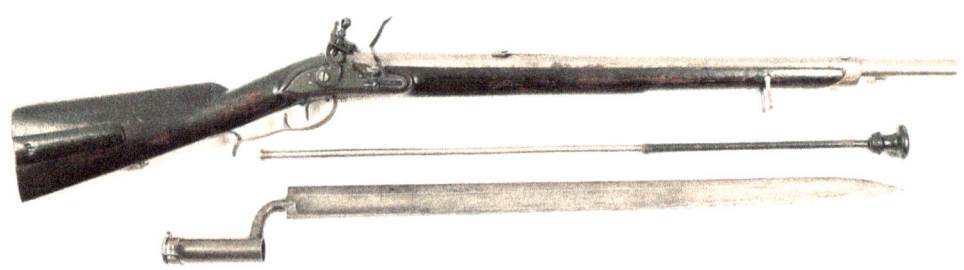

Model 1807 Jägerstutzen, ramrod (note leather sheathing) and M 1796 bayonet

Authors' Photo

The Model 1807 Jägerstutzen pictured above is a rifled flintlock with an octagonal barrel. The barrel is rounded at the muzzle to accommodate what was to become the characteristic Austrian wide blade socket bayonet, the M 1796 Haubajonet for Jäger, which utilized a lug on the underside of the barrel. Mounted, the bayonet was carried under the barrel. The lock plate was flat and the opening of the reinforced hammer was the heart-shaped "Unterberger" type. The barrel is attached to the stock by means of the tang screw, a bolt passing through a lug at the bottom of the barrel which also secures the forward sling swivel, and an additional short screw at the base of the nose cap. The stock is of walnut with a large cheek pad. There is a domed wooden-capped sliding patch box and a button for securing the sling at the butt end of the stock. The ramrod is carried separately and has a turned wooden knob to assist loading the tight patched ball. At the center of the knob is an insert used to start the ball. The opposite end was a steel tip with interior threading to accommodate ball pullers, cleaning jags and patch worms. The ramrod shown is sheathed in leather on the upper third, presumably to protect the bore. The rifle was

105 cm (46 inches) long, had a 13.9 mm (.54 cal) bore with 7 lands and grooves with a right twist, and weighs 3.55 kg (9 lbs). The sights consist of a front blade affixed to the barrel and a rear two-leaf sight in a dovetail. The example also contains a peep sight in the sight leaf.

The Model 1807 Jägerstutzen was one of two new weapons developed for Jäger troops. It was issued to Jäger of the 3rd rank and NCOs only. It was an accurate weapon with a considerable effective range and remained a standard Jäger armament, with modifications, until the appearance of the Model 1842 Jägerstutzen[13]

Pictured below is a variant of the M 1807 Jägerstutzen marked *"J. Albert in Wien"* fitted with what Gabriel[14] identifies as the right-hand lock of a M 1795 Doppelstutzen and a "slightly longer" barrel. Other elements conform to the M 1807. With the hurried expansion of the Jäger division cadres into full battalions beginning in late 1808 (see above, Chapter 3), and the consequent need to arm them, turning to gun makers who could fabricate 1807-type rifles utilizing existing stocks of Doppelstutzen parts may have been an expedient. Both the rifle Gabriel describes and the one below were the product of Vienna gun makers. Unlike the Jägerstutzen in Gabriel, this one is not fitted with a bayonet lug.

M 1807 Jägerstutzen variant with long Doppelstutzen lock by K. Albert, Vienna.

Authors' Photo

The Model 1807 Jägerkarabiner

The second Jaeger troops' arm adopted in 1807 was an updated model of the short musket described above intended for issue to Jäger of the first and second ranks. These henceforth seem to be referred to as *Jägerkarabiner*.[15] This was a flintlock smoothbore with a length of about 123 cm (47 in) in 17.6 mm (71 caliber) and with a weight of 3.55 kg (9 lbs.). It had the standard flat lock with a reinforced Unterberger hammer, the opening forming a heart shape. The barrel was round except for the sides being slightly flattened towards the breech. The Jägerkarabiner was sighted with a blade on the top barrel band and a single- leaf rear sight. The barrel was fastened to the walnut stock by means of the tang screw, and three barrel bands of which the first and third were secured by band springs. The stock had a cheek pad and the hardware was brass. Sling swivels were attached to the rear of the one piece, spurred trigger guard and to the middle barrel band. The ramrod was carried on the weapon and secured by a spring in the stock. The ramrod had a threaded hole in the tip to accommodate cleaning and unloading tools. A quadrangular fairly wide Austrian socket bayonet model 1799 (Stichbajonet) was utilized, fastening to the weapon with a spring catch and spur under the barrel

M 1807 Jägerkarabiner converted to Console ignition with its bayonet.

Courtesy of the Dorotheum, Vienna, Auction 09.11.2015

The Console and Augustin Conversions:
False Economy and Making the Best of it

In the 1830's most of the European powers were already experimenting with or adopting the percussion cap ignition system.[16] The Austrians were interested, but as usual limited by the lack of adequate funds to adopt a completely new series of weapons. As a result, in 1831, Giuseppe Console, an imperial financial bureaucrat from Milan, developed the "Console" lock. This lock used a "sausage," (i.e. tube-shaped) igniter that fit into a channel on the lock in a reconfigured pan. When struck it communicated the ignition through the touchhole to fire the charge in the breech.[17]

Guided by his understanding of the budgetary constraints, Console designed his lock so that it only required changing out three parts from the existing flint locks, allowed keeping the original stocks, and merely re-engineering the pan to accommodate the "sausage," adding a new pan cover, and fitting a steel striking plate between the beaks of the existing hammer to replace the flint. Fiscally it was a masterpiece.

The Army was at first resistant, but in 1835 agreed to test the system. The test was conducted by a captain and 8 Jäger from the 6th Feld-Jäger Battalion. The test was rigged in that the Console weapons were not measured against any cap ignition models, but only flintlocks. The Console weapons won hands down. General Vincenz von Augustin, later the chief of the state Arsenal in Vienna, embraced the design and conversions began in earnest. In 1836 600 guns were converted in Linz (presumably Jägerkarabiner) and shortly thereafter the decision was made to convert all Infantry weapons to the Console system. The Console design remained the K. u. K. conversion system until 1838.[18]

Agents from Bavaria and Württemberg got their hands on examples of the Console weapons. After testing, they sensibly rejected the design.[19] The percussion system the Prussians adopted in 1835 was vastly superior.

Prussian Jägerstutzen M 1810, percussion lock of the 1835 conversion.

AUTHORS' PHOTO

The M 1807 Jägerkarabiner was updated to Console ignition, making it the Model 1807/35. Early on problems were identified with the Console locks, the most serious being reliability after repeated use.

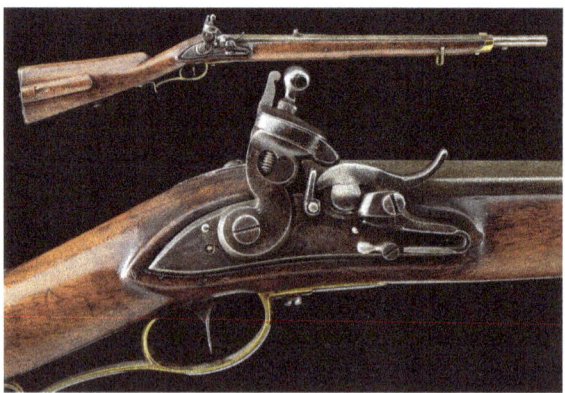

A converted M 1807 Jägerstutzen showing detail of the Console lock

Courtesy of Czerny's International Auction House S.r.l.

On 28 February 1835, Colonel Ignaz Freiherr Zephyris zu Greit, the Commander of the 6th Feld-Jäger Battalion in Eger wrote to his Division Commander in Prague that the "new" Console guns have been shown to throw igniter fragments into the eyes of the soldier, making the troops flinch ("*Feuerscheu*") and affecting accuracy. He requested permission to contact Console about the problems. Whether Colonel zu Greit's request was the precipitating factor or not, Console undertook a series of modifications including an outside pan cover. None were particularly effective.

On 29 April 1838, Kaiser Ferdinand I was persuaded of the need to replace the Console and ordered a replacement system advocated by General Augustin to be adopted. On 30 July 1838, 150 Console weapons were accepted at the K.u.K. Arsenal in Vienna for conversion to the Augustin system and tested at the Arsenal outer wall.

Upon conclusion of experimental alterations and testing, on 27 July, 1840, all K.u.K military weapons were ordered to be converted to the new Augustin system.[20]

Between 1840 and 1841, 80,000 guns were modified. The Model 1840 Infantry musket was the first Austrian arm newly- manufactured with the so called "Augustin (Large) Ignition Lock".[21]

The usual Austrian financial constraints slowed complete conversion to the Augustin system. Some weapons which had never been converted to Console were retained in the ranks as flintlocks. Others, including Infantry Models 1798, 1807, 1808, and 1828, were successfully converted and were redesignated as Models 1798/40, 1807/40, etc.

In service, the new Augustin lock on the 1840-41 guns did exhibit one serious design weakness: the "tooth" that struck the priming "sausage" (or tube as it was usually referred to in English-speaking countries) had to be machined perfectly. Too sharp and the sausage would be severed and block the ignition hole. On the other hand, if the tooth was machined too dull, or with wear, the sausage did not ignite at all. A further modification was needed, but before that could be initiated Augustin had to clear up a tangle of bureaucratic impediments.²²

A large source of difficulty in implementing the Augustin conversions was the Austrian tendency to embrace false economies, specifically the desire of the Imperial War Office to utilize old parts, including those from captured foreign weapons still on hand in the Vienna Arsenal. Augustin and his staff valiantly tried to comply, but finally, frustrated with the needless complexities and the concurrent negative effect on quality, Augustin requested and was granted permission to use completely new parts henceforward. He had also recommended another innovation, and this received imperial approval at the same time. On 29 April 1842 Augustin was authorized to begin manufacturing redesigned Augustin locks by machine at the Vienna Arsenal. The "Small Machine Lock" design was slimmer, had a rounded rather than pointed lock plate, and was easier and cheaper to fabricate. With a redesigned "tooth" or striker reliability was improved. The Model 1842 Infantry Musket and the Model 1842 Kammerbüchse incorporated the new system.²³ Thus "small" or "machine" locks are found on all firearms made after 1842, and remained the standard until the adoption of the Lorenz system in 1854.

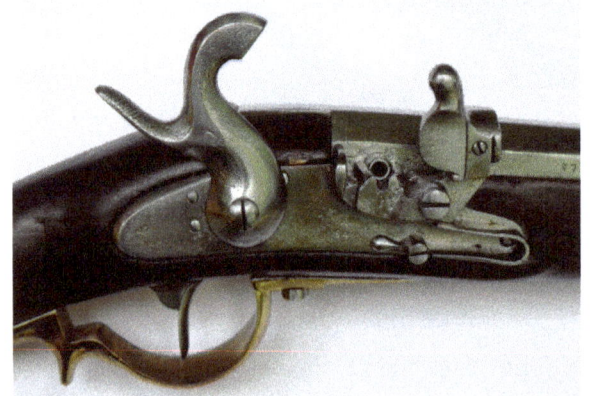 

Small Machine Augustin Lock on M 1842 Kammerbuchse (left) and Jägerstutzen cocked and uncocked. Note rounded ends of lock.

Authors' Photos

Augustin "sausage" or tube from a contemporary manual

With the lock issue settled, General Augustin turned his attention to the quest for increased accuracy. To this end, his design for the Model 1842 *Kammerbüchse* (chamber rifle) utilized, with modifications, the "patent chamber" concept developed by the French Captain Henri-Gustave Delvigne.

From the late 1820's Captain Delvigne sought a way for riflemen to load and shoot faster, and with greater accuracy. He developed a system that utilized a rifled barrel and a standard round ball, but undersized, with plenty of space between projectile and the interior of the bore, so that it loaded easily. Powder was poured down the muzzle and collected in a chamber in the breech slightly smaller in diameter than the bore. This shielded the powder from crushing as the bullet was rammed home. Crushing black powder under pressure changes its burn rate (the smaller the powder grain the faster the rate) thereby introducing ignition variables that would ultimately affect accuracy. In addition to shielding the powder, in theory, the chamber positioned the bullet to be pounded against the chamber rim with the heavy ramrod by the rifleman delivering several sharp raps, and in this way to expand (obdurate) it to more tightly engage the rifling. But Delvigne's system fell short in two ways: the chamber was difficult to clear of built-up fouling, and pounding with the rod did not produce enough expansion of the ball to improve accuracy sufficiently.

Baron Augustin tried to improve upon Delvigne's work. His Model 1842 Kammerbüchse would utilize only cold swaged lead balls, which therefore had no sprue (*Spiegel*) or flat spot created in the casting process. He also rounded the chamber reflecting the shape of the ball both for better deformation and easier cleaning.[24]

Officially, all available older Jägerkarabiner were supposed to be collected and converted to the 1842 Kammerbüchse pattern, including the new machine locks, as well as cutting down existing older Austrian Jägerkarabiner barrels from 84.73 cm to 79.33 cm.[25] How many actually were converted is not clear. We do know that some M 1842's were manufactured by the eminent Viennese master gun maker Ferdinand Frühwirth utilizing non-Austrian parts on hand. He used surplus brass furniture and some of the 47,000 captured French musket barrels then in storage in the Vienna Arsenal after 1815. The barrels, possibly acquired in 1815 from St. Etienne during the Austrian occupation, were, after inspection, cut down from around one meter to 84.5 cm and rifled. Cutting the barrel down won enough additional thickness to permit polishing and rifling. All things considered, the 1842 arms for Jäger troops represented major changes in terms of ignition mechanism, ammunition and even bayonet forms. While both improvements and economy may have been achieved with these M 1842 arms, it came at the price of much subsequent confusion for arms historians.

Models 1842 and 1844: More "*Heillose Confusion*" and Some Clarifications

The Model 1842 Kammerbüchse according to Götz was designed for issue to the 1st and 2nd ranks (*Glied*) to replace the Jägerkarabiner.[26] However, adoption of the '42 was envisioned as only the first step in providing one long arm for all three Jäger ranks, to be realized ultimately in adoption of a succeeding Model 1844 Kammerbüchse[27]. The confusion regarding subsequent arms may be attributable to this ambition never having been achieved. Instead, during the 1840's, an updated Augustin Jägerstutzen, designated as the Model 1842, with the small machine lock,[28] went to NCO's and to Jäger in the 3rd rank. (See below, p 144.) This deviation from plan may have subsequently created the impression that there was either a Model 1842 Kammerbüchse and Jägerstutzen or a Model 1844 Kammerbüchse, but not both, since most reliable authorities cite only one or the other.[29] In none of our research have we found any expert describing both models 1842 and 1844 Kammerbüchse as two discrete, if related, arms.

We have, instead, come to believe that in the case of the rifle for the first and second ranks, "Model 1842" actually refers only to those initial few thousand conversions utilizing foreign components by Frühwirth. We take the term "Model 1844" as indicating an entirely new-made Kammerbüchse incorporating all of the 1842 features with some additional significant updates.

As for the third rank's Jägerstützen, there are so few surviving, and so little evidence concerning these arms in the sources, we are inclined to designate all the Augustin- lock short rifles issued until the Lorenz models were adopted as the M 1842 Jägerstützen, and will treat them as such in this account. We are here following Ottenfeld's lead, as his plate illustrating "Feuerwaffen der Jäger" employs the rubric "Jäger-Stützen 1842-1848" for this arm.[30]

The Model 1842 Kammerbüchse

The Model 1842 is described as incorporating the small machine Augustin lock[31], and brass nose cap. All stocks were supposed to have been beech, but the rifle pictured below is in walnut. Like this one, stocks had a domed sliding wooden patch box for cleaning tools. Furniture is brass, and the iron ramrod has what becomes a typical Austrian feature, a brass band in the tulip head to ease wear on the rifling. Stock and barrel are attached by two brass barrel bands with retaining springs on the fore end and a double nose cap. There is small diameter ramrod spring retaining rod behind the lower barrel band. This rifle is in .71 caliber with 12 lands and grooves. Its sights consist of a domed half circular "*korn*" on the front barrel band and a rear spring-mounted flip sight graduated for 3, 4 and 500 paces with a standing open "V" battle sight for closer ranges at the rear of the sight assembly. The 1842-dated lock is in the white, with a small Austrian eagle. The other iron parts show some sign of having been blued. The trigger guard is brass with a spur finger rest. We suspect that this particular rifle is one of the conversions by Früwirth, as the barrel length conforms to what is known of the Früwirth guns, and the high quality of the workmanship overall suggests a product of the Früwirth shop. The formidable M 1842 Haubajonet, about 3 inches shorter than the M 1796, and without locking ring, is attached by means of a Laukart spring.[32]

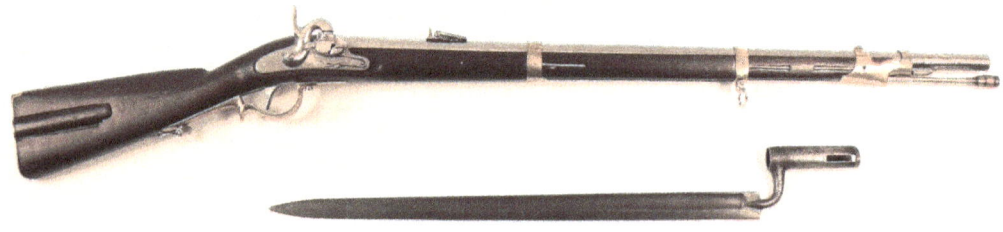

M 1842 Kammerbüchse and bayonet.

Authors' Photo

The Model 1842 Jägerstutzen

The Model 1842 Jägerstutzen is described[33] as being 105 cm long (41 in) with a 66 cm barrel (26 in), in 15.5 mm (.61 caliber) with four lands and grooves and a right twist. Its weight is 325 kg (7.2 lbs). The Jägerstutzen below conforms to these dimensions. The octagonal barrel is rounded 11 cm (4.3 in) from the muzzle to accommodate the large 79 cm long overall (31 in) wide blade socket bayonet which utilized a lug on the underside of the barrel. In this model the mounted bayonet sits underneath the barrel, as on the 1807, rather than to the right side. The Augustin lock is of the small machine type and is dated 1847 with the Austrian eagle at the end of the plate. The barrel is attached to the stock by means of the tang screw, a bolt passing through a lug below the barrel, and a second bolt which also passes through and secures the forward sling swivel. The stock is of good quality beech with a large cheek pad. There is a domed wooden sliding patch box and a button for securing the sling at the butt end of the stock. Butt plate, 1807-type trigger guard and nose cap are of brass. The heavy ramrod was carried separately (see above Chapter 4) and had a large 5.5 cm diameter (2.2 in) turned wooden walnut knob with a wide, flat brass center to assist in starting the round. The opposite end contains male threading to accommodate ramrod tip, ball pullers, cleaning jags and patch worms. Unfortunately with this sample arm all these appendages are missing. The sights consisted of a front brass blade in a dovetail and a rear two-leaf flip sight in a dovetail with a long flat finial extension similar to that of the M 1807.

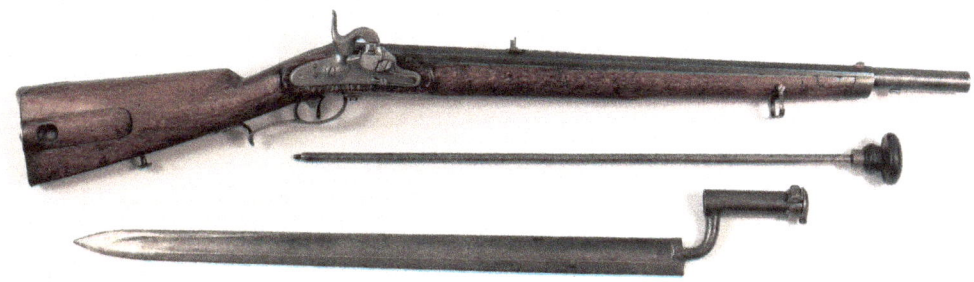

Model 1842 Jägerstutzen, bayonet (M 1796) and ramrod

Authors' Photo

The Model 1842 looked back and forward, to the Model 1807 and the Model 1854 Jägerstützen, with design elements of both.

The Model 1844 Kammerbüchse

The 1847-dated rifle pictured below is a little over 48 inches long (122.8 cm) and had a barrel of 84.5 cm (33.5 in). It is in 18.1 mm (.71 caliber), with 12 lands and grooves with a right twist and weighs 4.66 kg (10.1 lbs.) The barrel is octagonal in the rear to round moving towards the front. The front sight is a dovetailed small blade on a rectangle which is welded to the barrel. The rear sight has two flip-up leaves, with a standing battle sight on the rear, a significant characteristic that distinguishes 44's from 42's.

M 1842 Kammerbüchse sights. Note the similarity of the rear sight to that of the later M 1849.

M 1844 Kammerbüchse sights

Authors' Photo

Furniture is brass and the stock of beech with a cheek pad. The barrel is attached to the stock by means of three bands secured by band springs and the tang screw. There is a one piece trigger guard with a small finger support like the '42 and the rear sling swivel is attached at the rear or butt end of the trigger guard. The iron ramrod has a conical shaped recess and a hole for the "Zugstift", a small metal extension of the combination tool which allowed more torque to be applied to the rod while cleaning or removing a ball. The opposite end is threaded to accommodate ball pullers and cleaning jags.[34] Some M 1842-type brass-banded ramrods are also seen on these rifles, but as stocks of the older ramrods were used up, simple iron was deemed adequate since the new-made, as opposed to converted, barrels on the M '44's may have been judged more durable. A M 1842 Haubajonet was issued, fastened to the barrel with a Laukart system spring. Early models had a wooden covered sliding patch box on the right side of the stock, but it was eliminated from rifles like this made after 1847.[35]

Model 1844 Kammerbüchse, with original Augustin lock (top) and below as converted for export with a Model 1842 bayonet.

Authors' Photo

Documentary evidence suggests that by 1846 all Divisions and most Grenzers were supposed to have been equipped with the Model 1844 which would have replaced all Karabiner and Stützen.[36] However, shooting tests proved the superior accuracy of the M 1842 Jägerstutzen and, as suggested above, these were retained for the third Division Jäger and all NCO's for a number of years thereafter. They are seen in many representations of Jäger the Italian War of 1848-49.

It has been reported that some 6,000[37] to 10,000[38] M 1844's were bought by United States purchasing agents in Bohemia and other provinces of the empire in late 1861. Most were issued to troops in the Western theater in early 1862 and used until better weapons became available.[39] We suspect that what actually was purchased was a mixture of M1842, M1844 and M1849 rifles converted to percussion either in Liege, Vienna, Turin or in the US. In addition, up to 25,000 of these in their original Augustin configuration were imported by the Confederacy, all but 15,000 being ultimately converted to percussion in Confederate arsenals.[40]

The Model 1849 Kammerbüchse

The Model 1849 Kammerbüchse below is in most respects similar to its predecessor. The front sight consists of a blade attached directly to the barrel. The rear sight is a standing v-notched blade with a spring-assisted flip up sight graduated from 150 to 600 paces. Furniture, ramrod, and other details were like the Model 1844, except the front band, which is now simplified. Also on this rifle, the large, wide curved trigger guard with rounded finger grip first appears. This model reverts to a transverse rear "key" and front sling swivel bolt passing through an under barrel lug to secure the barrel to the beech wood stock.

The authors can find no hard evidence that the Model 1849 was ever issued to Jäger troops. It was specifically designed for the Imperial Danube/Sava Flotilla (Kaiserliche-und Königliche-Donau-Flotilla)" and other small units in the Austro-

Hungarian Imperial forces.[41]

Kammerbüchse Model 1849 converted to percussion for export to the U.S. (top) and below in original Augustin form with a M 1849 Haubajonet.

Authors' Photo

The Model 1849 was widely converted to percussion and imported into the United States during the American Civil War. Union records indicate that over 26,000 were purchased. It was also said to have been used by Italian nationalists in the 1850's and 60's and for this reason became widely known as the "Garibaldi" rifle, even being referred to by this name[42] by the U.S. Ordnance Department.

The Lorenz Era

Josef Lorenz was born in Vienna in 1814, the son of a master mechanic/locksmith in the employ of the K.u.K firearms factory in Vienna. When he was 17, Lorenz began his training in the 14-year apprentice program there.[43] In addition, the young man studied at the Vienna Polytechnic Institute and by 1846 was certified as an *Obermeister* gun maker, followed by further study and increasing status.[44]

In 1849, Lorenz developed a wall gun designed for use in fixed fortifications utilizing the percussion cap ignition system at a time when Austria was still manufacturing arms with the Augustin lock. The next year he also invented a prosthetic limb for amputees, for which he was awarded the "100-Florin Conventions Coin" by Emperor Franz Josef I.[45] Lorenz also became an honorary Lieutenant of Artillery,[46] another mark of professional distinction for his work.

After the retirement of the 70 year-old Baron von Augustin as Chief of the Austrian *Feldzeugmeisterei* (essentially the national arsenal command) in 1850, a new era of Austrian arms development dawned.[47] With a decision to alter all cavalry firearms to the percussion system, and reworking of various captured Piedmontese weapons[48] for use by auxiliary troops, Austria began the shift away from the Augustin tube-lock.

Conditions were now favorable for Lorenz to begin work on a new projectile which would become the foundation of a wholly new line of Austrian military firearms.[49] By 1852, he had a come up with a workable design.[50]

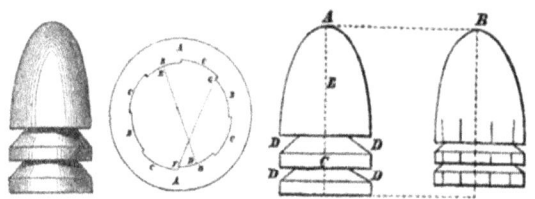

The undersized solid-based Lorenz compression bullet, like the Minie bullet, could be rammed down even a fouled bore. As the gases from the ignited powder expanded, the Lorenz bullet was pushed to the point where the two cutout portions were mashed upward (B), causing the bullet to widen enough to engage the rifling.

From the 1857 Austrian manual on the Lorenz infantry rifle for officers

Now that he had a bullet, Lorenz began to design a completely new series of weapons around it. The Lorenz system was officially adopted pursuant to the report to the Emperor of the Weapons Trial Commission of December 1853.[51] The resulting wholesale re-arming was unprecedented in Austrian military history. In the past updates and improvements had been piecemeal, often with modifications of existing out-of-date weapons. Now, however, the Emperor was convinced to adopt Lorenz's new series, which included a cavalry pistol, two models of the Jäger rifle, a short rifle for support troops (the so called "Extra-Corps), and two models of infantry rifle. Franz Josef accordingly approved a significant increase in the Army budget to speed adoption of the Lorenz system.[52] The Lorenz series of military arms would prove to be as good if not better than any other small arms systems adopted by the European powers of the day. The rapid-fire Prussian Needle Rifle could not match Lorenz arms in terms of durability, ease of maintenance, shooter-friendliness and accuracy.

Lorenz's new rifling was flat (easier to keep clean) with a slow right twist. The result was significantly increased range and accuracy over previous Austrian arms. The smaller bullet, and resulting somewhat lighter load, saved powder and lead. The solid-based bullet was easier to manufacture with steam swaging equipment than the hollow-based Minie or Burton bullet. Finally, the lighter rounds enabled the soldier to carry more ammunition on his person. Other South German states[53] decided to follow Austria's lead in adopting their own smaller bullets.

A rifle from one of the South German states that followed Austria's lead in adopting the 54 Caliber bullet. This is an Engineer rifle, the M 1864, from Nassau.

Authors' Photo

Josef Lorenz's inventiveness and relentless efforts in making the case for his designs earned him the Order of the Iron Crown, being named the *Oberwerksmeister* in the Vienna Arsenal and in 1862 being elevated to the nobility.[54]

But 12 years after Lorenz's design was adopted, war with Prussia confirmed the military desirability of breech loaders, and the Lorenz era came to an end. Joseph Lorenz died in Vienna on the 19th of November 1879, largely forgotten.

The Lorenz Firearms

Cavalry Pistol Model 1859

Authors' Photo

Model 1854 Extra-Corps Rifle and number-matching bayonet. Also manufactured was an alternate model with a fixed block rear sight and placement of the rear band spring on the butt side of the stock. The Extra-Corps utilized the Infantry rifle bayonet.

Authors' Photo

Model 1854 Infantry Rifle Type I (with fixed block sight) and bayonet

Authors' Photo

Model 1854 Infantry Rifle Type II (with adjustable flip-up sight) and bayonet

Authors' Photo

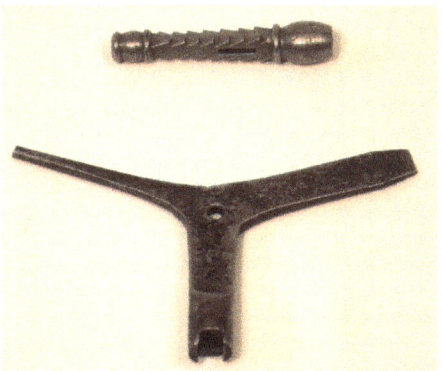

Combination tool and cleaning jag that were issued with Lorenz shoulder arms.

Authors' Photo

Lorenz Jäger Rifles

Model 1854 Jägerstutzen and ramrod, top, and Dornstutzen with M 1854 bayonet

Authors' Photo

Lorenz's two short rifles were issued exclusively to Jäger. With these new models a longer rifle, the Jägerkarabiner, was dispensed with entirely for Jäger. This standard Jäger rifle is 110 cm long (43.25 in) with a barrel of 71 cm (28 in) and intended for the first and second rank Jäger. It is, as were all of the Lorenz models, chambered for a 13.9 mm (.54 caliber) compression bullet. Rifling twisted to the right and consisted of four lands and grooves. The entire rifle weighs 4.08 kg (10.6 lbs).

The barrel is octagonal up to 11 cm from the bore where it is rounded to accept the bayonet socket. The barrel is attached to the stock by means of two transverse keys. The stock has a cheek piece and was generally made from walnut (as opposed to the other Lorenz infantry and Extra-Corps models with beech stocks). Sling swivels are located on the end of the stock and about 16.5 cm (6.5 in) from the nose cap with a screw passing through a lug at the bottom of the barrel that provides additional stability between barrel and stock. Furniture is iron and either browned, blued, or in the white. As in earlier Jägerstützen, the ramrod was not carried in the weapon, but separately. The rod tip is shaped to accommodate the head of the bullet without deforming it and has a brass ring to prevent damage to the rifling. The inside of the tip is threaded to accept a ball screw, cleaning jag or patch puller. The opposing end has a wooden knob referred to as the "pear." The adjustable sight was of the "Danish" design. The bowed, sight blade is marked from 300 to 1000 paces (300 - 750 meters).

These models were manufactured by the Vienna Arsenal and by a number of gunsmiths in Vienna and elsewhere and did not have interchangeable parts. Weapons examined for the K.u.K. military were stamped with inspectors' marks, and a small double headed eagle at the back of the lock plate and the last three numbers of the year on the lock plate below the bolster denote acceptance into Austrian service. As there were many of these manufactured for other German states, Jägerstützen can be encountered without these marks.

The second type, the so-called *"Dornstutzen"* (or thorn or pillar carbine, i.e. the Delvigne–Thourvenin system) was intended for use by the third rank sharpshooters for sniping. These Jäger worked the flanks and were placed in the rear to facilitate their fanning out behind the screen of the first two ranks. The Dornstutzen pictured is of the same dimensions as the Jägerstutzen. There is a nominal difference in weight. The "thorn" was designed to keep a small space between charge and bullet. It was thought that this provided a more even burning of powder and hence a more accurate shot for the third rank sharpshooters. Troopers were trained not to beat the bullet down onto the thorn, but to push it down gently until contact was made. The drawback of the Dornstutzen was difficulty in cleaning around the thorn. This model has a sight with a longer blade and marked from 400 – 1200 paces. The sight was mounted to the barrel on a longer base than that of the standard model and is recognizable by this feature.

Comparison of Jägerstutzen and Dornstutzen sights (Dornstutzen is on the right)

Author's Photo

Jägerstutzen Variants

Variant A is a standard stützen with a slot cut for the ramrod to be carried in the weapon. This alteration for accommodating a ramrod also included a sheet metal cone at the bore end of the channel to assist in getting the rod into the channel easily. In this model, 18.5 cm (7 in) of the ramrod is exposed. All other properties are unchanged.

Variant B also provides for carrying the ramrod on the weapon, but uses a cone farther back along the stock, exposing 30 cm (11.8 in) of the ramrod. This variation also used a different bayonet, similar to that used with the model 1849 rifle.[55]

Model 1854 Jägerstutzen, Variant A

Authors' Photo

Model 1854 Jägerstutzen, Variant B

Author's Photo

Model 1862

In 1862, at the urging of the Minister of War and Arsenal Commandant, August Graf Degenfeld-Schonburg, a new variant was developed.[56] This Model combined elements of the Jägerstutzen and the Extra Corps. At 62 cm (24.5 in) the barrel was shorter, with a total length of only 102 cm (40.25 in) as opposed to the 110 cm (43.25 in) of the Jägerstutzen. The weapon was lighter at 3.26 kg (7 lbs). It utilized the standard Lorenz flip up infantry sight graduated from 400 to 900 paces. The stock had no cheek piece; furniture was iron and included the standard Jäger finger grip behind the trigger guard. The barrel was attached to the stock with the tang screw, a barrel band and a small screw passing through the nose cap into a socket in the underside of the barrel. The sling swivels were on the barrel band and a few centimeters from the end of the butt. There was a small ring on the front side of the trigger guard which was probably used to secure a protector for the nipple, like that of the British P 1853 rifles, allowing dry firing with limited damage.[57]

Like all of the 1862 modifications, this weapon utilized the so called "small cap lock" (*Kleine Kapselschloss*). This was a slight modification of the original Lorenz lock which removed the front metal tab on the top of the lock. This made fitting the bolster to the lock much easier and made the lock plate easier and cheaper to produce.

Barrels for these Models, like all of the 1862 variants, were made from steel as opposed to the iron used in earlier models.[58]

The Model 1862 Jägerstützen was essentially a M1854 Dornstutzen with a ramrod channel (Variant A) and the "small cap lock."[59] There is no evidence that this weapon was ever placed into service with K.u.K. forces.

The Model 1862 Jägerstutzen, "*Leichter Art*" (light type) was significantly modified from the M1854. It had a ramrod channel (Variant B) and utilized the "small cap lock" found in all of the 1862 modifications. The barrel was steel and round except for back portion which was octagonal. This barrel configuration was the source of the reduced weight. The front sight consisted of a "Korn" or small pedestal with a half-ovoid button on the barrel upon which the bayonet attached (there was no additional bayonet lug). Slings attached to the front swivel and to a button on the rear of the butt of the stock.[60] The bayonet was a typical Jäger Haubajonet but only attaching to the front sight. There are also reports of this variant using a Stichbajonet as well.[61]

Finally, we can find no evidence that any one of these variations supplanted any earlier model until the Standardization Order of 1863. It seems that all variants were produced from their adoption throughout the service life of the series. Whether this is due to the individual desires of powerful Inhabers and Jäger officers with influence or just a lack of money remains unclear, but with some small variations we have seen, such as what appears to be an arsenal-removed bayonet lug on a rifle carrying marks of the 6th Feld-Jäger Battalion, we suspect at least some of the former.

Before leaving the subject of the Jägerstutzen, it should be noted that over time, the "pear" or knob of the Jägerstutzen ramrod assumed different profiles. Together below, for comparison, top to bottom, are the rods of the 1769, 1807, 1842 and 1854 rifles.

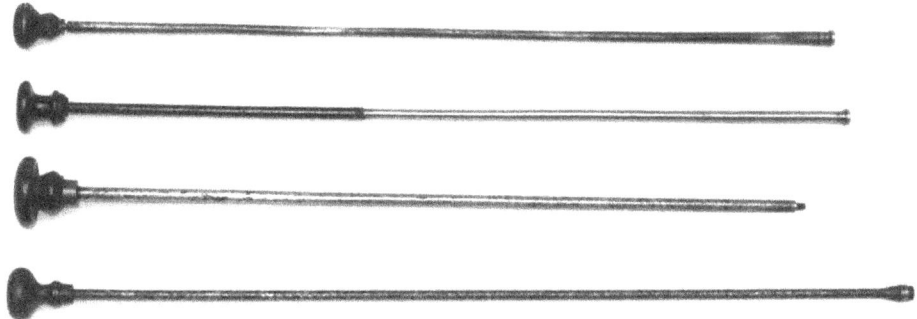

Authors' Photo

The Girandoni Air Rifle

No discussion of Jäger arms is complete without at least a mention of the air rifle. This weapon was developed by Bartholomäus Girandoni (1744-1799), an Italian gun maker from Tirol. The Girandoni was a rifled breech loading repeater utilizing tubular magazines with a 22-ball capacity. Loading was very quickly affected and compressed air was used to push the projectile down range. The system had been around for a while for hunting and target shooting.

In 1779 a report suggested the testing and possible adoption of an air rifle for the K.u.K. forces, and the Emperor Joseph II developed a keen interest in it. After a series of prototypes, the final military version was the Model 1780. A specially-designed air pump filled a flask which screwed into the base of the rifle. This air flask also served as the butt stock. There was generally enough pressure in one flask to shoot 20 to 30 lead balls accurately at a distance of 100 meters. The rifle was a little over 4 feet long (122.5 cm) and in 11.5 mm (.46 caliber). It had 12 right twisted lands and grooves, and weighed 4.6 kg (10.1 lbs).

Dr. Robert E. Beeman, a collector of historical air guns, and several associates have compiled an invaluable website[62] on the Girandoni, complete with a wealth of illustrations and rich in technical detail. He observes that:

> "The Girandoni system was adopted, in great secrecy, as the Austrian military repeating air rifle ... It has been recorded that the system was invented in 1779 or 1780, but deliveries of these guns to the Austrian army did not begin until between 1787 and 1791. Hoff's (1977) classic reference on antique airguns and Hummelberger and Scharer (1964/65) indicate that about 1500 Girandoni military airguns were produced. The eventual demise of these military airguns by about 1810 had little to do with their effectiveness, but was more involved with the logistics of keeping them charged in combat, the inability of contemporary gunsmiths to maintain the guns, and with the political implications of such

weapons which mistakenly were believed to be 'silent'. That the design was widely copied later in civilian circles indicates that it was well accepted by discriminating civilian gunsmiths and shooters and that such guns really were effective hunting arms. The system really was more suited to hunters who do not fire so many shots as a soldier, who can have the air reservoirs pumped up at leisure - even by a servant, and whose lives generally do not depend on the gun."

The Girandoni Repeating Rifle

Photo Courtesy of U.S. Army

The Girandoni, though ingenious and a tribute to the makers' skills, was simply too complex and prone to failure when not carefully handled to permit large numbers of troops to become proficient in their use, and required too much specialized equipment in the field to keep them operating. For example, in addition to the individual air pumps Girandoni developed large two-wheeled pumps to service five sharpshooters and even a special wagon to carry 100 filled air cylinders. The guns saw limited use in the field during Austria's last Turkish War, 1787-1792, issued to fusilier units, but produced so many problems that the Girandoni's greatest booster, the Emperor Joseph, was driven to complain,[63] "We appear to have a miserable bunch of riflemen, none of who is suitable for service with the air rifles." The Girandoni were withdrawn from the line troops by November of 1788, and issued on a limited basis to the Tiroler Scharfschützen, who reported them to be accurate and effective in action in the Turkish War. A few contemporary prints appear to show Girandoni-armed Jäger.

Regardless of this limited positive experience, with the overwhelming technical problems experienced in the field by these rifles, before the turn of the century the remaining 500 serviceable Girandonis were removed from service and consigned to storage. According to Beeman, it was likely a Girandoni that was carried west by Meriwether Lewis with the Corps of Discovery 1804-1806.

CHAPTER 8
"IF ONLY HE HAD BECOME AN UNTERJÄGER" A JÄGER STORY[1]

The story is set in Salzburg in the 1830's at Christmastime.
The narrator is a young Jägerkadet.

Wenzel had been a Kadet for over two years. He held the rank of Patrouillenführer (Gefreiter/PFC). As there was a current freeze in the advancement of officers in the entire Army, Wenzel had decided to actively pursue promotion to Unterjäger.

Christmastime is beautiful in Salzburg. This year, the weather was fine, we had no classes, no guard duty, and the Kadets were on the town. The day was so nice that the whole town was outside, a veritable caravan of "pilgrims."

Unterjäger and Oberjäger group of the 1860's. They wear the off-duty cap.

Authors' Photo

It seemed that the whole town was on the way to the "Leopoldskrone", an old castle. Near the castle was a lake for swimming or at this time of year, skating. Skates could be rented at the pub opposite the castle and we all took part. The lake was full of officers, dandies, priests and of course Kadets enjoying the day.

We skated like "Dutchmen" racing around and only taking breaks to drink the good Stiegel Beer.[2]

Around five o'clock, we began the march back into town with Wenzel shouting the commands. We laughed and were enjoying ourselves immensely.

Stopping at a monastery at the foot of the Mönchsberg, we sat at a table and drank a "Seidel" (pint) of wine at a total cost of four silver Grösschen. Wenzel then led us to the "Hypotrene" where we ordered "Windbeuteln" (Greek cream puffs).

So we sat around the big table talking. Topics of conversation were those normal to such groups of young soldiers: our leaders, pretty girls, the moods of the "Oberjäger", Meerschaum pipes, parades, acts of bravery, and finally about promotion, which we all desired.

Upon the introduction of this topic, Wenzel lost all of his good humor and declared: "The first in that line is me!" He then drank his wine, took his "Corsehut" from the peg on the wall, wished us a muted "good night" and stalked out of the room.

"Don't make much of that" lectured our beloved comrade, Kadet-Unterjäger Heidler. "You know he wants to pull his hair out with anger and frustration because our Major doesn't deem him properly prepared for promotion to "Herr Unterjäger. He is coming up on three years in the Guard Rooms, in the Company, and in the Kadet school. He has to salute every corporal and you know his father was an officer. Wenzel was even accepted in the Infantry as a "Kaiser-kadet". I don't blame him that he has had enough of this business."

"Nobody blames him!" echoed in the room.

As our happy mood was now gone, we decided to adjourn to the "Gablerbräuer" where we could meet up with friends from the town and some cavalry cadets we knew.

On the way, I began to feel poorly and as we passed our Kaserne, I begged off, was laughed at, but allowed to leave the group.

The Kadets in the Kaserne shared two rooms. One was for seven and the other for 12-15. The contingent from the 1st Division lived in the smaller room. Wenzel and I were assigned there and to the same Company.

Our "Kavallets" (iron beds) weren't in the middle of the room, but were separated by an abutment which jutted out from the stone wall. As a result, Wenzel and I couldn't see each other when we were in our bunks.

The Kaserne was empty, unguarded and dark. The bandsmen quartered next to us were out performing in one of the local churches. The Kadets were swarming over the city. The cannoniers, who were also quartered with us, old Salzburgers, were invited to their friends and families. No one was expected back until after midnight.

It was around eight when I entered our room in a cold sweat. Suddenly I met Wenzel who was coming toward me with his well-tuned guitar. After we got over our mutual shock, I said to him: "So you're also home early." "And not without reason" he responded.

"Do you want to be alone?" I asked. "Yes, that's what I want and you'd be doing me a huge favor by taking your hat, buckling on your belt, and going out to join the other Kadets and telling them what good company you are."

I responded that they already knew what good company I was and that I thought that I'd stay and see how pretty the person was that he was waiting on.

The effect of my answer on Wenzel was indescribable. Not only did I have to swim through a flood of curses, but also touching pleas and finally threats. These only hardened my resolve.

So I went to my bunk and began to undress.

I couldn't understand why Wenzel preferred the company of a guitar to a friend, but I figured he was just in a bad mood and heard no more from him.

I picked up a book out of my "Tornister" (a rucksack covered in pony fur) and headed for a stool by the oven, and in a short time British tragedy caused me to forget time, the world, everything.

I didn't pay much attention when Wenzel began playing Slavic and "half" German melodies with little devotional content on his guitar. I couldn't see Wenzel as he played and forgot his threats and coarseness.

All of a sudden it became very quiet in the room. I heard the last peal of the bell –

9 o'clock. The candle began to sputter so I got up to get the "Kerzenschere" (candle scissors – for trimming candle wicks). As I neared the balustrade, I had to stop in shock. There sat Wenzel with my Jägerstutzen.

I felt like I was seeing a frightening turn of events. In a moment, it would all make sense. Despite that, my heart was pounding and I was petrified with fright.

Wenzel was quicker than I. "Back! or I'll shoot!" In the blink of an eye, a bang and a blast and my own discharged Stutzen flew past me to the middle of the room.

I overcame my shock. Wide open, hollow, staring, two broken eyes in a face as white as a sheet – my friend was dead.

"That's it!" The powerful lead ball went through his heart and blood closed within, the pulse forever asleep. Everything finished, everything done. Wenzel was a good shot.

At the age of 17, a young soldier's no philosopher. I had a concept of the soul, the soul of the world, the changes of the dead, and that nothing is pardonable. That so young and vital and talented a person, one who could even write verse, finds himself in the place where a hand laid on the temple of the spirit results in a corpse: "Out of the place from which no traveler returns…"

Never in my life, even in firefights with the enemy did I move any faster as in this ghastly moment. I dressed quickly, but despite my haste and with my eyes averted, closed the eyes of my friend's corpse. Then I blew out the candle, slammed the Kaserne door so hard that the placards on the wall shook and I scrambled down the stairs to the street.

I stormed over the bridge, up the Linzestrasse to the "Gabler". There sat all of them, clueless, loud, and wreathed in pipe smoke, telling jokes. There was only one of us absent - absent forever!

"What's with this guy?" asked Kadet-Unterjäger Rolli as he looked up at me. I was white as a sheet; face bathed in sweat as I approached the table of this happy troop and prepared to make my speech.

"Gentlemen," I interrupted their impetuous questions. "I have very sad news to bring to you. Our good pal, our own good Wenzel has shot himself."

"Idiot!" screamed Kadet Heidler, "this sort of base prank is unacceptable. He who shoots his mouth off like cannon should just shut up, and under no circumstance challenge God with such sacrilege."

As they realized that I was serious, a huge noise broke out. We ran out, met at the bridge and divided into groups. One group went to the Main Guard House to report the incident. One group accompanied me to the quarters of our "Kadettenschulkommandanten" (Commandant of the Cadet School), and one group looked for the Captain of the "Garnison-Inspektion". A group went to pull the Auditor (JAG) away from his Christmas tree, children and guests. The remaining Kadets went to see the body.

After a few insignificant questions – I was asked how it could be that Wenzel shot himself with my Stutzen and further how it could be that the weapon was found so far removed from the body.

I had no way to answer, so remained quiet.

"As much as it pains me" began the Auditor after a long pause "but an unusual accretion of serious suspicions has forced me to consult with the "Oberstwächter (Major) and the arrest of this Kadet is ordered."

Upon this announcement, it seemed everyone was in motion, so that all could take in the scene. Every eye was fixed on me and then the severity of this painful situation finally hit me.

The auditor started in again: "Whether this is murder or suicide, we cannot determine at this point. What is known is that this Kadet went out with his comrades and was very anxious and distraught, which places strong suspicion on him. And that this same Kadet suddenly, as if in a dark, violent passion, was driven in a cold sweat and without motive to leave those comrades and return to the Kaserne. An hour later he reported that Kadet Wenzel had shot himself, in his presence, with this

Kadet's own Stutzen.

"No less serious is the fact that Wenzel, after being pumped by someone who spent an enjoyable day with him, displayed no signs of the suspect's description of his depression.

"Finally, suicides normally leave behind some indication of the reasons for their freely made decision to end their lives. Not only is this missing, but the chance that this body and the weapon lay so far apart brings me to the conclusion that this is murder."

The Major ordered my arrest. An Unterjäger and six Jäger from the Main Guard Room took me into their midst. We marched out of the door, climbed quietly up the mountain and into the "purgatory of Soldiers," the stockade on the Hohensalzburg.

We were greeted at the stockade by a surly, angry old "Kanonnenkrunzler" (Cannon cocker), the warden, who was less than happy at having his Christmas Eve disturbed. Sadly, at this point, I suspected that I would have a long relationship with this sinister "Knastenbart" (Old Jail Man).

As the commandant of my escort heard "murderer" all semblance of comradeship and friendliness disappeared, and he and his troop slouched away.

As a Kadet, I could not be imprisoned in the general population of the stockade. As a result, the Provost had an "Extra-Speckkammer" (bacon cabinet) ready for me. Upon reflection, he felt that as I was a murderer, that was too good for me and I spent the night in a creepy vault of the first class.

In fact, given my mood for Christmas Eve and Matins with the full weight of my 17 years, a more appropriate venue couldn't be imagined.

My cell was on the town side of the tower and of tiny proportions (1 Klaster x 1,5 Klaster) with walls of thick, impenetrable granite blocks. The only window was high on the wall and sheathed in iron bars as thick as your arm. A heavy, lead reinforced door with two giant locks and a heavy bolt confined me and I was guarded by an "Innviertler" (person from the quarter of the town along the Inn River) of the 59th

Regiment.

My stay in this thieves' nest at a freezing 12 degrees, on a thing which could only be ironically called a bed, in continuous fear of the appearance of diverse hidden "Galgenvögel (gallows birds) was, to say the least horrifying.

Enough. I experienced, with crying and chattering teeth, a lonely Christmas Eve, an experience I wouldn't ever wish on anyone. Fear, thirst, freezing cold, sleeplessness, and a thousand other small discomforts had worn me down to a nub. So imagine how I felt when at 9 o'clock in the morning the Provost entered and announced my immediate release.

Finally, when standing before the Auditor, I regained my senses. He filled me in on events subsequent to my arrest.

After a cursory search of the room revealed nothing, it was decided to look further, behind the beds and elsewhere. Behind Wenzel's bed, hidden under a loose tile, they finally found what they sought.

Wenzel left behind a large packet of letters and in them described his thought about breaking with life and the world. These thoughts had troubled him for more than eight days. He had finally decided to commit this act at 9 o'clock on Christmas Eve.

The K.u.K. Post also provided letters: one marked: "After my death to be opened by my comrades." This letter we were never allowed to read, so we never knew what he had written to us. (It became part of the official record and remained unavailable to us, locked away in the judge advocate files on the matter.)

One thing remained certain and that is that Wenzel killed himself because of his inability to achieve the rank of Unterjäger.

Incomprehensively, my inner fear and distraught state as well an overriding desire to go home and be free of the witnesses of this disaster resulted in my spending three weeks pale to the point of being unrecognizable and wandering around like a ghost.

The "legal post-mortem" was completed and the suicide put down to madness.

As a result, Wenzel received a Christian burial and rests in sacred soil.[3]

Madness! I know better. No one was healthier in mind and body than Wenzel, and even today he would be alive and happy – if only he had become an Unterjäger!!!

APPENDIX 1
JÄGER EDGED WEAPONS: WHAT WE KNOW AND DON'T KNOW

JÄGER

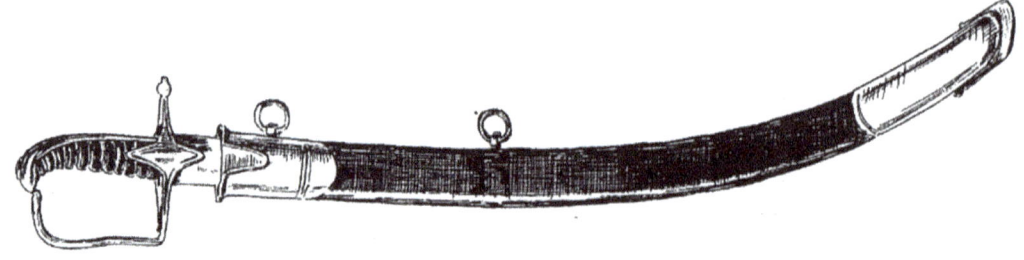

Officer saber for German Grenadier officers, 1820. Eduard Wagner identifies this same sword as the M 1811 as carried by Jäger officers

Print after Rudolf von Ottenfeld

From Wagner, Courtesy of Octopus Books

Officers' Swords

While from 1811[1] on Jäger officers' swords were required to conform to the succeeding regulation patterns in effect for all Austrian infantry officers, Ottenfeld[2] claims that before this time none was mandated above the regimental level. Ottenfeld does note a light infantry saber, M 1798 in one table, but nothing for the Jäger being prescribed before 1811. Pictured below are two shorter Austrian sabers from the later 18th and early 19th centuries, both somewhat narrower and lighter than the 1811 and similar in dimensions and weight to Revolutionary and Napoleonic-era French and Bavarian light infantry officers' weapons. Their blades are 9 cm (3 ½ in) shorter than the 77 cm (30 ⅝ in) M 1798 Saber for Light Infantry officers in Ottenfeld's table, but comparable in width. While they recommend themselves as lightened models suitable for the purpose, no direct association with a Feld or Freikorps Jäger officer can be claimed for them. With these as well as some other examples pictured in this section for which there is not irrefutable Jäger provenance, our aim is to illustrate basic types and, we hope, elicit further comment and foster more research on this aspect of Jäger arms.

Authors' Photo

Pictured below is a Hussar-type saber whose blade in both dimensions and form corresponds exactly to what became the M 1811, but with the older form brass lion's head hilt, guard and longer langets. It does not seem to be included in Ottenfeld's tables. This may suggest the appearance of one of the regimentally-adopted Jäger officer sabers predating the M 1811.

Authors' Photo

In the engraving of Colonel Kopal, Chapter 5, he is shown carrying the regulation M 1837 officer's saber like that above. But he also owned one, now in the Heeresgeschichtliches Museum and pictured in Ortner and Artlieb,[3] with the protective shell that was often retrofitted under the guard to provide better hand protection and a leather finger loop for improved handling.

Authors' Photo

As with firearms, enlisted Jäger edged weapons can be problematic. During the time frame under discussion here, Jäger troops could be issued bayonets, short swords or hangers, and in the 18th century, the specialized short knife/rifle rest called a *Krückenmesser*.

Bayonets

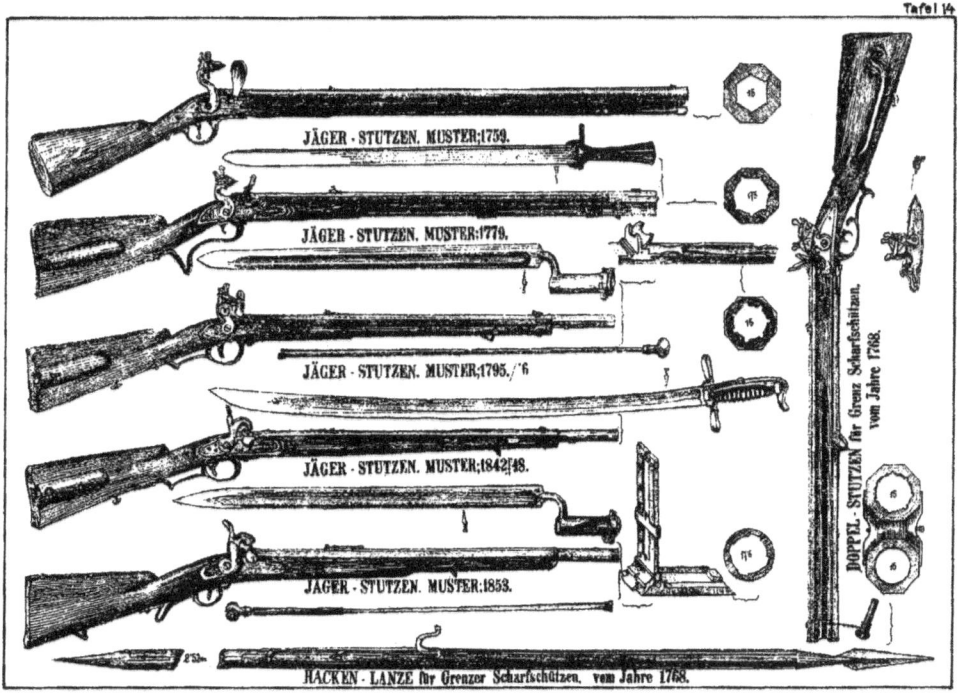

After Dolleczek

The most straightforward category is the bayonet, but even accounts of some of these raise questions. In his essential compendium Anton Dolleczeck pictures two bayonets in his Table 14, reproduced below, one of which we have seen in no other source on Austrian weapons, much less having encountered an actual example. For the Model 1779 Jägerstutzen, reportedly made from parts of captured Prussian weapons, he shows what looks to be a long, likely brass-hilted, bar-mounted Hirschfänger-type bayonet not unlike the Prussians' for their M 1810 Jäger rifle. The Austrian version as illustrated in Dolleczek is different from the Prussian in that the cross guard is asymmetric with one short arm, and also seems to feature a large semicircular langet or shell device under the guard. We are not aware of any surviving example of this bayonet, though the use of some form of Hirschfänger bayonet until adoption of the Haubajonet, and even afterwards, is also noted in Ottenfeld. The illustration of the M 1779 Jägerstutzen in Chapter 7 above from Ottenfeld also shows this bayonet.[4]

Downright bizarre is another bayonet in the same Table, which Dolleczek designates as M 1842-48 for use with the M 1842 Jägerstutzen. This unlikely design is a saber bayonet that seems as long as the stutzen itself, with what appears to be some form of attachment mechanism on the cross-guard and pommel and what may be a button to depress a spring on the grip. While the Haubajonet M 1796, in use until the adoption of the Lorenz series of firearms in 1854, is certainly the longest we have encountered, it has nothing else in common with this oddity, of which no example known to us or those authorities consulted exists. It is possible that there was some thought of replacing the old '96 bayonet for use with the new '42 Jägerstutzen. The French had adopted a brass-hilted saber bayonet in 1840 for their short *Chasseur* rifles, and it may be that this design was proposed, or even produced in limited numbers for trial, but not adopted.

After the Austrian Haubajonet was introduced, the only notable changes are in length, the configuration of the slot in the socket and the locking mechanism. (For full views of most bayonets see the illustrations above in Chapter 7.) The 1796 model is 80 cm long (31.5 in); the M 1849 for the Kammerbüchse is 72.6 cm long (28.6 in) and the M 1854 Haubajonet is 71 cm (28 in). Rather than the straight or L-shaped slot that prevailed in earlier models, the M 1854's forms a left-to-right diagonal pattern from the base of the socket to near the arm connecting the blade, a design common to all Lorenz bayonets. The first locking ring to appear on Jäger bayonets is that of the M 1796, carried forward to the 1854's, reflecting Unterberger's concern that the bayonet not be easily removable by an enemy.

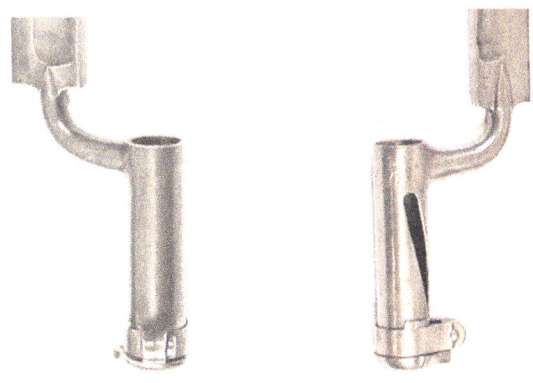

Socket details of M 1796 and M 1854 Jägerstutzen (Haub) bayonets

Authors' Photo

For Jägerkarabiner, the pre-1807 model illustrated below is a wide-bladed flattened cruciform profile bayonet, like the infantry M 1799 pictured by Dolleczek in his Tafel IX, 56 cm in overall length (31.5 in). The blade is 3 cm (1.2 in) at its widest point. It is fastened to the short spring catch under the barrel by means of a simple raised lip and slot in the socket. The bayonet is removed by simply twisting it to the soldier's left. This is by no means as secure a mounting as later models, but seems to have been retained up to 1842 for the First and Second Glied.[5]

Socket detail of the M 1799 Jägerkarabiner Stichbajonet

Authors' Photo

The Model 1842 Kammerbüchse Haubajonet is 72 cm long (28.3 in) with a straight, relatively short slot for the more secure Laukart catch. Finally in 1849 a locking ring was added to the Kammerbuchse bayonet.

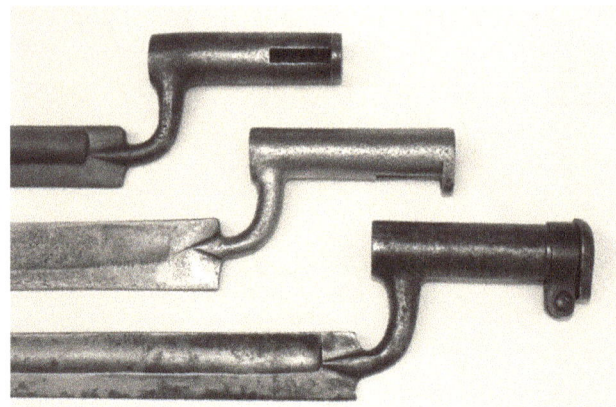

Kammerbüchse Haubajonet sockets, from the top, M 1842, 1844 and 1849

Authors' Photo

Sabers, Hangers, Hirschfänger

Short swords for enlisted Feld, Tiroler or Frei-Korps Jäger fall into two types: a.) either regular issue infantry hangers or, b.) Hirschfänger, similar to those used by hunters, either curved or straight, with either D or straight cross-guards. Some of these latter can be somewhat heavier than the civilian type. In his survey of Hunting Weapons, Howard Blackmore observed that many so-called hunting hangers of the seventeenth and eighteenth century "may have been made originally as military sidearms or for civilian defense."[6] Ottenfeld indicated that during the Seven Years' War, "Jäger" (whether Freikorps or Lacy's Feld-Jäger, is not specified) were armed with a short saber 50-55 centimeters long, very slightly curved, with a simple, "roughly-mounted" guard and brass roundels in the wood of the grip.[7] While he provides no illustration, Ottenfeld does picture a Sapper's hanger of 1769 with a short blade, Karabela-type hilt, grip fastened with rosettes or studs, a cross guard with short langets and a shallow hand-guard projection on the right side. This is a fairly common 18th-century hunting sword form, though beefier, and in the Sappers' case, with a saw back, that may, nevertheless, hint at the general appearance of the Jäger saber.

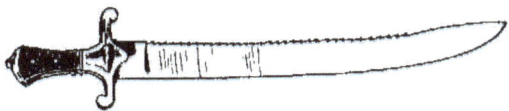

Print after Rudolf von Ottenfeld

Two hangers of type similar to M 1769 Sapper Saber above from Ottenfeld. The lower one is likely Swiss.

Authors' Photo

Ottenfeld claims that the Jäger saber was replaced by the regulation Fusiliers saber between 1767 and 1769. Since in fact the Feld-Jäger of the Staff Infantry Regiment provided for in the 1769 Generals Reglement were never re-activated, this may have been a theoretical change only. The circa 1792 illustration below seems to represent the period before the Generals Reglement, though the Imperial cipher is that of Joseph II.

This depiction of Pioneer and Jäger shows the former armed with a fusilier saber but the Jäger's hanger has a Hirschfänger-type hilt with D guard and grip fastened with rosettes or studs reminiscent of Ottenfeld's description above of a short Jäger saber. The artist erred with green facings on the Pioneer's jacket. These should be black, but he gets the white belts correct.

Anne S.K. Brown Military Collection, the John Hay Library, Brown University

While contemporary as well as authoritative modern representations of Austrian Jäger of the period 1763-1800 do show some armed with the fusilier saber, they are also depicted armed with a grenadier saber or some form of straight or curved Hirschfänger with a D guard, with or without a shell langet.

JÄGER EDGED WEAPONS: WHAT WE KNOW AND DON'T KNOW

A. Watercolor by Richard Knotel, B, C, D: NY Public Library

The illustrations above suggest the types of weapons Jäger carried c. 1763-1800. The following photographs provide a more detailed representation of each type. While they correspond to arms portrayed, none have a convincing Jäger provenance and therefore none is asserted here.

The first is a brass-hilted sword with a dog head pommel and straight, heavy blade measuring 62 cm (24 ¼ in) closely resembling the heavy hanger in illustration A above of a Le Loup (aka Dutch Jäger-Corps) Freikorps Jäger by Richard Knotel. Below it is an 18th-century short sword, likely of Central European origin, sometimes referred to as a Tessak. Its heavy 4.8 cm-wide (2 in) 56 cm (22 in) long blade is decorated with talismanic motifs and a representation of a Pandour. The brass cross guard carries a screwdriver head on one end and a flat, well-worn hammer head (or flint-knapper) on the other.

Authors' Photo

Next are two examples of D guard Hirschfänger with shell motif langets, seen in illustrations B and C above. The straight-bladed likely 18th century example with horn grip is embellished with simple, but well-executed decorative flourishes (non-

Talismanic) as well as a charging boar on one side and a deer on the other, with the motto *Nec timere nec timede* (Neither rashly nor timidly). The second example, with wood grip, is undecorated, with no discernible mark on its slightly curved blade.

Authors' Photo

Third is a Model 1784 Austrian Fusilier Saber. This is a flimsy, poorly-balanced weapon offering an unsteady grip--utterly useless against threatening cavalry, and is therefore an excellent argument for adoption of the Haubajonet. An earlier model, that of 1765, carried a straight cross guard, and the example we have examined is a bit more substantial, better balanced and superior overall.

Authors' Photo

Next, two Sabers for Corporal-Grenadiers of Hungarian Infantry, M 1770, like that in illustration D and also that carried by the noncom at the right in Ottenfeld's drawing of Light Infantry in Chapter 3 above. One is regulation length; the other has been shortened to Fusilier Saber length.

Authors' Photo

After the changes in Austrian weapons following Unterberger's commission on small arms improvements in the late 1790's, it was decided to stop manufacturing the fusilier saber. In their *With Drawn Sword*, the most authoritative modern compendium[8], Ortner and Artlieb note that most, "ordinary" fusilier sabers "of 1765 and 1780/84 [patterns] were…the last infantry troop sabers to be issued generally." NCO's and specialist or technical troops only continued to be issued sabers. They continue:

> "Countless different types of sabre were available, until, in 1824, a new (standard) sabre was introduced which had a blade very much like that of the Hussar's sabre in issue at the time. This was modified many times over the next few years until, in 1836, a new regulation sabre for fusiliers and grenadiers was introduced."

With respect to Jäger sabers or hangers it is difficult to say what prevailed after abandonment of the ordinary fusilier saber, but given straightened Austrian finances, and Jäger individualism in such matters, it was probably a mixed bag. Ottenfeld[9] indicates that in the immediate post Napoleonic Wars period Karabiner- Jäger were issued some form of saber, but it is not further described. A good possibility is the Model 1809 Grenadier saber pictured below.

The Model 1809 Grenadier Saber

Authors' Photo

In the Adjustierung of 1828[10] the non stutzen-armed Jäger are to be armed with a "Fusilier-Carpenter saber." None of our sources provide a description of this weapon. To further complicate matters, it must be noted that Jäger carpenters, as well as buglers, were not to be issued the Fusilier-Carpenter saber, but rather the Pioneer saber[11] with saw blade back.

Before the Adjustierung of 1828 took effect, or perhaps even until the new model 1836 infantry sabers were widely available, we can't be sure what kind of sabers the Karabiner- Jäger carried.[12] Without an officially-mandated model before 1828, it is reasonable to assume that Jäger unit commanders or Inhabers followed their own lead. In the hope of inspiring more research we provide the photograph below of four straight-bladed hangers. The first, for comparison, is the Danish Jäger hanger M 1788. The following three are unknown short swords of similar dimension and character all exhibiting some Austrian characteristics with respect to hilt details, including a partial langet, prima Plana-type lion's heads, shell guard reminiscent of earlier Jäger Hirschfanger and top nut (capstan) securing the tang— though none are exclusive Austrian features. Revolutionary-era French, Danish, Dutch and Swiss light infantry short swords share some of the same characteristics, though often they are slightly curved and, like the third hanger from the top pictured, carry basket guards. Of course, some Jäger may have carried captured blades including individual trophies. Whether any of these represent swords of the "countless different types," alluded to above is at best conjectural. To the degree it is relevant, Harold Peterson notes a straight-bladed brass bird head- hilted hanger with a D guard bearing similarities to our examples as being carried by German Jäger serving in North America in the 1770's,[13] while also observing "jaegers (sic.) were an elite corps, however, and it was not unusual for them to wear swords quite at variance with the accepted pattern."

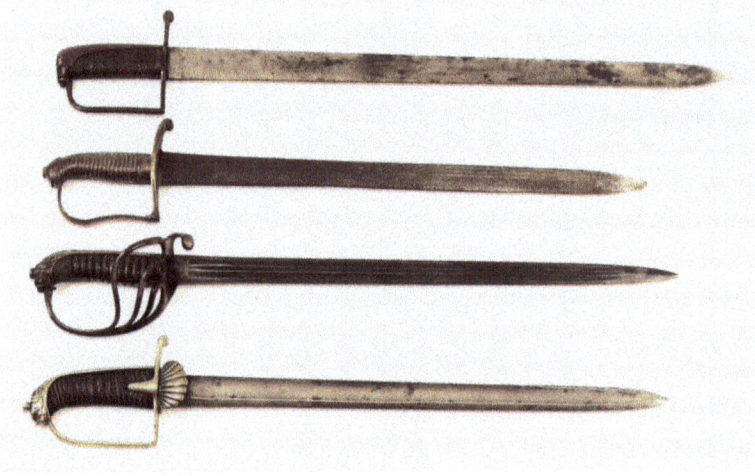

Authors' Photo

Finally, in the Heeresgeschichtliches Museum there is a series of late 19th-century drawings by Vincenz Lychdorff, one of which, labeled "*Detail zu Tyroler und Feldjäger Von 1820-1866*" includes the sword hilt of brass pictured below. Presumably, this represents at least one variant of the M 1824 carried by at least some Jäger.

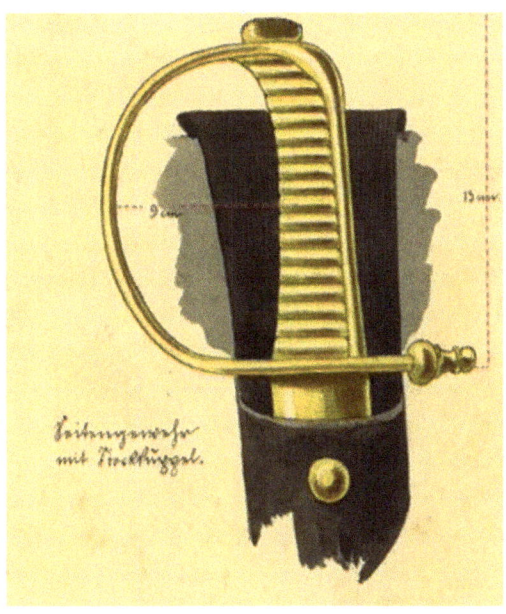

Heeresgeschichtliches Museum, Vienna

After its adoption the M 1836 infantry saber below was issued to Karabiner-Jäger (Jäger of the First and Second Glied.)[14] This was the final Jäger saber until adoption of the Lorenz Jägerstutzen and its Haubajonet for all Jäger troops after 1854. Carpenters, however, continued to carry the pioneer saber, as did hornists.[15]

JÄGER

Authors' Photo

The figure at the right shows the M 1836 infantry saber with its leather port-epee and the method of carriage by M 1842 or '44 Kammerbuchse-armed Jäger during the War of 1848-49. The left figure is a stutzen-armed Jäger. Drawing by Ilario Bailot from Massimo Zoppi, La Spada di Radetzky, 2011.

Courtesy of Itinera Progetti S.n.c.

M 1853 Pioneer saber (with 1853 horn grip, changed to wood in 1889.) After several unsuccessful attempts at finding a serviceable design, the M 1853 saber was introduced for Pioneer troops and issued to Jäger hornists and carpenters.

Authors' Photo

The Krückenmesser

Beginning with an article in 1894 by Captain Anton Dolleczek, Austrian military writers at the end of the nineteenth century refer to a *Krückenmesser*, probably the most mysterious of the Jäger edged weapons. The Krückenmesser is described as having been used in the 18th century by Jäger troops as a *Gewehrauflage*, a shooting rest. Dolleczek writes[16] that Lacy's Feld-Jäger Korps in the Seven Years' War, in addition to a Hirschfänger, were furnished the Krückenmesser. In fighting in wooded areas the Jäger stuck his Krückenmesser in a tree trunk to use it as a shooting rest, the Hirschfänger not being suitable for this purpose. We have consulted with museum curators and period weapons experts extensively, but have not been able to turn up additional information about, much less an example of, a Jäger Krückenmesser. In attempting to deduce what this specialized form of knife might have looked like, we have taken the word *Krück*, which can mean "crutch", to refer to its function rather than its form. Thus the Krückenmesser was used as a crutch to rest the Stutzen in the same way as would a convenient fork of a tree. We have reasoned that the blade needed an optimal profile to be strong—like a wedge-- and be as short as possible in order to survive being repeatedly pounded into the trunk with the small mallet[17] the Jäger carried to assist in loading, and removed without breaking. Pounding also necessitated some kind of durable pommel and hilt— a wooden grip over a full tang and iron or steel pommel would probably have been necessary. A relatively wide cross guard would have helped stabilize the Krückenmesser against the trunk and prevent it tipping down under the weight as well as cradle the rifle and protect the Jäger's hand as he levered it out of the trunk— so a simple patch knife would not do, nor would the kind of small utility knife found with other eating utensils attached to the traditional civilian Hirschfänger scabbard.

While we can, of course make no definitive claim to it, we suspect that the small 18th century spontoon-bladed knife pictured below satisfies all of the requisite characteristics and may give some indication of what a Krückenmesser would have looked like. As the second photo indicates it could also successfully support a Jägerstutzen.

Authors' Photo

JÄGER EDGED WEAPONS: WHAT WE KNOW AND DON'T KNOW

A Model 1769 Jägerstutzen supported by knife above

Authors' Photo

APPENDIX 2
THE VIENNA ARSENAL

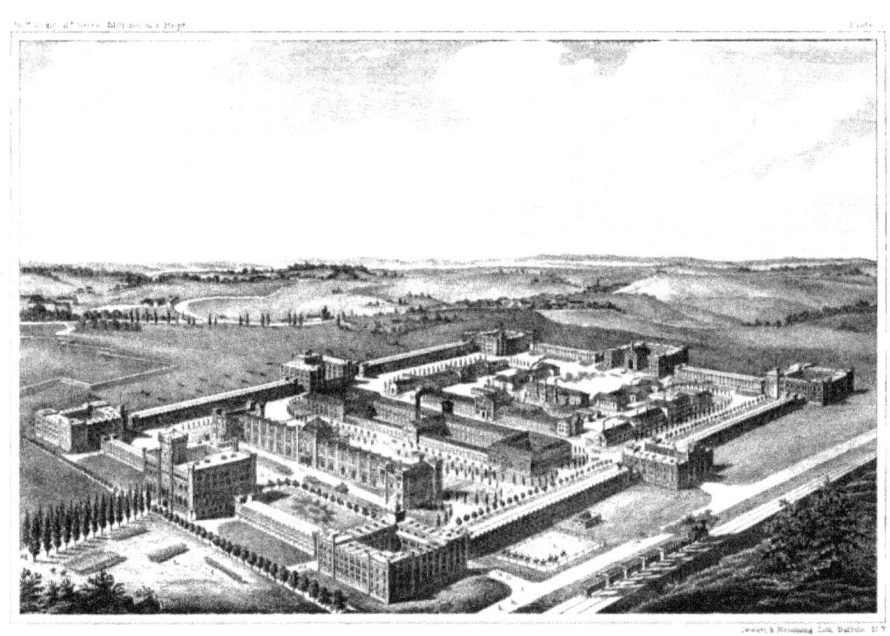

The Vienna Arsenal, c 1856 from Major Mordecai's report.

An Arsenal in some form or another had existed in Vienna since the 16th century. During the revolt of 1848 the Arsenal, then inside the city, was taken by the insurgents, arms were looted and distributed and it became the headquarters of their National Guard.

Storming of the old Vienna Arsenal, October, 1848

From an engraving by Franz Werner

Between 1849 and 1856 a new Arsenal complex was built on high ground in the Third District, which then was on the southeastern outskirts of the city. The complex was the first of several large fortified sites that replaced the old city walls, and included a

Museum, which survives to the present day as the Heeresgeschichtliches Museum.

Major Alfred Mordecai, an American ordnance officer on an official inspection tour of European armies and military facilities, visited the new Vienna Arsenal in 1856, just as production of the Lorenz series of arms had been initiated, "the new arms are all of the same caliber." He provided a detailed account of the facilities of this "magnificent establishment" and describes their functions in his report.[1]

Mordecai notes the citadel- like exterior designed to render the compound "secure from the assaults of a body of citizens, such as obtained possession of the military establishments in the city in the revolution of 1848."[2] In fact, some of the more serious security elements of the new complex[3] included an independent gas and water supply, and underground passages connecting the new arsenal to the Hofburg-- the imperial palace in the city, as well as the summer palace at Schönbrunn. The barracks could house as many as 10,000 troops, while the six artillery regiments assigned to the Arsenal could target the city in the event of a repetition of the 1848 unrest.

At the time of Mordecai's visit work was not completed on the foundry for artillery barrels but he did comment on the unusually high level of mechanization of the artillery carriage workshops for iron and wood work. An "extensive workshop for making harness and other leather work, &c." utlilizing American sewing machines is also noted.[4]

Mordecai found the steam-powered arms-making machinery to be up to date, but not significantly different from that used at comparable US facilities. Part of the hammer-making process involved use of a drop-hammer device patented by Colt. He observed[5] that the Austrian rifling equipment was not capable of producing progressive rifling mechanically -- relieving or increasing rifling depth had to be completed by a hand process utilizing cutters on long rods equipped with guides.

Generally, Mordecai notes "most of the parts being finally fitted by hand-filing." On the other hand Mordecai acknowledges the efficiencies and ease of manufacture afforded by the Austrian use of the compression bullet, eliminating the added complexity of the Minie round's hollow base.

The Arsenal did not do everything. Stocks were not made there, nor were lock plates or bridles, which were of annealed cast iron. Barrels were forged "in the iron regions, and are made chiefly of the excellent iron of Styria." [6]

At the Arsenal in addition to finishing, rifling and proofing of barrels, lock plates were punched and drilled for screw holes, internal parts and screws hardened as needed and locks assembled and fitted. Mordecai reports that at the time of his visit "the armory finishes from 2,000 to 2,400 arms a week." [7] After assembly, completed arms were tested on a well-appointed practice range "firing from one to five shots, from the shoulder, on a rest at 100 yards, in order to adjust the sights." [8]

After praising the "admirable solidity and massive construction of the buildings and machinery…as compared with ours, "Mordecai concludes his account by noting that a comparable "grand arsenal "is under construction in Verona, for the "assembling and repair of artillery carriages[and] equipments and for the assembling and repair of small arms." [9]

In his otherwise detailed account, while Mordecai makes clear that arms were assembled at the Arsenal, he unfortunately leaves us to surmise regarding the stages of inspection/acceptance and how these were registered generally, as well as specifically, how arms produced at the Vienna Arsenal were marked as distinguished from those by private contractors.

APPENDIX 3
MARKS ON AUSTRIAN FIREARMS

Maker's mark on M 1807 Jägerstutzen top flat: IOH SPÖ H I A NEUSTAT. The Spöck family of gun makers was active in Wiener Neustadt from 1765.

Authors' Photo

For arms historians as well as collectors makers' and acceptance marks are crucially important.

The earliest Habsburg military arms were marked prominently with the maker's name either in script or block letters on the flat of the barrel, usually along with the maker's location.

As procurement of military arms became bureaucratized, marks became more complex and varied.

Total parts interchangeability was not a fact of life through the Lorenz phase of Austrian weapons production and procurement. Most critical parts on Austrian military weapons, including bayonets, were therefore marked with a number indicating to which weapon they belonged. Bayonets were furnished by the gun maker, and interchangeability without a little hand fitting could not be assumed. As a result, units down to the battalion level often were authorized Armorers whose function it was to fit replacement parts onto weapons with broken or worn components.

Makers marked their arms with their names or initials, and in many cases the city in which they worked. The top flat of the barrel remained the most likely location for these marks. A list of those makers of Lorenz arms the authors have been able to identify follows.[1]

Beginning in the 1840's and continuing until the end of the period under consideration here, all arms accepted into service by Austrian military authorities had this acceptance registered by a small stamped double eagle on the tail of the lock plate, with the year of acceptance under the Augustin or Lorenz bolster with the "1" omitted. So, a weapon approved for service in 1855 would be stamped "855".

Since Austrian military weapons were manufactured or assembled at the Vienna

Arsenal, it is not unreasonable to assume that there would have been marks specific to that facility, but the sources and experts we have been able to consult are silent on the subject. One identifies the widely-encountered six –pointed star in a circle as seen on bayonets as "the Vienna Arsenal mark," but does not extrapolate this to firearms.[2]

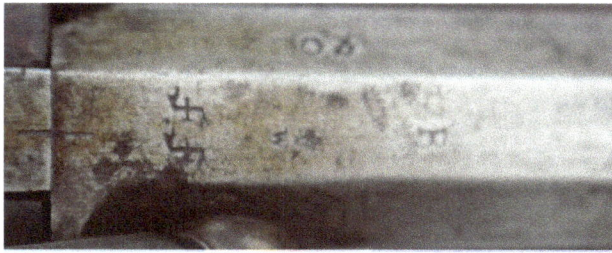

Bentz, Fruwurth and Pirko-made Lorenz model arms with W and eagle inspector marks

Authors' Photo

While of course plenty of individual Vienna inspectors' marks are encountered, we suspect that there was no Vienna Arsenal equivalent of a maker mark for firearms because it would have been extraneous. Other makers' products were inspected at the Arsenal, and when passed by individual inspectors were marked with that individual's stamp. At the end of this process acceptance was finalized by stamping the double eagle and date on the lock plate. Arms without individual makers' marks, but with inspector marks and the double eagle and date on the lock were, we believe, manufactured at the Arsenal rather than by a contractor. We have identified several of what we believe were individual Vienna inspectors' marks. These include W with a double eagle, W with a crown, W with 68, W with 69, F with a crown, E with a crown, and in the 1840's a five-pointed star or a crown in a circle.

Many familiar Austrian weapons surface today with no marks on the lock plate at all. There are several possible explanations: First, the Austrians sold large numbers of weapons to various European customers (Saxony and the city of Frankfurt, among others) as well as to both sides during the American Civil War. If these guns were manufactured for export, then in fact they were not accepted into service for the Austrian military and therefore never marked with the double eagle and date.

Weapons that were converted from the Console or Augustin ignition systems to percussion for export would have been reworked in an Austrian workshop, in Liege, Turin, or in the case of guns exported to the USA or CSA, at American facilities. These lock plates would likely have been cleaned and buffed after being machined for new components, with the possible resulting loss of marks, though examples of such exported conversions which retain the eagle do exist.

While we often encounter claims that many marks were lost due to the fact that the Austrian guns were made of "soft iron", this seems dubious, especially in light of the fact that weapons we have seen that spent a century in damp climates and pre-modern heating systems and subject to what often seems to us over-cleaning, manage to survive it all with most of their marks still intact.

Partial List of 19th Century Austrian Makers Marks

1. Anna Osterlein (Karl)/Vienna/1840-
2. "B" / ca. 1853
3. "B + C" / ca. 1857
4. "BG" / ca. 1853
5. Bollman / ca. 1859
6. Carl Heiser / ca. 1862
7. "CH" / ca. 1854
8. D.H. Rottmair / ca. 1854
9. Dojak (Josef, Elizabeth) / ca. 1820-1850's
10. E. Umfahrer / ca. 1850's
11. "EE" / ca. 1840's
12. Ferdinand Frühwirth (FF, F) / Vienna / ca. 1840-
13. F. Jescher / ca. 1854
14. G. Bentz (Gottlieb, Aloisa) / Vienna / ca. 1847-
15. G. Weigand / ca. 1864
16. Heiser, H, HH (Hilda, Karl) / Vienna / ca. 1850's
17. I. Florianschutz / Vienna / ca. 1840's
18. "IW"," S"," LP" / ca. 1847
19. IOS Drab / Vienna / ca. 1831
20. "KEG Fabrik" / ca. 1849
21. "LF", "W" / ca. 1861
22. Louise Bentz / Vienna / ca. 1850's

23. "MF a T / Vienna / ca. 1840's
24. Pirko / Vienna / ca. 1855
25. Zeilinger / ca. 1855
26. IH (Josef Heitzenberger / Vienna ca. 1859)
27. HF c1857

Other Marks of the Period

1. Double eagle over "LW": Indicates acceptance by the Landwehr[3]
2. Double eagle over "W": Vienna Arsenal acceptance mark (?)
3. Double eagle over "W 68": Unidentified[4]
4. Double eagle over "W 69": Unidentified[5]
5. IK, V
6. Crown over F in oval
7. Crown over E in oval
8. D, EE on stock
9. 5-pointed star in circle on lock plate c 1846: Vienna Arsenal?
10. 6-pointed star in circle: Vienna Arsenal?

ENDNOTES

CHAPTER 1 NOTES

1. Karl Goedeke, ed., Elf Bücher deutscher Dichtung: Von Sebastian Brant bis J. W. Goethe, Hahn'sche Verlbh., Leipzig, 1849 p.751.

2. W.W. Greener, The Gun and its Development, New Orchard Editions, Poole, Dorset, 1988, p. 620.

3. https://hessische-feldjaeger.hessen-militaer.de/hessische-feldjaeger.html Accessed May, 2017. https://de.wikipedia.org/wiki/Kurhessisches_J%C3%A4ger-Bataillon_Nr._11#1631%E2%80%931632, Accessed July, 2018.

4. The Emperor judged rifles' military utility so low that he ordered all withdrawn from service in 1807. This was not completely successful, as a return enumerating the shoulder arms on hand in the 14th Regiment of the Line in 1808-9 shows that among the 3115 arms there were 27 rifles still in service. Philip J. Haythornthwaite, Weapons and Equipment of the Napoleonic Wars, Cassell, London, 1996, pp. 25,

27. Regardless of the imperial prejudices, there were plenty of rifle-armed Jäger serving with Napoleon's German allied states including Westphalia, Wurttemberg, Saxony and Bavaria.

5. Hans-Dieter Götz, Militärgewehre und Pistolen der deutschen Staaten 1800-1870, Motorbuch Verlag, Stuttgart, 1996, pg. 159.

6. Ibid.

7. Gregory D. Bereiter, "Campaigning in America: Captain Johann Ewald's Hessians in the American Revolution," Constructing the Past: Vol. 3: Iss. 1, Article 4. (2002), p.10, http://digitalcommons.iwu.edu/constructing/vol3/iss1/4. Accessed June, 2017.

8. Miriam J. Levy, Governance and Grievance, Habsburg Policy and Italian Tyrol in the Eighteenth Century, Purdue University Press, Lafayette, Indiana, 1988, p.15.

9. Ibid., p.48.

10. Enrico Acerbi, http://www.napoleon-series.org/military/organization/Austria/ArmyStudy/c_AustrianArmyRecruiting.html Accessed July 2, 2017.

11. http://www.gemeindegut.at/da-boarische-rummel/ Accessed July 2, 2017.

12. R. J. W. Evans, Austria, Hungary, and the Habsburgs: Central Europe C.1683-1867, Oxford University Press, Oxford, 2006, pp. 123,124.

13. Michael Hochedlinger, Austria's Wars of Emergence 1683-1797, Routledge, London and New York, 2013, pp.323, 324.

14. Ibid., pp.297, 298.

15. Ibid., pp. 318, 319. http://www.journal.forces.gc.ca/vo11/no4/48-ouellet-eng.asp, (Vol. 11, Nº. 4) Accessed June, 2017. Jérôme Lacroix-Leclair and Eric Ouellet, Canadian Military Journal, "The Petite Guerre in New France, 1660–1759: An Institutional Analysis, " "*Petite guerre*… is described as '… all the movements that merely back up the operations of an army [translation].' Today, it can be compared to the actions carried out by commandos or Special Forces, as it shares the same characteristics. Historically, *petite guerre* was the specialty of regular light troops who harassed the enemy, gathered intelligence, and carried out deep strikes. They were organized into small groups called 'parties,' and terrorized the enemy's rear party. Thus, *Petite Guerre* was the way in which those light troops were used in Europe within the military institution." A Hungarian hussar Mihály Lajos Jeney, a commander of wide experience in the Turkish wars and later with the French, Prussian and Austrian armies in the last half of the 18th century, published a widely-circulated practical guide on *Petit Guerre* that emphasized well-disciplined light infantry-type functions. First appearing in French in 1759, it was soon translated into English as The Partisan: Or the Art of Making War in Detachment, Translated from the French of Mr. De Jeney by an Officer in the Army, R. Griffiths, London, 1760, (modern reprint by Gale ECCO Print Editions, no date.) With its emphasis on the importance of thorough reconnaissance, operational security, combined infantry/cavalry task forces and the necessity for perfect intelligence of enemy positions and strength, as well as the special qualities required for officers and troops engaged in this service, it foreshadowed much future Jäger practice. George Washington is known to have recommended it to American officers, Kevin J. Hayes, George Washington, A Life in Books, Oxford University Press, Oxford, 2017, p. 182.

16. Hochedlinger, p. 321.

17. Gunther E. Rothenberg, Napoleon's Great Adversaries, The Archduke Charles

and the Austrian Army, 1792-1814, Indiana University Press, Bloomington, 1982, p.53.

18. See Phillip Elliot-Wright, Rifleman, Elite Soldiers of the Wars Against Napoleon, Military Illustrated, London, 2000, p.12. As Wright observes tapping "Frontier wild men" as a source of irregular troops for *petit guerre* was hardly unique to Austria. In the mid eighteenth century the British in the Highlands, and both French and British in North America used frontier provincials for the same work. In fact, the first shots of the Seven Years' War were fired by North American provincial troops on the frontier. For a comprehensive account see Ian McCulloch, "Within Ourselves, the Development of British Light Infantry in North America during the Seven Years War." Canadian Military History, Vo. 7, 1998. McCulloch notes the influence of a key foreign officer: "Their commander was an experienced Swiss officer, recruited from the Dutch service to be one of the four original Royal American battalion commanders. [Henri] Bouquet had devoted his training abilities to 'combining the qualities of a scout with the discipline of a trained soldier' in all soldiers coming under his command. During his seven years in theatre he had strived to develop his men literally as "hunters" (a direct translation of the German "Jaegers") so they would be as adept as their Indian and *coureur de bois* adversaries. " http://docplayer.net/100605919-Within-ourselves-the-development-of-british-light-infantry-in-north-america-during-the-seven-years-war.html Accessed July 2017.

CHAPTER 2 NOTES

1. Christopher Duffy, Instrument of War, the Austrian Army in the Seven Years War, Emperor's Press, Rosemont, Ill., 2000, Volume 1, p.299.

2. See the detailed observations and source commentary on the *Deutsches Feld-Jäger Corps* in the Seven Years' War by Richard Couture at: https://www.kronoskaf.com/syw/index.php?title=Deutsches_Feldj%C3%A4gerkorps, Accessed July 2017. Mr. Couture has expanded significantly on our knowledge of Seven Years' War armies drawn from primary materials with valuable information hitherto unavailable in the standard published sources. Originally 50 Jäger were attached to each of the four Pioneer companies, later the Jäger were grouped in two companies of their own and detached as needed to support the Pioneers. There appears also to have been a contingent of mounted Jäger (*Jäger Corps zu Pferde*) raised in 1758 as well. The 1762 collection of uniform drawings known as The Bautzen Manuscript (modern edition Die Österreichische Armee im Siebenjährigen Krieg, Lars-Holger Thümmler, ed., Brandenbürgisches Verlagshaus, 1993,) features a caption to a plate showing "a mounted officer and a man, giving the following (translated) caption: *'This was raised in 1758 and consists of all trained marksmen. They serve as escort (or guard) and also are used as couriers.'* "

3. "For the War of the Austrian Succession in 1745, the *Deutsche Jäger-Compagnie* (under a Captain Pfeiler) was raised, which went to the Netherlands theatre. It was dissolved in 1746… The first trace of a… *Feldjägerkorps* in the Seven Years' War can be seen in the fall of 1756, when a group of some 50 Jäger assembled in northern Bohemia. These had volunteered (or 'been volunteered' by their quasi-feudal employers) for armed duty against the Prussian invasion. Their participation would have been even more welcome because they would have had local connections and knowledge. " Ibid.

4. Duffy, p.241.

5. Anton Dolleczek, Monographie der KUK oster.-ung. Blanken und Handfeuer-Waffen, Wien, 1896, (Reprinted Akademische Druck-u. Verlagsanstalt, Graz, 1970,)

p.77.

6. Duffy, p.241.

7. By 1763 the Pioneers and the Jäger had been incorporated into the Staff Infantry Regiment (*Stabs-Infanterie-Regiment*), another Lacy creation. The staff regiment, including the Jäger, was disbanded at the end of hostilities, but the 1769 staff manual produced while Lacy was top military advisor to the Crown, prescribed its reconstitution in time of war. Generals-Reglement, Wien, 1769, p.17. Web edition,

8. Couture, https://www.kronoskaf.com/syw/index.php?title=Deutsches_Feldj%C3%A4gerkorps https://www.kronoskaf.com/syw/index.php?title=Pionier_Korps#Uniform Accessed July, 2017. Ottenfeld, p.330. Peter Krenn, et. al., Die handfeuer-Waffen des Österreichischen Soldaten, Akademische Druck-u. Verlagsanstalt, Graz, 1985, p. 28, note that the Deutsches Feld-Jäger Corps were not issued paper cartridges, but utilized a powder measure and powder horn only in loading, which helps explain their subsequent retention of these items as valued marks of distinction.

9. On subsequent Jäger actions during the last years of the war we are following Couture's account.

10. Most notably among more recent works, Acerbi, David Hollins, Austrian Auxiliary Troops, 1792-1816, Osprey, London, 1966; Lubomir Uhlir, "Jager in the Austrian Army during the Coalition Wars," (Google translation from Hungarian) http://www.primaplana.cz/news/myslivci-v-rakouske-armade-za-koalicnich-valek/, Accessed September 2017; Uhlir's work essentially tracks Austrian Major Wrede's account written at the end of the nineteenth century: Alphons Freiherrn von Wrede, Geschicte der J. und K. Wehrmacht, Vol II, L. W. Seidel & Sohn,

Wien, 1898, pp. 504-542. Rothenberg, op. cit., pp.33, 49, 50; Ernst Konzett, Die Jägertruppe - Ursprung und Geschichte, http://www.bundesheer.at/truppendienst/ausgaben/artikel.php?id=1819 Accessed July, 2017.

Notwithstanding these more recent efforts, Ottenfeld, pp. 591-621, remains the most comprehensive account, and certainly should be the starting point for further work on these volunteer units. For the key role Lacy and Laudon played, "forerunners of a new era," in transforming the better Freikorps into an effective military force see p. 595. Rudolf von Ottenfeld and Oscar Teuber, Die Österreichische Armee von 1700-1867, Akademische Druck und Verlagsanstalt, Verlag von Emil Berte & Cie. Und S. Czeigner, Wien, 1895. We are aware that in more recent scholarly citations of this work Teuber, as author of the text, often receives top billing. Stipulating that, we have nevertheless chosen for clarity and ease of reference for the general reader to refer to the work in the traditional form—Ottenfeld—and in the singular. https://www.scribd.com/doc/82557579/Ottenfeld-Teuber-Die-Osterreichische-Armee-von-1700-bis-1867 provides convenient Internet access to Ottenfeld prints.

11. Oskar Crist, Kriege unter kaiser Josef II. Nach den feldakten und anderen authentischen quellen bearbeitet in der kriegsgeschichtlichen abteilung des K. und K. Kriegsarchivs, Wein, 1904, Verlag von L. W. Seidel & Sohn , pp. 256, 264. Also note that Andreas Graf Thürheim, in his comprehensive Gedenkblätter aus der Kriegsgeschicte de K.K. Armee, Wien und Teschen, Verlag der Buchhandlung fur Militär-Literatur, 1880 does not identify formations of Austrian Jäger troops until the establishment of the post-1801 units.

12. Uhlir, p. 2; Wrede, Vol. II, p.507.

13. See below, Chapter 3.

14. Uhlir, p.5. Wrede Vol. II, pp. 507,521.

15 Hochedlinger, pp. 367-369. https://weaponsandwarfare.com/2016/07/06/the-war-of-the-bavarian-succession/ accessed October, 2017. Robert B. Asprey, War in the Shadows: The Guerrilla in History, Universe 2002, Volume 1, p.53.

16. Uhlir, p.2; Wrede, Vol. II, p.509.

17. Ibid. pp.2,3. Wrede, Vol. II, p. 511.

18. Hochedlinger, p.401.

CHAPTER 3 NOTES

1. Rory Muir, Tactics and the Experience of Battle in the Age of Napoleon, Yale University Press, New Haven, 1998, p.51.

2. For welcome, if brief accounts of the character and appearance of this decidedly mixed bag see Hollins, Austrian Auxiliary Troops, pp. 13-16.

3. Enrico Acerbi, http://www.napoleon-series.org/military/organization/Austria/ArmyStudy/c_AustrianArmyJagers.html, Accessed July 2017 and Lubomir Uhlir, http://www.primaplana.cz/news/myslivci-v-rakouske-armade-za-koalicnich-valek/ 2007. Accessed September, 2017. In Google translation.

4. Geert van Uythoven quoting his own article: "The Battle of Aldenhoven / Aix-La Chapelle, 1793" First Empire N°. 68, Jan/Feb 2003. http://www.napoleon-series.org/cgi-bin/forum/archive2003_config.pl?md=read;id=15192 Accessed September, 2017.

5. Guillaume Philibert Comte Duhesme, Essai historique sur l'infanterie légère, ou Traité des petites opérations de la guerre, à l'usage des jeunes officiers ,3rd Edition, Paris, 1864, p. 67. Authors' translation.

6. Rothenberg, p.33 and Hollins, p. 6.

7. Bernhard Voykowitsch, Castiglione 1796, Helmet Military Publications, Maria Enzersdorf, Austria, 1998, p.36.

8. David Hollins, Austrian Frontier Troops, 1740-98, Osprey, London, 2005, p.22.

9. Hollins, Austrian Auxiliary Troops, pp.3, 5. For example, the Warasdin-Kreuz and Ottocac Grenzers successfully conducted the final rearguard action after Marengo permitting significant numbers of Austrians to reach their bridges over the Bormida. See David Hollins, Marengo 1800, Osprey, Oxford, 2000, pp.49, 95 for examples of tenacious fighting by Grenzers.

10. Instruktionspunkte für die k. k. Armee zur Campagne des Jahres 1794, Valenciennes, 12. 3. 1794, in Beiträge zur Geschichte des österreichischen Heerwesens, Vol 1, Wien 1872, p. 127.

11. See the extended and spirited, if sometimes uneven, web discussions of Austrian practice in this period, some citing periodical sources unfortunately no longer readily available, such as the defunct magazine First Empire. http://www.napoleon-series.org/cgi-bin/forum/archive2003_config.pl?md=read;id=15173 Accessed July 2017, and http://www.napoleon-series.org/cgi-bin/forum/archive2003_config.pl?md=read;id=14747 Accessed July 2017.

12. Duhesme, p.72 (Authors' translation).

13. Peter Paret, Yorck and the Era of Prussian Reform, 1807-1815, Princeton University Press, Princeton, 1996, p.74.

14. Observationspunkte fur die Generale bei der Armee in Deutschland in Jahre 1796 in Beiträge zur Geschichte des österreichischen Heerwesens, Vol 1, Wien, 1872, pp 136-142. These instructions are attributed by contemporary authorities to either to Archduke Karl or General Karl von Mack; see Paret, Ibid. Note that Lee W. Eysturlid nowhere in his study of the Archduke's military thought attributes these to Karl. Lee W. Eysturlid, The Formative Influences, Theories, and Campaigns of the Archduke Carl of Austria, Greenwood Press, Westport, Ct, 1996.

15. Rothenberg, pp.107, 111.

16. Ottenfeld, p. 268.

17. Ottenfeld, Ibid. Wrede, Vol. II, p.377.

18. Wrede, Vol. II, pp. 378-394.

19. Rothenberg, pp. 54, 74.

20. Wrede, Vol II, p.392.

21. August Gräffer, Geschichte der Kaiserl. Königl. Regimenter, Corps, Bataillons und anderen Militär-Branchen, Seit ihrer Errichtung bis zu Ende des Feldzuges 1799, Vol 1, Wien, 1804.

22. Gräffer, pp. 371, 372, 374, 383, 384; for an apparent fiasco see p.379. David Hollins, Marengo 1800, Osprey Publishing, Oxford, 2000, pp.27, 29, 34,41,62,63 notes the presence of light infantry battalions and Freikorps Jäger in the Marengo

campaign.

23. F.Schneidnwind and Dr. Wilhelm Wägner, Das Buch vom Feldmarschall Radetzky Fur Heer und Volk, Verlag von Otto Spamer, Leipzig, 1859, pp. 38,39. See also Hollins, Marengo, pp. 68, 69 for an account of the incident. The Jäger were likely from the four companies of Mariassy-Jäger, (Italienische Feldjäger-Korps) a Freikorps unit, attached to Frimont's advance guard. Dr. Alfred Herrmann, Marengo, Druck und Verlag der Aschendorffschen Buchhandlungm, Münster i.W., 1903, pp. 75, 76.

24. "You should not tell a recruit: "I will make you a Jäger!" You must instead take them from the forests. They should know how to perch on a rock, how to conceal themselves in one of those fissures which open in the ground after a great drought, or hide behind a mighty oak. They must make their way slowly and softly, so as not to make any sound, and in such a way they can creep up on a post and take it by surprise, or shoot down the enemy generals." Prince Charles-Joseph de Ligne, who commanded a regiment of Netherlands infantry in the Seven Years' War, from his Mélanges Militaires, Litteraires et Sentimentaires, Dresden 1795-1811, cited by Christopher Duffy, Instrument of War, p.241.

25. Wrede, Vol. 2, p.397

26. Frederick W. Kagan, The End of the Old Order, Da Capo Press, Boston, 2006, pp. 406-408.

27. Kagan, p. 440.

28. Wrede, Vol. 2, p.398.

29. Wrede, Vol. 2, p 397.

30. Kagan, p. 660. John H. Gill, 1809 Thunder on the Danube: Napoleon's Defeat of the Habsburgs, Vol. 1, Frontline Books, London 2008, xiii.

31. Rothenberg, p.103.

32. Ibid., p. 105.

33. Kagan, p. 526.

34. Rothenberg, pp. 111,112.

35. Rothenberg noted that "As Radetzky observed in September [1813], 'fighting *en tirailleure* should be done only in very restricted fashion because neither the Russians nor we have mastered the *maniere de tiraller*,'" p. 184. This should be read for what it is and no more—namely, Radetzky, as chief of staff of the main Austrian army under FM Prince Schwarzenberg, echoing the regulations' prescription for line troops. The curt 1813 note from which the Radetzky comment has been drawn (Alte Feldakten Kt 1536, 1813-X-436b, fol.02r) is not exactly an extended military treatise. Nevertheless it has at times been used to support excessively broad inferences about Austrian lack of appreciation for light troops and tactics, including Jäger, e.g. Phillip Haythornthwaite, Austrian Army of the Napoleonic Wars (I): Infantry, Osprey Publishing Ltd., London, 1986, pp. 10, 11. Moreover, George Nafziger observes in his exhaustive treatment of Napoleonic-era European tactical regulations that, even for the French, "universal employment of their line infantry as skirmishers…began to decline after the Revolutionary Wars and became less frequent as time went on." George Nafziger, Imperial Bayonets: Tactics of the Napoleonic Battery, Battalion and Brigade as Found in Contemporary Regulations, Greenhill Books, London, 1996, p. 132.

36. Kandelsdorfer, Karl, Streuffleurs Österreichische Militärische Zeitschrift, 3rd

Volume, Vienna, 1897, p. 215. Philip J. Haythornthwaite, Austrian Armies of the Napoleonic Wars, Vol. 1: Infantry, Osprey Publishing, London, 1986, pp. 35, 36.

37. Kandelsdorfer, pg. 215. Austria's depleted economy's inability to sustain an expanded regular army also caused the Archduke to put aside his long-standing opposition to a national militia or Landwehr. A month before the Jäger divisions were authorized, an imperial order created a Landwehr infantry force, for political reasons effectively limited to the German-speaking lands, with a similar annual three-week training camp. Service was compulsory for men between 18 and 45, though there were exemptions which would have applied to recruits for the Jäger divisions as well as the generally better-heeled volunteer (*freiwillige*) Landwehr units like the Archduke Karl Legion and Vienna Volunteers. Hollins, Austrian Auxiliary Troops, pp. 16-18.

38. Kandelsdorfer, p. 215.

39. Ibid. p. 215.

40. Ibid. p. 215.

41. ibid p. 217.

42. Ibid. p. 218.

43. Ibid. p. 218.

44. Rothenberg, p.123.

45. Kandelsdorfer, p. 218. Karl later wrote (in the third person) of this period: "the archduke recognized that the ministry had brought things to a state where war was

inevitable, and concerned himself from then on with the requisite preparations in order to contribute as much as possible to success." Gill, Vol. 1, p. 12.

46. Gill, Vol. 1, xiii. For a different view of the Archduke and his work see Richard Basset, For God and Kaiser: The Imperial Austrian Army from 1619 to 1918, Yale University Press, New Haven, 2015, p. 250: "Another two years, perhaps even another eighteen months, and most of [Archduke Charles']reforms would have borne fruit. However, fate dictated that Austria would wage war once again against the Archduke's wishes and before she was ready. But that the campaign of 1809 was fought with such glory for Austrian arms is entirely due to the Archduke Charles."

47. Kandelsdorfer, pp. 218-219, Rothenberg, p. 114.

48. Kandelsdorfer, pp. 218-219.

49. Rothenberg, p. 112. See Chapter 4 for a description of unofficial manuals.

50. Kandelsdorfer, pp. 223-224.

51. Gill, Vol 1, xiii. Also attributed to the Emperor, but likely apocryphal: "You did not see the Austrians at Essling, and therefore you have seen nothing."

52. Ibid., p. 311.

53. Ibid., pp. 140-141. Andreas Graf Thürheim, Gedenkblatter aus der Kriegsgeschichte der K.K. Österreichischen Armee, Verlag de Buchhandlung fur Militär-Literatur Karl Prochaska, Wien und Teschen, 1880, vol I, pp.489, 492, 496. The irritated commander was Ferdinand Peter Hennequin, Graf von Fresnel und Curel (1762-1831) General of Cavalry, later Field Marshal. https://commons.wikimedia.org/wiki/File:Ferdinand_Peter_Hennequin_Litho.jpg Accessed January

2018.

54. Gill, Vol. 1, p. 297. The 7th Battalion had another bad day at Palestro in 1859, see below Chapter 5. F. Lorraine Petre noted how in the Ratisbon campaign the best French line troops could perform effectively in wooded country as skirmishers: "Some of Davout's battalions were entirely broken up into groups of skirmishers" as compared to the Austrians, whose field instructions circumscribed skirmishing by line units very closely. F. Loraine Petre, Napoleon and the Archduke Charles, 1909, new ed., Greenhill Books, Barnsley, 2017, p. 205. Clearly, for this kind of work the Austrians depended upon their Jäger.

55. J. Strack, Das Kopal-Denkmal in Znaim und das K. K. 10. Feld-Jäger Battalion, Der K-K Hof und Staatsdrückerei in Commission bei Wilhelm Braumüller, Wien, 1864, p. 5. Then Captain Kopal also led the Light Division's advance guard at Leipzig in the storming of Baumsdorf, p. 6. The 6th Feld-Jäger Battalion in 1815 was assigned to the brigade in the Austrian Reserve Army commanded by Major General Max Freiherr von Paumgartten, author of *Abhandlung über den Dienst de Feldjäger zu fuss*.

56. Thürheim, p.494. An Oberjäger and Unterjäger were personally cited by the Archduke Karl for their bravery, including capture of a captain of the French Imperial Guard, and promoted to Lieutenant in the battalion. See also pp.396, 7 and p. 511 for 3rd and 7th Jäger employed like regular infantry.

57. James B. Arnold, Napoleon Conquers Austria: The 1809 Campaign for Vienna, Praeger, Westport, Ct., 1995, pp. 128-130. Bassett, p.270.

58. Petre, pp. 357-362.

59. Gill, Vol II, pp.209, 237.

60. Ibid., p.236

61. Thürheim, pp. 517,520

62. Petre, pp. 392,393.

63. Bassett, p. 284; Stephen Herold, MA, PhD. "The Austrian Campaign under FM Schwarzenberg in 1812," The Société Napoléonienne, http://www.antiquesatoz.com/habsburg/1812/campaign.htm Accessed October, 2017

64. Thürheim, pp 502, 511.

65. George Nafziger, Napoleon's Dresden Campaign, Emperor's Press, Chicago, 1994, pp. 167, 168: "Colloredo personally led the 1st and 2nd Jäger Battalions forward to storm Redoubt 3. Led by Oberstleutnants Luz and Schneider, the two battalions moved through a hail of canister and musket fire, leapt into the ditch, climbed over the palisades and into the breast works, where they captures six cannons about 5:00 pm. By 5:00 pm, a heavy musketry battle had begun from the barricades to the city spitting fire into the advancing allies. The French had been obliged to evacuate Redoubt III, after firing off all their cartridges and withdrew behind the Machzinsky garden....M. Lichtenstein's 1st Light Division pushed forward to the Machzinsky Gardens and encountered an 8 foot high wall. The passage through the wall was defended by a ditch and palisade. The French stood in this strong position and fired volley after volley, into the advancing Austrians. The Austrians fell back, regrouped and advanced again to storm the wall. A position battery was placed 200 paces from the palisade and began firing. The Jägers pushed into the French position, but were pushed out before too long."

66. Thürheim., pp. 489,492,509-10.

67. Anonymous, Reminiscences of an English Cadet in the Austrian Service, 1848-c1854, Duncan Rogers, ed., Helion & Company, Solihull, UK, 2006, p.11. (Originally published as a series of articles in The Cornhill magazine, 1867.)

CHAPTER 4 NOTES

1. George Nafziger and Marco Gioannini, The Defense of the Napoleonic Kingdom of Northern Italy, 1813-1814 Praeger, Westport, Ct, 2002, p. 16. Oswald von Gschließer, (1954): Zur Geschichte des stehenden Heeres in Tirol, II, Die Zeit von 1813-1848. Veröffentlichungen des Tiroler Landesmuseums Ferdinandeum 34, p. 69.

2. Thürheim, p. 481.

3. Gschließer, II, p. 70. https://de.wikisource.org/wiki/BLK%C3%96:Schneider_von_Arno,_Karl_Freiherr Accessed Nov. 2018. Colonel Schneider's severe leg wound from Dresden must have limited his activity in the campaign against Murat, and Pirquet seems to have, at least for Neipperg, served as de-facto Lt. Colonel of the Fenner-Jäger.

4. R. John Rath, The Provisional Austrian Regime in Lombardy–Venetia, 1814–1815, University of Texas Press, 1969. pp. 328-339. For a good account of the campaign see Robert Matteson Johnston, The Napoleonic Empire in Southern Italy and the Rise of the Secret Societies, Vol. 1, Macmillan, London, 1904, pp. 350-376.

5. Ennino Ferretti, La Battaglia di Cesenatico, privately printed, Cesenatico, 2010 http://phoenix.tuwien.ac.at/Cesenatico/Cesenatico_Ferretti.pdf, Accessed December, 2017, pp. 34-38. A local historian and citizen of Cesenatico, Ferretti was

granted access by descendants of Major Pirquet to his unpublished diary, notes and other documents. Pirquet had previously served with a Feld-Jäger battalion. For other comparable use of Jäger by Neipperg and other commanders in this campaign see, Graf Alberti de Poja, Geshichte des k. und k. Feldjägerbattalions Nr. 11, Druck von Rudolf Brzezowsky & Söhne in Wien, Köszeg, 1905, pp. 30-35, 37, 42.

6. Ferretti, p.44. Cf. Thürheim, p. 482 who says there were 200 prisoners, but including a general and 300 Neapolitans killed.

7. Thürheim, p. 518. Johnston, Volume 1, p. 374. In an indication of the practice of posting Jäger well to the front of Austrian forces, the Neapolitan general Guglielmo Pepe, who served with Murat's army at Tolentino, in his memoirs described how on the first day of the battle a *"battaglione di Tirolesi"* was in an exposed enough position to be nearly captured by Italian cavalry, but were saved by the absence of Neapolitan infantry support. Guglielmo Pepe, Memorie, Vol. 1, Paris, Baudry Libreria Europea, 1847, p.287.

8. Johnston, p. 372.

9. Ferretti, pp. 39, 46.

10. Ibid., p.47. In 1843 Pirquet was named Second Inhaber of the Regiment, with the Kaiser continuing as First Inhaber, Thürheim, p. 481.

11. Ibid., pp. 39, 40.

12. Ibid., p. 44.

13. Ibid., pp. 39, 40.

14. Thürheim, p. 482.

15. Ibid., p. 518.

16. Ottenfeld, p. 389.

17. Thürheim, p. 481. In the broader political context, re-establishment of the regiment and the Emperor's personal association with it was consistent with a postwar program of official patriotic sentiment and imagery incorporating themes of Austria triumphant, legitimacy restored and loyal Tirol rejoining an Austria increasingly referred to in national, as opposed to purely dynastic terms. Laurence Cole, Military Culture and Popular patriotism in Late Imperial Austria, Oxford University Press, Oxford, 2014, pp. 35-37.

18. Gschließer, II, p. 76. http://www.kaiserjaeger.com/at/TKJ/Die_geschichte_der_tiroler_kaiserjaeger.htm Accessed November, 2017. http://de.metapedia.org/wiki/Fenneberg,_Franz_Philipp_Fenner_von Accessed November, 2017

19. Ottenfeld, p. 389.

20. Thürheim, p. 482.

21. Ibid., pp. 523,528. At least in the case of the 10th Feld-Jäger Battalion, duties included small detachments pursuing and suppressing bandits. Strack, pp.78, 79.

22. Darko Pavlovic, The Austrian Army 1836-66 Vol. 1, Infantry, Osprey Publishing, Oxford, 1999, p. 35.

23. Ottenfeld, pp. 398,399.

24. Pavlovic, p.35.

25. Ibid.

26. Ibid.

27. Max Sigismund Armand Josef von Paumgartten, Abhandlung über den Dienst der Feldjäger zu Fuss, Self published,. Vienna, 1802.

28. Ibid., See especially pp. 225-259.

29. Ibid., e.g., pp. 301-317.

30. Leopold Freiherr von Unterberger, *Wesentliche Kentnisse der Infanterie-Cavallerie Feuergewehre zum Gebrauch der Offiziere der k.k. österreichischen Armee*, Christian Friedrich Wappler und Beck, Wien, 1807. Then Feldmarschalleutnant Unterberger had a solid military career and also was something of a cerebral soldier and ordnance expert, serving both as mathematics tutor to Erzherzog Maximilian and Kronprinz Ferdinand, and heading an army commission on needed small arms improvements that resulted in adoption, among other innovations, of the Model 1796 bayonet for Jäger and the reinforced hammer for flintlocks. Peter Krenn et. al., *Die Handfeuer-Waffen des österreichischen Soldaten*, Akademische Druck-u Verlagsanstalt, Graz, 1985, p. 16.

31. Unterberger, p. 67.

32. Ibid., p. 77.

33. Ibid., p. 67.

34. Ibid., p 38. Unterberger advocated longer and more frequent target practice for Jäger troops. He also advised that the new Jäger recruit should be well trained

in the disassembly, maintenance and reassembly of his weapon. This included emphasis on a well-maintained lock and bore. The new Jäger should be trained to protect his weapon and never use it roughly.

For Unterberger specific marksmanship training goals included accustoming recruits to aiming higher or lower depending on distance, as well as training in judging distances accurately. Unterberger also included tips on shooting over large bodies of water (makes distance to the target seem closer) and the importance of taking front, back, and crosswinds into account. Finally he advocated that the Jäger learn to lead targets moving at various speeds.[20]

Unterberger believed that since the Jäger engaged single, widely dispersed targets and not massed formations usually, that he must be capable of hitting smaller targets in training than the normal Infantryman. His standards for Jäger qualification were:

- At 100 paces   Hit a man/surface of 6 "Schuh" by 2 "Schuh and never miss

- At 200 paces   Hit a surface 6 Schuh by 3 Schuh with more hits than misses

- At 300 paces   Hit a surface 6 Schuh by 4 Schuh at least $\frac{1}{8}$th of the time

Authors' Note: A Schuh is slightly less than 12 inches.

For recruits unaccustomed to fairly stiff military loads, Unterberger recommended a period during which the trooper shot half loads at a distance of 50 paces. This allowed the new Jäger to get accustomed to recoil, learn proper trigger pull, and avoid flinching and becoming recoil-sensitive. Once the instructor was satisfied that these tasks were mastered, the recruit could graduate to normal loads at prescribed distances.

Unterberger placed much emphasis on proper loading and prescribed a detailed series of steps to be followed in loading the Stutzen. His appreciation for accuracy led him to even suggest that lead balls be carried in a small, tightly-tied bag to prevent them rubbing together in the ammunition pouch and becoming deformed, thus degrading accuracy. See Unterberger, pp. 66, 67.

35. Freiherr Constant Villars' career later included service with the 11th Feld-Jäger Battalion in Austria's 1815 war against Murat's Italian kingdom. A unit history reveals him as an energetic officer, frequently engaged in detached duty, commanding extended mixed-unit reconnaissance patrols, leading Jäger in advance guard, raids and even delivering a clandestine message to the tiny neutral city state of San Marino. Constant Villars was awarded the Order of St. Ferdinand from the restored Bourbon King. Poja, pp. 32, 33, 34, 37, 42.

36. August von Constant Villars, Handbook ueber des Vorposten-Dienst zum Gebrauche des Jäger-Officiers im Felde, Akademischen Kunst Musik und Buchhandlung, Linz, 1812.

37. Ibid, pp 43, 44.

38. Ottenfeld, pp. 387, 398.

39. Cf. Rothenberg: "the [Napoleonic era] Feldjäger operated without receiving any instructions specifically designed for their service," p. 112.

40. Ottenfeld, p. 398.

41. Ibid., p. 400.

42. Ibid.

43. Ibid.

44. Ibid., p. 503.

45. Ibid., p. 400.

46. Ibid.

47. Ibid.

48. Ibid. p. 398.

49. Ibid.

50. Ibid. p.400.

51. Ibid.

52. Unterberger, pp. 42-44. Unterberger proposed other ideas for better preparing the Jäger for survival in exposed situations. He recommended the use of a reusable brass cartridge to facilitate faster loading in emergencies. Each Jäger would carry 12 of these in a pouch on his "middle". Contemporary muzzle-loader shooters will recognize this as a "speed loader." The cartridges had a short end containing the patch and ball with the ends of the patch being exposed. The long end carried one shot of powder sealed with oakum or a piece of rag. To use this cartridge, the Jäger removed the stopper from the long end and primed the pan. He then closed the pan and covered it with a leather cap (*Käppel*) which acted to prevent accidental ignition when ramming the ball home. Remainder of the powder was then shaken into the bore and the patch and ball removed from the short end of the cartridge. The ball was then placed onto the crown of the bore over the patch. The ball and

patch were then pushed down into the bore using the button on the knob of the ramrod. Once the ball was firmly in the bore, it was forcefully rammed home until there was no space between patched ball and charge. The Käppel was then removed and the piece ready to shoot.

53. Ottenfeld, p. 400.

54. Ottenfeld, p. 207.

55. Muscovy leather involved an additional step in the tanning process whereby birch oil was rubbed into the back face of the leather producing more hard durable, supple, water resistant leather which also resisted insect damage.

56. Ibid, p. 207.

57. Ottenfeld, p. 390.

58. Ibid.

59. Ibid, p. 390.

60. Ibid, pp. 390-391.

61. Napoleon at War, Austrian Infantry, Osprey/ Del Prado Publishers, Madrid, 1986/1998, pp. 9, 11, 15.

62. Napoleon at War, Austrian Auxiliary Troops, Osprey/Del Prado Publishers, Madrid, 1996, p. 10.

63. Ottenfeld, p. 264.

ENDNOTES

64. Ibid., pp. 390, 391.

65. Ibid., p. 390.

66. Ibid.

67. Ibid.

68. Ibid.

69. Ibid.

70. Ibid.

71. ibid., p 389.

72. Ibid.

73. Ibid.

74. Ibid., p. 390.

75. Ibid., p. 391.

76. Ibid., p. 392.

77. Ibid., p. 391.

78. Ibid.

79. Ibid.

80. Ibid.

81. Ibid., p. 392.

82. Darko Pavlovic, The Austrian Army 1836-66, (i) Infantry, Osprey Publishing, Ltd., Oxford, 1999, pp. 37,38.

83. Ottenfeld, p. 394.

84. Pavlovic, pp. 37, 38.

85. Ottenfeld, p. 394.

86. Pavlovic, pp. 39, 40.

87. Ibid.

88. Ibid., p. 40.

89. Ottenfeld, p. 504.

90. Ibid., pp. 503,504,506. See also Abrichtungs-Reglement für die k. k. Jäger, Wien, Verlag von Leopold Sommer, 1851, Plate XV.

91. Götz, p. 179. Cf. illustrations in Pavlovic, pp. 38, 39. See also Ottenfeld, pp. 506, 507. Note the powder horn and the alteration in method of attaching cartridge box and sling.

CHAPTER 5 NOTES

1. A mixed conscript/volunteer force with a long professional tradition, comprising one Guards Brigade, nine brigades of line infantry, two rifle-armed light infantry battalions (*Bersaglieri*), six regiments of cavalry, and competent artillery and technical troops, numbering around 65,000 men, which a prickly Prussian officer who served with them described as "on the whole good." Michael Embree, Radetzky's Marches: The Campaigns of 1848 and 1849 in Upper Italy, Helion & Company, Solihull, UK, 2010, p. 49.

2. A young English volunteer serving with the Jäger in 1848 later wrote: "Like every other man that served, I quickly contracted an ardent respect and devotion for our chief, Radetzky. We were delighted when he came among us with *"Grüss Euch Gott, mein Jäger,"* and smiled at our hearty response *"Grüss Ihnen Gott Fader* (sic.)" for the old man was always known as Father Radetzky by the troops. To the attachment he inspired, and the thorough co-operation between officers and men with him, no doubt part of his success was due. And he deserved it all, for owing to his almost paternal care, never, to my knowledge, except when actually under fire, were we one day without our full ration." Anonymous, Reminiscences of an English Cadet in the Austrian service, 1848- c1854, p. 5. Laurence Cole, in Military Culture and Popular Patriotism in Late Imperial Austria, devotes an entire chapter to Radetzky as "father figure of the army" in the last half of the nineteenth century, noting, for example, that "reputedly it was Radetzky's doing that senior officers began to address their junior colleagues with the more informal and comradely *Du* (thou) rather than the polite form, *Sie* (thee)." See pp. 63-107, especially pp. 66, 90, 106.

3. Alan Sked, Radetzky: Imperial Victor and Military Genius, I. B. Tauris & Co. Ltd., London, 2011, p. 79.

4. Sked, op. cit., pp. 80, 83-86. Within a short time Radetzky's presence was felt

in the army in Italy. An anonymous British observer's report in the United Service Journal describes large-scale maneuvers conducted in 1833 which simulated an attack by a "Western Army" along the Mincio immediately to the south of Lake Garda." The observer notes approvingly the "active and offhand style of manoevre; large bodies moving with rapid combinations, marches of great length and continuance over mountainous country; and every other characteristic of the adoption, in the Austrian system, of the most approved principles of tactics." In the early phase of the action an Austrian retreat is ordered requiring a brigade commanded by then Brigadier Peter Martin Pirquet, comprising three battalions of Tiroler-Jäger, two squadrons of Hussars and six guns, to serve as a rear guard. United Service Journal, Part 1, Henry Colburn, London, 1834, pp. 184, 187, 188, 190.

5. Differences among Italians respecting the rebellion included those serving in the Austrian army. Less than half of the Italian troops in Austrian service went over to the enemy when the war broke out. As Lawrence Sondhaus notes: "The thirty-one battalions of infantry and regiment of cavalry raised in Lombardy and Venetia accounted for a total of 30-35,000 men in the spring of 1848. In late April, five weeks after his retreat from Milan, Radetzky's deserters numbered 10,860 men and two officers. Almost all of these were Italian and, since the initial desertions from his army accounted for over three-quarters of all Italian defections in 1848-49 (nine battalions plus parts of three others out of a total of ten battalions and parts of six) the final tally of army deserters from Lombardy and Venetia must have numbered well under 15,000 men. Thus between one-half and two-thirds of the troops from these provinces remained loyal, and if the six battalions of the Trieste Regiment and the hundreds of *kaisertreue* Italians in the Tyrolese Kaiser-Jagers are counted, the overall proportion of disloyal Italians becomes still smaller." Lawrence Sondhaus, In the Service of the Emperor: Italians in the Austrian Armed Forces,

1814-1918. East European Monographs, Boulder, CO, 1990, p. 42. The defections included four companies of Italians serving in the 8th (largely Lombard) Feld-Jäger Battalion. Two companies deserted immediately after hearing of the rising in Milan, while on the withdrawal to Vicenza two other companies briefly took their commanding officer prisoner but released him before departing to join enemy. The two remaining companies continued on to Vicenza with their commander, and went on to distinguish themselves in June in retaking that city. Embree, p. 44; Thürheim, p.514.

6. Embree, op. cit.

7. Anonymous, *Kriegsbegebenheiten bei der kaiserlich österreichischen Armee in Italien, Ein wortgettreuer Abdruch der offiziellen Ausgabe*, 4 Parts, Verlag von Karl Hözel, Wien, 1854.

8. Embree, pp. 360,361,377, 381.

9. The exception was volunteers armed with so-called "Swiss Carbines." These were the Cantonal precursors of what later became standardized as the famous 1851 Swiss Federal Rifle-- heavy, highly-accurate small-bore short rifles, many with double-set triggers. The Piedmontese army valued these volunteers, or at least their rifles, so highly that Lombards armed with them were ordered to join their regular forces concentrating against Radetzky. Some carbine-armed Swiss volunteers remained in the South Tirol, among the more formidable opponents the Austrians faced there. Embree, pp.75, 80.

10. Ibid, pp. 77-79.

11. Ibid., p. 85.

12. Ibid., pp. 82, 85, 86.

13. Ibid., pp.79, 87.

14. Ibid., pp. 84, 85.

15. Ibid., p.104.

16. Josef Strack, *Das Tiroler Jäger-Regiment Kaiser Franz Josef I. in den Jahren 1848 und 1849*, Verlag von Leopold Sommer, Wien, 1853, pp. 111,112.

17. *Carinthia: Ein Wochenblatte fur Vaterlandskunde, Belehrung u. Unterhaltung*, No. 11, Simon Martin Mayer, ed., Klagenfurt, 1856, p. 43.

18. Embree, p. 104. See, for instance, Österreichischer Soldatenfreund, Zeitschrift fur militärische Interessen, No. 35, March, 1851, pp. 1-4.

19. *Österreichischer Soldatenfreund*, p. 3. Cf. Strack, p.157.

20. Embree, pp. 206-208. In the engagements around the bridge at Goito on April 9, another "Kaiser-Jäger" of distinguished ancestry, the grandson of Andreas Hofer, was killed. *Kriegsbegebenheiten*, I, p.88.

21. Strack, *Denkmal*, pp. 98-99.

22. Embree p.113.

23. Ibid.

24. Strack, *Denkmal*, pp. 100, 101.

25. Embree, p. 120.

26. ibid., pp. 384, 385.

27. Ibid., p. 168. Baron Augustin, who was responsible for the lock mechanisms on the Austrian soldiers' firearms in 1848, had also studied foreign armies' use of rocket batteries extensively.

28. The stone *Villa Rotunda*, in the plan of a symmetrical cross with each arm terminating in a two-story Doric pediment and columns , the center crowned by a dome, is considered one of the masterpieces of the Renaissance architect Giovanni Palladio, and survives to this day. It was defended by the Roman University Battalion and the Bersaglieri of the Po. Infantry Regiment Prohaska (N°. 38) stormed the place at a loss of 11 men killed and 30 wounded and missing.

29. Strack, Denkmal, p. 108.

30. Ibid, pp. 109, 110.

31. Embree, p. 186.

32. Strack, Denkmal, p.114; Thürheim, p.527.

33. On the Kopal Monument see https://www.jgbnoe.at/kopaljaeger/?lng=de&sekt=7&txt=7 . After the founding of Czechoslovakia as an independent republic in 1918, all Imperial inscriptions and decorations were removed from the obelisk, but in 2010 these, including the Jägerstutzen with Haubajonet and signal horn, were restored.

34. Strack, Denkmal p. 114.

35. Anonymous, *Kriegsbegebenheiten bei der kaiserlich österreichischen Armee in Italien*, 4 Parts, II, pp. 40-42.

36. Ibid., I, pp. 52, 78, 84, 85, 131.

37. Ibid., II, p. 41. III, pp. 28, 60, 61, 103, 111. Embree, pp. 228, 9. For the employment of Jäger at the big battles of Custozza and Novara supporting this distinction see Embree, especially pp. 211, 229, 232,233,247, 250,292,293,295,296,302,303,310,311.

38. Frederick C. Schneid, The Second War of Italian Unification, 1859-61, Osprey, Oxford, 2012, pp. 25, 26, 34. One of Gyulai's first acts on taking command had been to order all troops to dye their facial hair black to provide a uniform appearance. Richard Brooks, Solferino, 1859, Osprey, 2009, p.8.

39. Schneid, pp. 44-46. He might have been well advised to do so. The spurned staff chief, Colonel Franz von Kuhn, had suggested a strategy worthy of Hess and Radetzky: move quickly and decisively against the Piedmontese; destroy them or at least knock them back seriously, and defend the Alpine passes to slow their French allies' concentration by forcing them all to come by sea. Bassett, p.315.

40. See the orders of battle, Brooks, pp.15-17.

41. Ibid., p. 11.

42. Sondhaus, p. 50, Brooks, p. 11.

43. Schneid, pp. 32, 44.

44. Giovanni Cerino Badone, "Not an Easy Day, The Austrian and the Sardinian

Armies at the Battle of San Martino, 24th June, 1859," XVIIIe Symposium International D' Histoire et de Prospective Militaires, 1er mars 2014, Le Centre Général Guisan, Pully, Switzerland, p. 8. By the Battle of Solferino some Austrians seem to have mastered long-range fire with their Lorenz rifles, resulting in higher losses among French gunners, including a general, than had been experienced at Magenta weeks earlier. Brooks, p.88.

45. Badone, p.7., Geoffrey Wawro, The Austro-Prussian War: Austria's War with Prussia and Italy in 1866, Cambridge, Cambridge University Press, 1996, pp. 11, 12. The previous Field Instructions, those of 1847, still advocated the use of relatively narrow-fronted Napoleonic attack columns in appropriate circumstances, but with adjustments that permitted bringing linear firepower to bear (pp. 184, 300,). The 1847 Instructions also devoted considerable space to the kind of skirmishing, patrolling and detachments, especially in broken, mountainous or wooded terrain, which were realized and, in fact, extended by the small combined arms task forces employed in 1848-49. *Feld-Instruction fur die Infanterie, Cavallerie und Artillerie*, Vol. II, Olmutz, 1847, pp. 34, 35, 67-81, 143, 150, 161, 164, 165, 182, 186, 229, 268, 275, 281, 282. Likewise, the Abrichtungs-Reglement für die k. k. Jäger of 1851 emphasizes that the training it lays out is based on the assumption that the Jäger will likely be making initial contact with the enemy, "*in einzelngefecte*" and in open order, though requiring him to be skilled in conventional tactics as well. Abrichtungs-Reglement für die k. k. Jäger, Verlag von Leopold Sommer, Wien, 1851, p. ix.

46. Thürheim, p. 484.

47. See order of battle, Brooks, pp 15-17. Essentially the same kind of distribution of Jäger units prevailed at Solferino at the end of the month.

48. Brooks, pp. 26, 27.

49. Typically for the Austrians in this war, elements of three corps, V, VIII and IX, were mixed in this relatively small engagement. Proceedings of the Royal Artillery Institution, Vol II, Woolwich, 1861, p. 218; Thürheim, pp. 497,498.

50. Adolphus Lance, Struggles for Freedom, or the Liberation of Italy with the Successful Campaign in Lombardy and the Heroic Deeds of Garibaldi in Sicily and Naples, Resulting in the Formation of a United Kingdom of Italy, London, James Hagger, 1859, p. 126.

51. Brooks, p.29.

52. Lance, p.128.

53. Thürheim, p. 546.

54. Lance, p. 152; Schneid, p. 42.

55. Brooks, pp. 32, 33. We have followed Brooks' narrative for this account generally.

56. Thürheim, p. 511.

57. Jäger are credited with bringing down a French Division commander, Charles Espinasse, and members of his staff, see Basset, p. 316, "beating with his sword pommel on the door of a house full of Austrian Jäger, whose accurate fire caused many casualties." Brooks, p. 45. Thürheim, p. 494 identifies them as the 2nd Feld-Jäger Battalion.

58. Badone p. 5.

59. Brooks, pp. 16, 17.

60. Badone, p. 13.

61. Schneid, p. 56.

62. Badone, p.10.

63. Basset, p. 320.

64. Tait Keller, Apostles of the Alps, Mountaineering and Nation Building in Germany and Austria, 1860-1939, Chapel Hill, University of North Carolina Press, 2016, pp. 95, 96.

CHAPTER 6 NOTES

1. Bassett, 323-325 Thürheim, p. 519. Rothenberg notes: ""One Prussian officer noted that the Austrian *Stosstaktik* resulted in prohibitive casualties. Even some Austrian officers realized that the emphasis placed on all-out attack caused unacceptable losses and Feldzeugmeister Franz Ritter von Hauslab proposed more intensive use of artillery to prepare for infantry assaults. Such dissenting opinions, however, were largely discounted in Vienna. Instead, as the future Austrian Chief of Staff, Lieutenant Colonel Friedrich Beck, noted, the Danish campaign was used to prove the contention that everything could be achieved with the bayonet and that the army was now prepared to face all comers." Gunther E. Rothenberg, The Army of Francis Joseph, West Lafayette, Indiana, Purdue University Press, 1998, p. 65.

2. Rene Chartrand, Richard Hook The Mexican Adventure, 1861-67, Osprey Publishing, London, 1994, p. 35. Für Kaiser Maximilian nach Mexiko, http://www.

zapfenstreich.at/mexiko.freikorps/freikorps.html, accessed April 2018.

3. Rothenberg, The Army of Francis Joseph, p.63.

4. Gordon A. Craig, The Battle of Königgrätz, University of Philadelphia Press, Philadelphia, 2003, p.17.

5. Rothenberg, The Army of Francis Joseph, p.70.

6. Bassett, pp.334, 335.

7. Ibid., p.351."Unlike Benedek, who conferred half his *corps d'armee* on inept protégés and aristocratic mentors, and needlessly divided his headquarters into four independent chanceries, Albrecht peremptorily closed South Army to dilettantes and rigorously centralized all his staff and adjutant functions in the hands of a single, talented staff chief…Albrecht then entrusted his three infantry corps and his reserve cavalry to able, non-noble professional soldiers, all with combat experience." Geoffrey Wawro, the Austro-Prussian War, Cambridge University Press, Cambridge, 1996, p. 67.

8. Keller, pp. 95, 96.

9. H. M. Hozier, The Seven Weeks' War, Second Edition, London and New York, Macmillan and Co., 1871, p. 457.

10. A later Prussian observer had a decidedly different view: "The brief course of the campaign of 1866, in which our infantry acted mostly on the offensive, gave the Jäger an opportunity for profitable employment only where, contrary to accepted notions, they fought side by side with the rest of the infantry." He concluded from this experience that: Since the introduction of accurate breech

loading weapons, and their use by all infantry, Jagers- and riflemen have no tactical excuse for existing, except where they are specially trained in mountain warfare... While Jager-battalions are at present employed like the rest of the infantry, they are retained by us as such because of tradition... Since the war of 1866 the demand for special employment of Jäger has ceased." Tactics by Balck, Colonel, German Army, [sic.] Volume I, Introduction and Formal Tactics of Infantry, Translated by Lt. Walter Krueger, Fourth ed., U.S Cavalry Association, Fort Leavenworth Kansas, 1911, p. 23.

11. Craig, p. 7.

12. Hozier, pp. 512-518.

13. Craig, p.60.

14. Hozier, p. 230.

15. Ibid, pp. 237,238.

16. Ibid. However, in describing the field following the battle Colonel Hozier notes: "Wherever the Austrians fought unprotected by cover, and wherever the Prussian riflemen armed with the Needle-Gun could see their enemies, the disproportion of the dead became immediately apparent." P. 267.

17. Ibid. p. 238.

18. Ibid. p. 260.

19. "How the Prussian Guards were allowed to get into Chlum appears inexplicable," Hozier, p. 264. Craig, pp. 132, 145-147.

20. Anon., The United Service Magazine, Vol XXXI, New Series, London, William Clowes and Sons, Ltd., 1905, p. 452.

21. Captain C. Francis Clery, Minor Tactics, London, Henry S. King & Co, 1875, p. 28.

22. Clery, pp. 29, 30.

23. Wawro, p. 89.

24. Alexander Hold, History of the 1866 Campaign in Italy, Translated by Stuart Sutherland, 2010, Helion and Company, West Midlands, England, p. 51.

25. Ibid., p. 49.

26. Clery, pp. 31, 32.

27. Hold, p. 53.

28. Clery, p. 36.

28. Wawro, p. 96.

30. Ibid. p. 103, 122.

31. Hold, p. 69.

32. Wawro, p. 115.

33. Hold, pp.72, 79.

34. Echoing some contemporary participants' opinion, Archduke Albrecht

has been soundly criticized by modern historians for failing to follow-up his victory: "At Custoza, Albrecht stood on high ground observing the wild flight of a demoralized, largely unarmed Italian army. The fate of the fledgling Italian state was in his hands." Albrecht's able Chief of Staff, Franz John cited Albrecht's being mistakenly restraining by undefined "political considerations," Wawro, pp. 116-121. Whether these included the knowledge that "The decision to cede Venetia to Napoleon III, who would in turn give it to Italy, had already been taken in Vienna," Bassett, pp.350, and an unwillingness, reminiscent of his father's, to take more losses when the army might very well be needed to preserve the dynasty in the event of reverses in Bohemia, we can only speculate.

35. Ibid., pp. 103-105.

36. Ibid., p. 104.

37. Ibid., pp.112, 117, 118, 119, 121, 123, 125.

38. Ibid., p.163.

39. Ibid., pp. 112, 113.

40. Ibid., p. 109.

41. Ibid., pp. 115-119. "There was no more water…At 3pm there appeared an enemy parliamentary. [11th IR Lt.] Preu climbed through the embrasure to meet him, and was delivered the following message: 'General Garibaldi has instructed me to congratulate you on your brilliant defence of the work, which he had not believed would hold out for so long, and to request you lay down your arms in order to spare the lives of so many brave men.' Preu refused and proposed he be allowed to depart with the honors of war. The officer led him behind a ledge, showed

him many thousands of volunteers covering the road and conducted him to the headquarters of General Haugh, who assured Preu that he would not assault but would have the defenseless work bombarded into a pile of rubble. In addition, Preu was convinced that the new battery was fitted with 24-pounders. Last…he learned that the entire valley was in the hands of the Garibaldians. Thus he decided in concert with the other three officers to surrender the fort, the officers being allowed to retain their sabres. As the garrison was conducted down the road from Ampola…it was rendered the honours of war by the several thousand men drawn up there." Franz Jaeger, ed., War in the Tyrol, The History of the 11th Austrian Infantry regiment during the Campaign of 1866, translated by Stuart Sutherland, Helion & Company, Solihul, West Midlands, 2010, pp. 26,27.

CHAPTER 7 NOTES

1. Dolleczek, p. 77.

2. D. Bailey, British Military Flintlock Rifles, 1740-1840, Andrew Mowbray, Lincoln, RI, 2002, p. 65.

3. Dolleczek, p. 77.

4. Erich Gabriel, Die Hand – und Faustfeuerwaffen der habsburgischen Heere, Wien 1990, p.37.

5. Dolleczek, p. 77. See Appendix 1 for a discussion of Jäger edged weapons.

6. Gabriel, p.37. Authors' Note: All technical descriptions of these weapons are translated from the Gabriel text throughout the remainder of this chapter, unless otherwise indicated.

7. Eugene Heer Der Neue Stockel, Internationales Lexicon de Büchsenmacher, Feurwaffenfabrikanten und Armbrustmacher von 1400-1900, Journal-Verlag Schwend GMBH, 1979, Vol 2, p. 1207.

8. Ottenfeld, p. 270.

9. See above, p. 56.

10. Dolleczek, pp. 77,120.

11. Ottenfeld, p.271.

12. Ibid, p.204. Also see the pen-and-ink drawing of the Doppelstützen, sacke, and pike, p. 202. Ottenfeld pictures a Doppelstützen-armed Jäger of 1778, p.207. David Hollins, Austrian Auxiliary Troops 1792-1816, Osprey Publishing Ltd., London, 1996, maintains that "only" 2,500 were manufactured and suggests they were intended primarily for Grenzers. Following Ottenfeld, he also notes that each Grenzer Regiment was officially supposed to include a detachment of 256 trained sharpshooters, but that some were definitely armed with "rifles" rather than Doppelstützen, pp.5, 9.

13. Dolleczek pg. 120.

14. Gabriel, p.228.

15. Dolleczek, p. 91.

16. Gabriel, p. 37.

17. Gabriel, p. 72.

18. Hans-Dieter Götz, Militärgewehre und Pistole der deutschen Staaten 1800 – 1870, Motorbuch Verlag, Stuttgart, 1970, pp. 144-146.

19. Götz pp. 45, 46.

20. Gabriel, pp. 74, 75.

21. Götz, p. 153.

22. Ibid., pp. 142-153. For clear illustrations of the large and small machine locks see, pp. 149,150.

23. Ibid., p. 154.

24. Ibid., pp201-213 http://kapszli.hu/en/the-story-of-the-augustin-tube-lock-ignition-system/ Accessed November, 2017.

25. Dolleczek, pp. 92, 93.

26. Götz, pp. 210-212.

27. Ottenfeld, p. 397.

28. Dolleczek, pp. 92,93, 120; Götz, pp. 210, 211; Todd, p130; Whisker, et. al., pp. 77, 78; Gabriel, pp. 64, 82, 83; Darko Pavlovic, The Austrian Army 1836-66, Vol. 1 Infantry, Osprey Publishing Ltd., Oxford, 1999, p. 36.

29. Dolleczeck, p.120. Krenn et. al., p. 79.

30. Ottenfeld, Vol 3, Tafeln, n.p.

31. Gabriel, p. 268.

32. Cf. Götz, p. 211, Gabriel, p.268.

33. Gabriel, pp 268-269.

34. Gabriel, p. 270.

35. This is the rifle described in Krenn et. al., p.79 as the M 1842 Kammerbüchse. The rifle pictured is later production, without the patch box. See Gabriel, pp. 92,158, 543.

36. Dolleczek, op. cit., pp. 92-93, Ottenfeld, p. 397. Clearly, it is not always easy to determine definite timelines on adoption and issue of K.u.K. arms. A ubiquitous and busy bureaucracy had a role in creating some of the ambiguities we encounter. As befitted a wide flung, multilingual, polyglot empire overseen by an army of bureaucrats, Austrian government clerks kept endless records on everything. With a huge volume of data being collected, orders dispatched and reports received from offices and military commands from Poland to Italy, information was not always collatable, and therefore accuracy for our purposes a century or more removed cannot always be assumed. We suspect there are also ambiguities introduced by the very need for bureaucratic precision—for example, different contracts, drawing funds from different budget lines for new- made arms, as opposed to converting and updating arms already in stock, leading to confused model designations and even phantom or seemingly undocumented weapons. In all, 100% identification and description of many models is problematic at best, and we have tried whenever possible to base our discussion on arms we can hold in our hands.

37. Frederick P Todd, American Military Equipage, Charles Scribner's Sons, New York, 1980, p. 130.

38. James B. Whisker et. al., Firearms from Europe 2nd Ed., Tom Rowe Books, College Station, PA., 2002, p. 78.

39. Ibid. p. 77.

40. Todd, op. cit., p. 130.

41. Dolleczek, p. 93, Ottenfeld, p. 867.

42. Whisker et. al., op. cit., pp 77-78. In fact, nothing makes the Austrian M 1849 particularly deserving of this appellation. The Colt Revolving Rifle, various British arms, Prussian Potsdam muskets, ancient East India Company arms, small-bore American and Swiss rifles, Austrian stützen as well as large bore rifles like the '49, and American M 1816 muskets originally converted by Colt under a contract with Russia, were also employed by the Italians. See G. M. Trevelyan, Garibaldi and the Making of Italy, Longmans Green and Co., London, 1911, Appendix on Arms, pp. 326-330. To us, frankly, this Garibaldian attribution sounds more like clever marketing by the arms brokers to give these particular Austrian offerings some special aura and perhaps justify a higher price. Garibaldi was a major international celebrity, much admired in the US at the time, and there was an extensive international campaign, the "Garibaldi Rifle Fund," to raise money to purchase one million rifles for the Italian nationalists. See, Jasper Ridley, Garibaldi, Phoenix Press, London, 1974, p. 419.

43. http://www.biographien.ac.at/oebl_L/Lorenz_Josef_1814-1879.xml. Accessed 29 Jun 2017

44. Ibid.

45. Ibid.

46. Ibid.

47. Götz, p. 255.

48. Dolleczek pp. 94, 121. Götz, p. 255.

49. In 1851 the Swiss had adopted a relatively small compression bullet-- 10.5mm (41 caliber) for use in their newly-standardized short rifles, earlier larger-bore Cantonal versions of which as "Swiss Carbines," were used effectively by Italian and Swiss volunteers against the Austrians in 1848-49. Shortly afterwards, Lorenz in Austria and Henry Wilkinson in England began work on compression bullet designs. Writing in 1860, journalist Frederick Engels, best known today as Karl Marx's collaborator, but at the time a widely-published commentator on contemporary military affairs, noted that Wilkinson and Lorenz," simultaneously, but each independently of the other, invented another method of making a loose-fitting elongated bullet increase its diameter by the forces of the explosion, so as to make it fit the bore closely and follow the turn of the grooves. This method consisted in making the explosion compress the bullet lengthways, instead of expanding it." Wilkinson's bullet was submitted for approval to the British Army, but never adopted. Friederich Engels, "The History of the Rifle," [Part] V, Volunteer Journal, Vol. i, Nº. 17, pp. 223-4, December 29, 1860, reprinted in W. H. Chaloner and W.O. Henderson, Engels as Military Critic, Articles by Friederich Engels reprinted from the *Volunteer Journal* and the *Manchester Guardian* of the 1860's, Manchester University Press, Manchester 1959, p. 56.

50. Dolleczek, p.96, Götz, p. 257.

51. Gabriel, p. 59.

52. Gabriel, p. 90.

53. With respect to firearms for their armies the so-called German Bund, a loose confederation of large and small German states established in 1815, chose to go in two different directions in the later 1850's. The northern, mostly smaller states, opted for the Prussian Needle-Gun with its relatively large 15.43mm bullet, while in the south, in addition to Austria, Bavaria, Württemberg, Baden, Hessen-Darmstadt, Bavaria, Nassau, and Saxony decided to continue with muzzle loaders and their own smaller Austrian 13.9 mm-sized bullets. As a result, some excellent military muzzle-loading arms were produced by these states. These "southern" states made up the majority of the army of the German Confederation with 350,000 troops, and by adopting the smaller bullet opened a world of improved accuracy and performance in their small arms. Accuracy was improved by higher muzzle velocity with the smaller bullet. Since the traditional large, heavy bullets had a bell shaped trajectory, like an artillery round, they required accurate adjustments of relatively complicated sights to achieve any level of longer-range accuracy. The new, lighter bullet's flatter trajectory enabled accuracy achievable with simpler sights. Götz, pp. 253, 254.

54. Gabriel, p. 88.

55. Ibid., 306.

57. Ibid., pp. 95, 320-321.

58. Ibid., pp. 94-99.

59. Ibid., pp. 95, 320, 321.

60. Ibid., pp. 95, 322-325.

61. Ibid., p. 95.

62. http://www.beemans.net/Austrian%20airguns.htm accessed August, 2017.

63. Ibid. Girandoni's experimentation with improvements in firearms was not confined to the air rifle. Ottenfeld, p. 844, illustrates two Jägerstutzen designs by Girandoni, a breechloader and a repeater utilizing a tubular magazine like that of the air rifle, both dated 1779. In the collection of the Heeresgeschichtliches Museum are two other experimental Jägerstutzen, one, of 1850 incorporating what looks similar to the Prussian lock design of 1835 and the other a pin-fire ignition system: HGM Bezugsnummer 3582/2008, and 4180/2009 respectively.

CHAPTER 8 NOTES

1. Translated and abridged from: Jacob F. Neitzschner, Österreichischen Soldatenwelt, Band I, Verlag der J.B. Messler'schen Buchhandlung, Stuttgart, 1852, pp 35-50.

2. Stiegel Beer is still brewed in Salzburg and on its own, a good enough reason to visit this beautiful city.

3. Sadly the topic of suicide among young soldiers which was a problem in the 1830's, remains one today. The pressures on men scarcely teenagers who find themselves away from home, many for the first time, away from family and community support, and in a high pressure world, both physically and mentally, has driven many to this tragic end. A suicide rate of 23.8 per 100,000 was reported by DOD studies for the US Army in 2014. This capped a number of years of increasing suicides among active and reserve component troops – See: Stars and Stripes, 9, February 2016.

APPENDIX 1 NOTES

1. Dolleczek, pp. 27,28, Eduard Wagner, Cut and Thrust Weapons, English Edition, The Hamlyn Publishing Group, Ltd., London, 1967, pp. 354,355, 413, Ottenfeld, p. 824.

2. Ottenfeld, p. 828. For light infantry saber see table p. 830.

3. M. Christian Ortner, Erich Artlieb, With Drawn Sword, Austro-Hungarian Edged Weapons from 1848 to 1918, 2006, Verlag Miltaria, Edition Stefan Rest, Vienna, p. 102.

4. Ottenfeld, pp. 270, 825: logical in that Dolleczek collaborated with Teuber and Ottenfeld on this work. American historical artist Don Troiani shows a similar bayonet in an unpublished depiction dated 2014, of a Brunswick Jäger circa 1777, but with a symmetrical cross guard.

5. Dolleczek, Tafel 15.

6. Howard L. Blackmore, Hunting Weapons, Walker & Company, New York, 1971, pp. 28, 29. "In most European armies the small brass-hilted hanger was adopted first as a sidearm for infantry and then specialized corps such as pioneers and riflemen…hangers of suitably superior quality were also worn by many military and naval officers. Portraits…show a number of naval officers carrying both plain and ornate hangers indistinguishable from hunting swords."

7. Ottenfeld, pp. 825. Ottenfeld is not clear on whether this hanger's "roughly-mounted guard" was a "D" or simple cross-guard; the illustration of the Pioneer and Jäger from 1792 suggests the former. For Sapper Saber M 1769 see Ottenfeld p. 826. See also Dolleczek, Tafel IV. Ottenfeld, p. 602, notes that in the 1770's at least

one Freikorps Jäger unit carried a hanger which in a pinch could be used as a plug bayonet. The hilt was pewter and cast to conform to the barrel.

8. Ortner & Artlieb, p. 70.

9. Ottenfeld, p.389. There should certainly have been plenty of alternatives around. Depending upon supply, the sabers for Artillery and Miners, Models 1774, 1805, which Ottenfeld shows on p.826, could have been possible choices, in addition to any surplus 1802 NCO/Grenadier or 1809 infantry sabers.

10. Ibid., p. 392.

11. Ottenfeld, p. 392, Pavlovic, p. 46.

12. Ortner, Artlieb, p.70. Ottenfeld suggests that the 1824 design was based on the M 1809, p. 824.

13. Harold L. Peterson, Arms and Armor in Colonial America, 1526-1783, Bramhall House, New York, 1956, pp. 257, 261.

14. Ottenfeld, p. 396.

15. Ottenfeld, p. 504, Ortner, Artlieb, p.304.

16, Anton Dolleczek, Die Entwicklung de Handfeuerwaffen im osterrichischen Heer, Minerva: illustrierte militär-wissenschaftliche Zeitschrift, Vol. 2 Dreisel & Gröger, Wien, 1894, p. 458. See also Karl Kandelsdorfer, et. al. österriechischer militärische Zeitschrift, Folge 74, Vol.III, XXXVII, Wien, 1897, p. 234, and Folge 75, Vol. III, XXXIX, Wien, 1897, p. 160.

17. Ottenfeld, I, p. 390; Philip Haythornthwaite, Austrian Army of the Napoleonic

Wars (I) Infantry, Osprey Publishing, Ltd., London, 1986, p.46.

APPENDIX 2 NOTES

1. Military commission to Europe in 1855 and 1856. Report of Major Alfred Mordecai, Ordnance Department, 1861, p. 96.

2. Ibid., p. 95.

3. Laurence Cole, Military Culture and Popular Patriotism in Late Imperial Austria, Oxford University Press, Oxford, 2014, pp. 50, 51.

4. Military Commission, p. 97.

5. Ibid., p. 95

6. Ibid, pp. 95, 96. Mordecai notes average failure rates of barrels at proofing "about two percent, but are sometimes as high as fifteen percent. If one third of those delivered at one time fail, the whole are rejected."

7. Ibid., p. 95.

8. ibid., p. 96.

9. ibid., p. 97.

APPENDIX 3 NOTES

1. For a good list of Austrian makers of Lorenz series arms drawn from an archival

source see Marc Schwalm, Klaus Hofmann, European Arms in the Civil War, Mowbray Publishing, Woonsocket, RI, 2018, p. 91.

2. David Noe, Joseph Serbaroli, Jr., European Bayonets of the American Civil War, Andrew Mowbray Publishing, Woonsocket, RI, 2013, pp. 81, 82, 89, 95, 97.

3. Found on a rifle maker marked "KEG Fabrik" / Dorotheum Auction 01.03.2018, Item 240V

4. .Found on a rifle maker-marked "Bollman" with acceptance date of "859", Dorotheum Auction 02.05.2017, Item 183.

5. Found on a rifle maker-marked "B+C" with acceptance date of "857", Dorotheum Auction 12.12.2016, Item 245.

BIBLIOGRAPHY

Abrichtungs-Reglement für die k. k. Jäger, Wien, Verlag von Leopold Sommer, 1851.

Alte Feldakten Kt 1536, 1813-X-436b, fol.02r, Kriegsarchiv, Wien.

Feld-Instruction fur die Infanterie, Cavallerie und Artillerie, Vol. II, Olmutz, 1847.

Generals-Reglement, Wien, 1769.

Instruktionspunkte für die k. k. Armee zur Campagne des Jahres 1794, Valenciennes, 12. 3. 1794; Observationspunkte fur die Generale bei der Armee in Deutschland in Jahre 1796, Beiträge zur Geschichte des österreichischen Heerwesens, Vol 1, Wien 1872.

Anonymous, Kriegsbegeheiten bei der kaiserlich österreichischen Armee in Italien, Ein wortgettreuer Abdruch der offiziellen Ausgabe, 4 parts, Verlag von Karl Hözel, Wien, 1854.

Anonymous, The Partisan: Or the Art of Making War in Detachment, Translated from the French of Mr. De Jeney. By an Officer in the Army, R. Griffiths, Bookseller, London, 1760. Gale ECCO Print Editions, no date.

Anonymous, Reminiscences of an English Cadet in the Austrian Service, 1848-c1854, Duncan Rogers, ed., Helion & Company, Solihull, UK, 2006. (Originally published as a series of articles in The Cornhill magazine, 1867.)

Anonymous, Instruktionspunkte für die k.k. Armee zur Campagne des Jahres 1794, in Beiträge zur Geschichte des österreichischen Heerwesens, Nº. 1, Wien, 1872.

Arnold, James, Napoleon Conquers Austria: The 1809 Campaign for Vienna, Praeger, Westport, Ct., 1995.

Bailey, D., British Military Flintlock Rifles, 1740-1840, Andrew Mowbray, Lincoln, R.I., 2002.

Basset, Richard, For God and Kaiser: The Imperial Austrian Army from 1619-1918, Yale University Press, New Haven, Ct., 2015.

Brooks, Richard, Solferino, 1859, Osprey, 2009.

Chartrand, Rene, and Houk, Richard, The Mexican Adventure, 1861-67, Osprey Publishing, London, 1994.

Captain C. Francis Clery, Minor Tactics, London, Henry S. King & Co, 1875.

Cole, Lawrence, Military Culture and Popular Patriotism in Late Imperial Austria, Oxford University Press, Oxford, 2013.

Von Constant Villars, August, Handbook ueber des Vorposten-Dienst zum

Gebrauche des Jäger-Officiers im Felde, Akademischen Kunst Musik und Buchhandlung, Linz, 1812.

Craig, Gordon A., The Battle of Königgrätz, University of Philadelphia Press, Philadelphia, PA., 2003.

Crist, Oskar, Kriege unter Kaiser Josef II. Nach den Feldakten und anderen authentishen Quellen bearbeitet in der Kriegsgeschichten Abteilung des K. und K. Kriegsarchivs, Verlag der Buchhandlung für Militär-Literatur, Wien, 1880.

Dolleczek, Anton, Monograph der K. u. K. österreichische – ungarische Handfeuer Waffen, Wien, 1896 (Reprinted by the Akademische Druck und Verlegungsstalt, Graz, 1970).

Duffy, Christopher, Instrument of War, the Austrian Army in the Seven Years War, Volume I, Emperor's Press, Rosemont, Il., 2000.

Guillaume Philibert Comte Duhesme, Essai historique sur l'infanterie légère, ou Traité des petites opérations de la guerre, à l'usage des jeunes officiers, 3rd Edition, Paris, 1864.

Embree, Michael, Radetzky's Marches: The Campaign of 1848 and 1849 in Upper Italy, Helion and Co., Solihull, 2010.

Evans, R. J. W., Austria-Hungary and the Habsburgs: Central Europe c. 1683-1867, Oxford University Press, Oxford, 2006.

Eysturlid, Lee W., The Formative Influences, Theories, and Campaigns of the Archduke Carl of Austria, Greenwood Press, Westport, Ct, 1996.

Fichenbauer, Peter and Ortner, M. Christian, Eds., A History of the Austrian Army From Maria Theresa to the Present Day, Verlag Militaria GmbH, Vienna, 2015.

Gabriel, Erich, Die Hand – und Faustfeuerwaffen der habsburgischen Heere, Wien, 1990.

Goedeke, Karl, ed., Elf Bücher deutscher Dichtung: Von Sebastian Brant bis J. W. Goethe, Hahn'sche Verlbh., Leipzig, 1849.

Greener, W.W., The Gun and its Development, New Orchard Editions, Poole, Dorset, 1988.

Götz, Hans-Dieter, Militärgewehre und Pistolen der deutschen Staaten 1800-1870, Motorbuch Verlag, Stuttgart, 1970.

Gill, John H., 1809 Thunder on the Danube: Napoleon's Defeat of the Habsburgs, Vol. 1, Frontline Books, London 2008.

Gräffer, August, Geschichte der Kaiserliche-Königliche Regimenter, Corps, Bataillons und anderen Militär-Branchen seit ihrer Errichtung bis zu Ende des Feldzeuges 1799, Vol. I, Wien, 1804.

Hayes, Kevin J. George Washington, A Life in Books, Oxford University Press, Oxford, 2017.

Haythornthwaite, Philip J., Austrian Armies of the Napoleonic Wars, Vol. I, Infantry, Osprey Publishing, London, 1986.

Heer, Eugene, Der Neue Stockel Internationales Lexicon der Büchsenmacher, Feuerwehrfabrikanten und Armbrustmacher von 1400-1`900, Journal-Verlag

BIBLIOGRAPHY

Schuend GmbH, 1975.

Herrmann, Dr. Alfred, Marengo, Druck und Verlag der Aschendorffschen Buchhandlungm, Münster i.W., 1903.

Hochedlinger, Michael, Austria's Wars of Emergence 1683-1797, Routledge, London and New York, 2013.

Hold, Alexander, History of the 1866 Campaign in Italy (Translated by Stuart Sutherland), Helion and Company, West Midlands, 2010.

Hollins, David, Austrian Auxiliary Troops, 1792-1810, Osprey Publishing, London, 1966.

Hollins, David, Austrian Frontier troops 1740-98, Osprey Publishing, London, 2005.

Hollins, David, Marengo 1800, Osprey Publishing, Oxford, 2000.

Hozier, H.M., The Seven Weeks' War, MacMillan & Co., London, 1867 (Reprinted by Oakpast Ltd., 2012.)

Jaeger, Franz, ed., War in the Tyrol, The History of the 11th Austrian Infantry regiment during the Campaign of 1866, translated by Stuart Sutherland, Helion & Company, Solihul, West Midlands, 2010.

Johnston, Robert Matteson, The Napoleonic Empire in Southern Italy and the Rise of the Secret Societies, Volume 1, Macmillan, London, 1904.

Kandelsdorfer, Karl, Streuffleurs Österreichische Militärische Zeitschrift, Vol. 3, Wien, 1897.

Keller, Tait, Apostles of the Alps, Mountaineering and Nation Building in Germany and Austria, 1860-1939, University of North Carolina Press, Chapel Hill, N.C., 2016.

Krenn, Peter et. al., *Die Handfeuer-Waffen des österreichischen Soldaten*, Akademische Druck-u Verlagsanstalt, Graz, 1985.

Lance, Adolphus, Struggles for Freedom, or the Liberation of Italy with the Successful Campaign in Lombardy and the Heroic Deeds of Garibaldi in Sicily and Naples Resulting in the Foundation of a United Kingdom of Italy, James Hagger, London, 1859.

Levy, Miriam J., Governance and Grievance, Hapsburg Policy in Italian Tirol in the Eighteenth Century, Purdue University Press, Lafayette, IN., 1988.

Military commission to Europe in 1855 and 1856. Report of Major Alfred Mordecai, Ordnance Department, 1861.

Muir, Rory, Tactics and the Experience of Battle in the Age of Napoleon, Yale University Press, New Haven, CT, 1998.

Nafziger, George, Imperial Bayonets: Tactics of the Napoleonic Battery, Battalion and Brigade as Found in Contemporary Regulations, Greenhill Books, London, 1996.

Nafziger, George, and Gioannini, Marco, The Defense of the Napoleonic Kingdom of Northern Italy, 1813-1814 Praeger, Westport, Ct 2002.

Neitzschner, Jacob F., Österreichischen Soldatenwelt, Band I, Verlag der J.B. Messler'schen Buchhandlung, Stuttgart, 1852.

Noe, David et. al., European Bayonets of the American Civil War, Andrew Mowbray Publishers, Woonsocket, R.I., 2013.

Ortner, Christian, et. al., With Drawn Sword, Austro-Hungarian Edged Weapons from 1848-1918, Verlag Militaria, Vienna, 2006.

Von Ottenfeld, Rudolf and Teuber, Oscar, Die Österreichische Armee von 1700-1867, Akademische Druck und Verlagsanstalt, Verlag von Emil Berte & Cie. Und S. Czeigner, Wien, 1895.

Paret, Peter, Yorck and the Era of Prussian Reform, 1807-1815, Princeton University Press, Princeton, NJ, 1996.

Von Paumgarten, Max Sigismund Armand Josef, Abhandlung über den Dienst der Feldjüber den Dienst der Feldjäger zu Fuss, Self Published, Wien, 1802.

Pavlovic, Darko, The Austrian Army 1836-66, Volume 1, Infantry, Osprey Publishing, Oxford, 1999.

Guglielmo Pepe, Memorie, Vol. 1, Baudry Libreria Europea, Paris, 1847.

Peterson, Harold L., Arms and Armor in Colonial America, 1526-1783, Bramhall House, New York, 1956.

Petre, F. Loraine, Napoleon and the Archduke Charles, 1989, new edition, Greenhill Books, Barnsley, 2017.

Philibert, Guillaume Comte Duhesme, Essai Historique sur l'infanterie Légère ou Traité des petites Operations de la Guerre, a l'Usage des jeunes Officiers, 3rd Edition, Paris, 1864.

De Poja, Alberti, Geshichte des k. und k. Feldjägerbattalions Nr. 11, Druck von Rudolf Brzezowsky & Söhne in Wien, Köszeg, 1905.

Rath, R. John, The Provisional Austrian Regime in Lombardy–Venetia, 1814–1815, University of Texas Press, 1969.

Rothenberg, Gunther E., Napoleon's Great Adversaries, the Archduke Charles and the Austrian Army, 1792-1814, Indiana University Press ,Bloomington, IN, 1982.

Rothenberg, Gunther E., The Army of Francis Joseph, Purdue University Press, West Lafayette, IN, 1998.

Schneid, Frederick C., The Second War of Italian Unification, 1859-61, Osprey, Oxford, 2012.

Schneidnwind, F. and Wägner, Dr. Wilhelm, Das Buch vom Feldmarschall Radetzky Fur Heer und Volk, Verlag von Otto Spamer, Leipzig, 1859.

Schwalm, Marc, et al, European Arms in the Civil War, Mowbray Publishing, Woonsocket, RI, 2018.

Sked, Alan, Radetzky: Imperial Victor and Military Genius, I. B. Tauris & Co. Ltd., London, 2011.

Sondhaus, Lawrence, In the Service of the Emperor: Italians in the Austrian Armed Forces, 1814-1918, East European Monographs, Boulder, CO, 1990.

Strack, J., Das Kopal-Denkmal in Znaim und das k.k. 10. Feld-Jäger Batallion, der k-k Hof und Staatsdrückerei in Commission bei Wilhelm Braunmüller, Wien, 1864.

Josef Strack, *Das Tiroler Jäger-Regiment Kaiser Franz Josef I. in den Jahren 1848 und*

1849, Verlag von Leopold Sommer, Wien, 1853.

Thürheim, Graf Andreas, Gedenkblätter aus der Kriegsgeschichte der k.k. österreichischen Armee, Verlag der Buchhandlung für Militär-Literatur Karl Prochaska, Wien und Teschen, 1880.

Todd, Frederick P., American Military Equipage, Charles Scribner's Sons, New York, 1980.

Von Unterberger, Freiherr Leopold, Wesentliche Kentnisse der Infanterie-Cavalerie Feuergewehre zum Gebrauch der Offiziere der k.k. österreihischen Armee, Christian Friederich Wappler und Beck, Wien, 1807.

Voykowitsch, Bernhard, Castiglione 1796, Helmet Military Publications, Maria Enzeudorf, 1998.

Wagner, Eduard, Cut and Thrust Weapons, English Edition, The Hamlyn Publishing Group, Ltd., London, 1967.

Wawro, Geoffrey, The Austro-Prussian War: Austria's War with Prussia and Italy in 1866, Cambridge University Press, Cambridge, 1996.

Whisker, James B., et al, Firearms from Europe, 2nd Ed., Tom Rowe Books, College Station, PA, 2002.

Wrede, Alphons Freiherrn von, Geschicte der J. und K. Wehrmacht, Vol II, L. W. Seidel & Sohn, Wien, 1898.

Zoppi, Massimo, La Spada di Radetzky, Itinera Progetti Bassano Del Grappa, 2011.

ARTICLES AND WEBSITES

Anonymous, "Austrian Review on the Mincio," United Service Journal, Part 1, Henry Colburn, London, 1834.

Anonymous, Review of H. M. Hozier, The Seven Weeks War, Proceedings of the Royal Artillery Institution, Vol II, Woolwich, 1861.

Anonymous, http://kapszli.hu/en/the-story-of-the-augustin-tube-lock-ignition-system/ (Accessed November, 2017).

Anonymous, http://www.kaiserjaeger.com/at/TKJ/Die_geschichte_der_tiroler_kaiserjaeger.htm (Accessed November, 2017).

Anonymous, *Carinthia: Ein Wochenblatte fur Vaterlandskunde, Belehrung u. Unterhaltung*, Nº. 11, Simon Martin Mayer, ed., Klagenfurt, 1856.

Anonymous, Österreichischer Soldatenfreund, Zeitschrift fur militärische Interessen, Nº. 35, March, 1851.

Anonymous, https://www.jgbnoe.at/kopaljaeger/?lng=de&sekt=7&txt=7 (Accessed December, 2017).

Anonymous, http://www.biographien.ac.at/oebl_L/Lorenz_Josef_1814-1879.xml (Accessed September, 2017).

Acerbi, Enrico, http://www.napoleon-series.org/military/organization/Austria/ArmyStudy/c_AustrianArmyJagers.html (Accessed July 2017).

Acerbi, Enrico, http://www.napoleon-series.org/military/organization/Austria/

ArmyStudy/c_AustrianArmyRecruiting.html(Accessed July 2017).

Badone, Giovanni Cerino "Not an Easy Day, The Austrian and the Sardinian Armies at the Battle of San Martino, 24th June, 1859,"XVIIIe Symposium International D' Histoire et de Prospective Militaires, 1er mars 2014, Le Centre Général Guisan, Pully, Switzerland.

Beeman, R. Robert E. http://www.beemans.net/Austrian%20airguns.htm (Accessed August, 2017).

Bereiter, Gregory D. "Campaigning in America: Captain Johann Ewald's Hessians in the American Revolution," Constructing the Past: Vol. 3 : Iss. 1, Article 4. (2002) http://digitalcommons.iwu.edu/constructing/vol3/iss1/4 (Accessed June, 2017).

Couture, Richard, https://www.kronoskaf.com/syw/index.php?title=Deutsches_Feldj%C3%A4gerkorps; https://www.kronoskaf.com/syw/index.php?title=Pionier_Korps#Uniform (Accessed July, 2017).

Dolleczek, Anton, Die Entwicklung der Handfeuerwaffen im österreichischen Heer, Minerva Illustrierte militär-wissenschaftliche Zeitschrift, Vol. 2, Dreisel & Gröger, Wien, 1894.

Engels, Friederich "The History of the Rifle," V, Volunteer Journal, Vol. i, No. 17, reprinted in W. H. Chaloner, W.O. Henderson, eds., Engels as Military Critic, Articles by Friederich Engels Reprinted from the *Volunteer Journal* and the *Manchester Guardian* of the 1860's, Manchester University Press, Manchester 1959.

Ferretti, Ennino, La Battaglia di Cesenatico, privately printed, Cesenatico, 2010 http://phoenix.tuwien.ac.at/Cesenatico/Cesenatico_Ferretti.pdf (Accessed December, 2017).

Gschließer, Oswald von,: Zur Geschichte des stehenden Heeres in Tirol, II, Die Zeit von 1813-1848. Veröffentlichungen des Tiroler Landesmuseums Ferdinandeum 34, (1954).

Stephen Herold, MA, PhD. "The Austrian Campaign under FM Schwarzenberg in 1812," The Société Napoléonienne, http://www.antiquesatoz.com/habsburg/1812/campaign.htm (Accessed October, 2017).

Lt. Walter Krueger, "Tactics by Balck, Colonel, German Army," Volume I, Introduction and Formal Tactics of Infantry, Translated by Fourth ed., U.S Cavalry Association, Fort Leavenworth Kansas, 1911.

Konzett, Ernst, Die Jägertruppe - Ursprung und Geschichte, http://www.bundesheer.at/truppendienst/ausgaben/artikel.php?id=1819 (Accessed July, 2017).

Lacroix-Leclair, Jérôme and Ouellet, Eric, Canadian Military Journal "The Petite Guerre in New France, 1660–1759: An Institutional Analysis, "http://www.journal.forces.gc.ca/vo11/no4/48-ouellet-eng.asp, (Vol. 11, Nº. 4) (Accessed June, 2017).

Uhlir, Lubomir, "Jager in the Austrian Army during the Coalition Wars," (translation from Hungarian) http://www.primaplana.cz/news/myslivci-v-rakouske-armade-za-koalicnich-valek/, 2001. (Accessed September, 2017).

van Uythoven Geert, "The Battle of Aldenhoven / Aix-La Chapelle, 1793" First Empire Nº. 68, Jan/Feb 2003. http://www.napoleon-series.org/cgi-bin/forum/archive2003_config.pl?md=read;id=15192 (Accessed September, 2017).

INDEX

A

von Appiano General Carl 114

Archduke Albrecht of Austria 111, 115, 116, 117, 240, 242, 243

Archduke Johann of Austria 35, 44, 45

Archduke Karl of Austria 36, 37, 38, 39, 40, 44, 45, 54, 57, 111, 214, 217, 219

D'Aspre, FML Konstantin Ghilian Karl 23, 35

Arminius 2

von Augustin, General Vincenz xiii, 137, 139, 140, 141

Austrian Army Units

   Grenzer Troops xvii, xix, xxiii, 8, 9, 10, 15, 16, 25, 26, 28, 102, 130, 131, 148, 213, 245

   Imperial Danube/Sava Flotilla 148

   Infantry Regiment Nº 4 (Hoch und Deutschmeister) 114

   Infantry Regiment Nº 19 (Schwarzenberg) 89

   Infantry Regiment Nº 46 (Chasteler) 33

   Light Infantry Battalions

     Establishment and record 28, 29, 30

     Light Infantry Battalion Nº 12 (Rubenitz) 30

   Pioneers 13, 14, 15, 18, 31, 32, 41, 42, 64, 65, 209, 210, 252

Austrian Edged Weapons

  Bayonets

    Haubajonet xviii, 54, 62, 101, 120, 133, 134, 144, 147, 149, 159, 178, 180, 185, 189, 235

    Laukart system xx, 129, 144, 147, 180

    Stichbajonet xxiii, 54, 130, 136, 159, 179

  Fusilier-Carpenter saber 187

  Jäger officer saber M 1811 174, 176

  Krückenmesser xx, 176, 191, 192

  M 1765, 1784 Austrian Fusilier saber 185, 186

  M 1798 saber for Light Infantry officers 29, 175

  M 1809 Grenadier saber 187, 253

  M 1836 Infantry saber 187, 189, 190

  M 1837 Infantry Officer saber 176

  M 1853 Pioneer saber 191

  Sabers for Corporal-Grenadiers of Hungarian Infantry, M 1770 186

  Sapper's hanger of 1769 181

  Short swords (infantry hangers) 125, 176, 180, 187, 188

Austrian firearms

  Doppelstutzen xv, xxiii, 10, 13, 25, 130, 131, 135

    M 1807 Jägerstutzen variant utilizing Doppelstutzen lock and stock 135

  Girandoni Air Rifle 160

  Jägerstützen and Jägerkarabiner

    Console conversion, 1836 137, 138, 139

    Early *Jägerstutzen* 124

    Jägerkarabiner (Musqueten) xix, 129

    M 1769 126, 127, 128, 131, 132, 133, 159, 181, 193, 252

    M 1779 128, 132, 177, 178

    M1807 126, 134, 135, 139, 144, 145, 199

INDEX

M 1807 *Jägerkarabiner* 129, 130, 136, 138, 179

M1842 *Jägerstutzen* 135, 144, 145, 148, 178

   Jägerstutzen ramrods 159

M 1842 *Kammerbüchse* 52, 140, 141, 142, 143, 144, 146, 180, 247

M 1844 *Kammerbüchse* 142, 143, 146, 147

M 1854 *Dornstutzen* 158

M 1854 *Jägerstutzen* 154, 179

   Variants 157

M 1862 *Jägerstützen* 158

M 1840 Infantry musket 139

M 1849 *Kammerbüchse* (Garibaldi" rifle) xvi, 148, 149

  Augustin (Large) Ignition Lock 139, 150

  Augustin Small Machine Lock xxi, 140

  Console Lock xiv, 138

  Percussion conversion for export to US 148, 149, 202

  Pillar breech (*Dorn*) xv, 155

  Powder chamber (*Kammer*) 149, 178

  Wesentliche Kentnisse der Infanterie-Cavallerie Feuergewehre zum Gebrauch der Offiziere der k.k. österreichischen Armee 56, 224

M 1854 Extra-Corps Rifle 152

M 1854 Infantry Rifle Types 1 and 2 101, 153

Austrian Jäger

  Freikorps units

    Abortive volunteer Jäger force, 1789 16, 18

    Boer'sche Scharfschützen-Korps 18

    Deutsches Jäger-Corps (originally an amalgam of Sinzendorff and Dandini units) later a.k.a. Geppert, Dandini, Mahony, Plank, D'Aspre and Kurz Feld-Jäger 19, 28

    Dutch Jäger-Korps, a.k.a. Le Loup Feld-Jäger 23, 24, 28, 33, 184

Green Laudons 17, 25, 28, 182, 183

  Italienische Feldjäger-Korps, a.k.a. Mariassy-Jäger 215

  Lombard Jäger-Korps, a.k.a *Würmserische-Frei-Korps*, and *Lombardisches Jäger-Korps Corti* 23

  Moravian-Silesian *Gebirgsjäger* 16

Jäger organization, manuals and tactics

  Abhandlung über den Dienst der Feldjäger zu Fuss 56, 129, 219, 224

  Abrichtungs-Reglement für die k. k. Jäger 1851 77, 230, 237

  Detachments 14, 15, 35, 43, 44, 45, 46, 57, 59, 86, 89, 90, 91, 96, 114, 116, 120, 223, 237

  Einzelkämpfer 33

  Generals-Reglement 1769 25, 210

  Glied xvii, xix, xxiii, 142, 179, 189

  Handbuch ueber des Vorposten-Dienst zum Gebrauche des Jäger-Officiers im Felde 57

  Kette xx

  Kettenglied xx, 62

  Kleiner Krieg (Petit Guerre) xx, 9, 16, 56, 88, 207, 208

  Klumpen xx, 61

  Piquet xxi

  Unit organization 54, 55

  Vorposten xxiv, 59, 99, 226, 258

  Zerstreute Fechtart xxiv, 62

Jäger training regime

  Geschichtlichkeit 62

  Jäger training regulations, 1841 59, 62, 63

  Marksmanship, 56-63

    Marksmanship cord, 60

  Raschheit, 62

Jäger uniform and equipment

  Adjustierung, 1811, 1836 xiii, 68, 73, 175, 187

INDEX

Cartridge Box 65, 71, 72, 76, 77, 230

Cords (*Achselschnur*) xiii, 68, 69, 70, 71, 79

Corsehut xiv, xv, 41, 42, 67, 69, 73, 74, 76, 78, 102, 111, 165

Federbusch xv, 67, 68, 69, 73, 75, 76

Gaiter xvi, 65, 68, 73

Haselstock xviii, 68

Kaskett xix, 42 (illustration)

Mannschaftsvorschrift, 1828 73

Powder horn xiii, 69, 70, 71, 77, 79, 210, 230

Tornister xxiv, 65, 69, 166

Regular Army units

1st *Feld-Jäger battalion* 43, 45

2nd *Feld-Jäger Battalion* 43, 45, 48, 238

3rd *Feld-Jäger battalion* 43, 57, 79, 88, 103

4th *Feld-Jäger Battalion* 53, 114

5th *Feld-Jäger Battalion* 45

6th *Feld-Jäger Battalion* 43, 45, 137, 139, 159, 219

7th *Feld-Jäger Battalion* 43, 45, 105

8th *Feld-Jäger Battalion* 43, 48, 55, 233

9th *Feld-Jäger Battalion* 44, 48, 51, 52, 109

10th *Feld-Jäger Battalion* 43, 54, 93, 94, 96, 98, 116, 122, 223

17th *Feld-Jäger Battalion* 114

Deutsches Feld-Jäger Corps 13, 209, 210

Fenner-Jäger-Corps 48, 49, 51, 52, 221

Jäger Regiment Nº 64 36, 38

Tiroler Jäger Regiment, 1801 33, 54

Tiroler Jäger Regiment, 1816 (*Kaiser Jäger*) ix, xv, xix, xxiii, 47, 52, 53, 54, 73, 74, 87, 102, 109, 117, 118, 120, 121, 234

Tiroler Scharfschutzen-Corps 24

Austrian tactical doctrine and commanders' field instructions

   1806-9 Reforms and Light Infantry 33, 36, 38

   Field Instructions of 1847 237

   Observationspunkte 1796 27, 214

   Radetzky on fighting *en tirailleur* (1813) 216

   Stosstaktik 63, 101, 109, 110, 117, 239

B

Battles, smaller engagements

   Amberg 43

   Ampola blockhouse 121, 244

   Aspern 43, 44

   Cesenatico 49, 50, 51, 90, 221

   Custoza 86, 99, 117, 118, 120, 243

   Dresden 45, 48, 215, 220, 221

   Königgrätz 113, 114, 118, 240

      Chlum 114, 241

   Leipzig 45, 47, 205, 215, 219

   Magenta 102, 104, 106, 237

   Marengo 30, 31, 32, 213, 214, 215

   Montebello 103, 104

   Mt. Suello 120

   Novara 83, 86, 99, 104, 236

   Occhiobello 49

   Palestro 104, 105, 219

   Pastrengo 89, 90, 93

   Regensburg 42, 43

Rivoli 83, 91, 92, 96

Santa Lucia 43, 89, 93, 94, 95, 97, 117

Solferino 104, 106, 107, 236, 237

  San Martino 106, 107, 237

Stockach 30

Strub Pass 45

Tolentino 49, 51, 222

Ulm 35

Vicenza 43, 91, 95, 96, 97, 98, 99, 233

Wagram 43, 44, 84

  Baumersdorf 44

Wenzelberg 113

von Benedek, FML Ludwig August, Ritter 110

Bersagliere xiii, 107

C

de Chasteler de Courcelles, FML Gabriel, Marquis 34, 44

Compression (Minie or Burton) bullet 101, 150, 151, 154, 198, 249

Console, Giuseppe xiv, 137

von Constant Villars, Oberleutnant August, 57, 226

D

Delvigne, Captain Henri-Gustave xiv, 141, 155

F

Fenner von und zum Fennerberg, FML Phillipp, Ritter 34, 48

French skirmishers (*Tirailleurs*) xxiii, 22, 24, 33, 219

Frühwirth, Ferdinand 142, 143, 203

G

von Gablenz FML Ludwig 110

Garibaldi, Giuseppe xvi, 104, 119, 120, 243, 248

Grünne, FML Karl, Graf 100, 108

Gyulai FZM Franz, Graf 100, 104, 108, 236

H

von Hess, FM Heinrich 100, 101, 236

Hessian Jäger 4, 5, 65, 123

J

Jelačić, General Franz 35

K

Kaiser Ferdinand I xv, 139

Kaiser Franz I xvi, 36

Kaiser Franz Josef 107, 150, 151, 234

Kaiserin Maria Theresa xxi, 5, 12, 13, 34, 48, 92, 124

Kaiserjägermuseum 53

Kaiser Joseph II 5, 160, 181

Kopal, Colonel Karl 43, 93, 97, 98, 117, 176, 219

von Kuhn, Major General Franz, Freiherr 119, 122, 236

L

von Lacy, Franz Moritz, Graf 12, 18

von Lichtenstein, FML Moritz, Prince 98, 220

Lorenz, Josef xxi, 149, 150, 151, 152, 249

M

INDEX

Military Frontier (*Militärgrenze*) 8

Mordecai, Major Alfred 195, 197, 198, 254

Murat, Joachim, King of Naples and Marshal of France 47, 48, 49, 51, 52, 54, 81, 221, 222, 226

N

von Neipperg, FML Adam Albert, Freiherr 49, 51

P

von Paumgartten, FML Max Sigismund Armand Josef 56, 129, 219, 224

Peace of Camp Formio 28

Peace of Luneville 29, 32

Pirquet von Merdaga, Anton, Freiherr 90, 91, 92, 93

Pirquet von Merdaga, FZM Peter, Freiherr 48, 49, 50, 51, 90

von Preu, Oberleutnant Anton 121

Prussian Dreyse Needle Rifle 101, 112, 113, 151, 250

Prussian Jäger
   Prussian Jägerstutzen Conversion, Model 1810/35 138

Q

Quadrilateral, The 82, 85, 88, 89, 99, 110, 115, 116, 118

R

Radetzky von Radetz, FML Johann Josef Wenzel Anton Franz Karl, Graf xv, 31, 32, 82, 83, 84, 87, 88, 95, 97, 99, 100, 101, 102, 108, 112, 114

S

Saxe-Coberg, Josias, Prince 25

Schneider, Colonel Karl, Freiherr von Arno, 48, 220, 221

von Strassoldo, General Julius Cäser 89, 93, 94, 96

T

Teutoburg Forest 2
Tirol Landlibell 6
Treaty of Schönbrunn 42, 45

U

von Unterberger, FZM Leopold, Freiherrn 56, 57, 62, 101, 178, 186, 224, 225, 226, 227
von Urban, General Karl 104

V

Vienna Arsenal xiii, xxi, 140, 142, 152, 155, 195, 196, 197, 198, 200, 201, 202, 204

W

Welden, FML Ludwig 88, 89
Wilhelm V. Landgrave of Hesse 3, 4
von Wohlgemuth, General Ludwig Freiherr 89

Z

Zephyris, Captain Adolf, Baron 120
Zephyris zu Greit, Colonel Ignaz, Freiherr 139

ABOUT THE AUTHORS

JAMES V. CAPUA

James V. Capua is Managing Partner and co-founder of Fides Philanthropic Management and Advisory Services, LLC, which administers charitable foundations for its clients.

Mr. Capua earned his MA and Ph.D. in medieval English history at the University of Chicago, where he was a Danforth Graduate Fellow, and his BA at the University of Rochester.

In addition to scholarly publications in English legal and constitutional history, Mr. Capua has written on maritime art, antique firearms, and philanthropic issues.

He has also served as associate producer for segments of *Firing Line with William F. Buckley*, and has been a frequent contributor to *American Thinker, Liberty Nation* and other public affairs websites.

Mr. Capua has served on the boards of the New York City Commission on the Bicentennial of the Constitution, the American Society of Marine Artists, and the Friends of the National Parks at Gettysburg.

A collector and shooter of antique arms, Mr. Capua is a Life Member of the National Rifle Association and competes with the 49th Virginia Infantry of the North-South Skirmish Association.

COL. CARL M. KRUGER, USA, (ret.)

Colonel Carl M. Kruger was born in Munich Germany and has been conversant in German from his earliest days. He graduated from the US Military Academy with the class of 1972, earning a BS in Engineering with an emphasis on Ordnance Engineering. He entered active duty with the 82nd Airborne Division. He served as a Rifle Platoon Leader, Weapons Platoon Leader, Company Executive officer and as a Battalion Operations LNO in the 1st Battalion (Airborne) 504th Infantry. He transferred to the Quartermaster Corps to pursue his passion for all things parachute and commanded B Company, 407th S&S Battalion (Airborne) and E Company (Aerial Delivery) 407th S&S Battalion (Airborne).

Col. Kruger attended Fairleigh Dickinson University and earned a DMD degree in May 1981. He served as a staff dental officer at the Fort Bragg and Walter Reed Dental Activities, commanded B Company 7th Medical Battalion, 7th Infantry Division (Light), was the Chief Clinician in Kirchgoens, Germany supporting the 1st Brigade, 1st Armored Division, and commanded the USA Dental Activity in Japan and the Hanau Clinic Command in Germany, providing dental health support for some 20,000 US Army Soldier and family beneficiaries.

He is a graduate of the Infantry Officers' Basic Course, Basic Parachute Course, Jumpmaster Course, Parachute Rigger Course, AMEDD Officers' Advanced Course, the Advanced Trauma Life Support Course, the Combat Casualty Care Course, and the Command and General Staff College.

His awards include the Master Parachutists' Badge, Expert Infantry Badge, Parachute Rigger Badge, Legion of Merit, Meritorious Service Medals, Army Commendation Medals, Army Achievement Medals, German Proficiency Badge in Gold with numeral "5", and is a member of the Army Medical Department Order of Military Medical Merit.

Retiring from the US Army in 2005, Col. Kruger has maintained a lifelong interest in arms collecting and military history, and is a member of the 49th Virginia Infantry of the North-South Skirmish Association.

Col. Kruger is the author of a forthcoming illustrated history of the Prussian Model 1809 musket.

www.ingramcontent.com/pod-product-compliance
Lightning Source LLC
Chambersburg PA
CBHW061147070526
44584CB00034B/4451